D0058135

THE MINDFUL THERAPIST

DANIEL J. SIEGEL, MD

THE MINDFUL THERAPIST

*A Clinician's Guide to Mindsight
and Neural Integration*

W. W. NORTON & COMPANY

New York • London

For information about permission to reproduce selections from this book, write to
Permissions, W. W. Norton & Company, Inc., 500 Fifth Avenue, New York, NY 10110

For information about special discounts for bulk purchases, please contact W. W. Norton
Special Sales at specialsales@wwnorton.com or 800-233-4830

Manufacturing by World Color, Fairfield Graphics
Production manager: Leeann Graham

Library of Congress Cataloging-in-Publication Data

Siegel, Daniel J., 1957–
The mindful therapist : a clinician's guide to mindsight and neural
integration / Daniel J. Siegel.—1st ed.
p. ; cm.— (Norton series on interpersonal neurobiology)
Includes bibliographical references and index.
ISBN 978-0-393-70645-1 (hardcover)
1. Mindfulness-based cognitive therapy. I. Title. II. Series: Norton
series on interpersonal neurobiology.
[DNLM: 1. Psychotherapy—methods. 2. Awareness. 3. Brain—physiology.
4. Mind-Body Relations (Metaphysics) 5. Professional-Patient Relations. WM 420
S5705 2010]
RC489.M55S54 2010
616.89'1425—dc22
2009049383

ISBN: 978-0-393-70645-1

W. W. Norton & Company, Inc., 500 Fifth Avenue, New York, N.Y. 10110
www.wwnorton.com
W. W. Norton & Company Ltd., Castle House, 75/76 Wells Street, London W1T 3QT

6 7 8 9 0

To my parents, Sue and Marty,
and my brother, Jason:
Thank you for growing me up in Carthay Circle
and inspiring me to dream
of triangles of well-being and
planes of possibility

CONTENTS

CONTENTS

ACKNOWLEDGMENTS
ACKNOWLEDGMENTS

As my wife says, this work has taken a lifetime to develop before I ever placed fingers on keyboard to enable the words and the worlds to be expressed here. In this way, I am also grateful for a lifetime of support from many wonderful people who have graced this journey with their presence. From the beginning with my mother, father, and brother, I have been encouraged to "think on my feet" and to not take anything for granted. My friends in my youth, Jon Fried and Yves Marton, have likewise nourished this propensity to question everything with a curious mind. As I grew through my formal education, elementary, junior high, high school, and college teachers have variously inspired and pushed me to look beyond what was in plain view. Through medical school, Leston Havens was a mentor in this same vein; and in psychiatry training through my clinical and research years, Gordon Strauss, Joel Yager, Denny Cantwell, Robert Stoller, Donald Schwartz, Regina Pally, Marian Sigman, Mary Main, Erik Hesse, Chris Heinicke, and Robert Bjork all contributed to my growth as clinician and academician. I thank them all. Now, in my work at UCLA, Sue Smalley, Diana Winston, Marv Belzer, Susan Kaiser-Greenland, and the gang at the Mindful Awareness Research Center along with the assembly of wonderful thinkers at the Foundation for Psychocultural Research/UCLA Center for Culture, Brain and Development continue to stimulate my creative thinking about our human lives. My close connections with Diane Ackerman, Lou Cozolino, Jon Kabat-Zinn, Jack Kornfield, Allan Schore, and Rich Simon continue to offer me sustenance, as I feel blessed by their wisdom and our relationships. At the Mindsight Institute, Stephanie Hamilton, Eric Bergemann, Tina Bryson, Adit Shah, and Aubrey Siegel make working at the interface of ideas, interventions, and education in the world of compassion and brain science a wonderful adventure. Stephanie's husband, Chris, was a tremendous help in putting my ideas of the plane of possibility into visual form. The other drawings were done by MAWS & Company, for which I am much appreciative. Deborah Malmud, Kristin Holt-Browning, and Vani Kannan have been a pleasure to work with at W. W. Norton and Gabe Eckhouse has been helpful in the final proof editing of the manuscript. At home, my two children have inspired me to be present as they move forward in their own journeys, exploring their passions and bringing me great joy and wonderment with their growth. And, as always, my wife Caroline Welch remains a steady and attuned partner whose support, advice, and role modeling continue to nurture my life and my work.

INTRODUCTION
INTRODUCTION

You and I are the subjects of this book. I invite you to join with me in the chapters that follow, written as a conversation between two clinicians, as we explore the nature of how we connect with others in healing relationships. This dialogue is organized in both breadth and depth with the goal of being useful for experienced practitioners, as well as for those new to their education in the healing arts.

Research suggests that our presence as medical or mental health clinicians, the way we bring ourselves fully into connection with those for whom we care, is one of the most crucial factors supporting how people heal—how they respond positively to our therapeutic efforts. Whatever the individual approach or clinical technique employed, the therapeutic relationship is one of the most powerful determinants of positive outcome in a range of studies of psychotherapy (see Norcross, Beutler, & Levant, 2005).

In this book we'll be addressing these findings by asking ourselves this basic question: Why is our presence—not just the interventions we offer or the theoretical stance we take—the most robust predictor of how our patients respond? What is "presence," and how can we cultivate this in ourselves? In *The Mindful Therapist*, we will be exploring the possible answers to these fundamental questions that emerge from a scientific journey into the art of healing. In this *Clinician's Guide to Mindsight and Neural Integration*, we'll be diving deeply into a professional view of the fundamental way that we sense and shape energy and information flow in our lives—a process called *mindsight*. With mindsight, we are given the tools of empathy and insight to more deeply sense and understand ourselves and others within relationships, the process of our ever-changing brains, and even how our mind itself functions. This inner clarity can help us to modify the flow of energy and information within our own lives and in our interactions with others in a very specific manner. The power to move our lives from nonintegrated states of rigidity or chaos toward the more flexible and harmonious flow of an integrated system is what we create when we intentionally cultivate neural integration in our lives. This creation reveals how we can be intentional in nurturing, first, the differentiation of aspects of our relationships and our nervous system, and then linking those separate elements to one another to cultivate integration. In essence, we use mindsight to foster neural integration as we move our lives toward health.

Now more than ever we can harness the insights from scientific research to enhance our own effectiveness as clinicians in helping to cultivate both the objective health and subjective well-being of others. Physicians who are more empathic, for example, have patients who heal faster from the common cold and have more robust immune functions to fight infections (see Rakel et al., 2009). And studies also reveal how becoming more attuned to ourselves and others with mindfulness practice can improve our own sense of well-being and our attitudes toward our patients. Learning to be mindful has been demonstrated in research with primary care physicians to prevent burnout and promote positive attitudes toward patients, as it bolsters resilience and well-being in the challenge of caring for others (see Krasner et al., 2009). What these studies share in common is the notion that our presence—with others and with ourselves—promotes empathy and self-compassion, which both cultivates well-being in our mental lives and in our bodily health. And so this conversation will be focusing upon two important dimensions of understanding: the scientific knowledge derived from various disciplines of research and the direct subjective insights attained by immersion in personal experience through focused exercises, which we will be exploring throughout this book.

If it were not possible to change our own capacity for presence as clinicians, there would be no real point in reading (or writing) this book. Fortunately, it turns out that we can actually transform the way we are and how we communicate—to the benefit of all concerned. This is the aim of our journey together in the following pages. The brain continues to develop throughout the life span, and with the proper focus of our minds we can actually strategically change our brains in a helpful way. As you'll see, the conceptual framework, brain basics, and practical exercises contained within each chapter offer a way for us to enhance our own lives as we develop resilience, strengthen the focus of our attention, and create resourcefulness in our selves. These are some of the many traits within our own way of being that support the presence, empathy, and compassion essential in helping others.

A BRIEF BACKGROUND

When I was first learning to become a physician and later training to be a pediatrician and then a psychiatrist, I would have loved to have a literary companion along the journey to help me develop the inner knowledge and interpersonal skills necessary in becoming an effective clinician. As I moved toward a research focus on relationships between parents and their children, I was struck by how the caring, attuning communication between adult and child could promote healthy development. Yet in my training as a therapist, little was available to help our own development as individuals, beyond electing to engage in personal psychotherapy of varied type and with mixed results. In those days, nothing seemed to be available to develop empathy, compassion, or self-regulation for professionals in our own training. I had so many questions about what healing involved, about how to deeply connect and comfort others—and myself. I wondered how we could develop a way to communicate with others and feel compassion for their situation, yet also be able to soothe the suffering that may emerge with empathizing with their distress. What were the tools that could give us the strength and the skills as clinicians to know ourselves so deeply that we could maintain our own equilibrium while bringing clarity to others' confusion and tranquility to their turmoil? Like so many in clinical training, I just did the best I could, scraping together whatever I could lay my hands on to make my way in the journey from student to practitioner. But now in the healing arts we can do better than that to support the growth of those of us who have decided to devote our lives to helping others.

My hope is that this book can be a deep dialogue between you and me that deals directly with how being mindful offers us inner resilience and the power to create the healing presence that research has demonstrated to be such a robust predictor of a client's improvement in therapy. "Being mindful" is defined in various ways in both practice and scientific discussions. One way of conceptualizing mindfulness is that it is intentionally focusing attention on moment-to-moment experience without being swept up by judgments or preconceived ideas and expectations (see Kabat-Zinn, 2005). This is the notion of mindfulness that embraces a caring conscious experience that often emerges with contemplative practice. Another way of defining mindfulness is in avoiding premature closure of possibilities that often come with a "hardening of the categories" (Cozolino, 2002) by which we filter and constrain our perceptions of the world (see Langer, 1989, 1997). By keeping our mind open in this way, we promote creativity in school, work, and our everyday lives. And even in our everyday use of the word *mindful*, we have the connotation of being thoughtful, considerate, and aware (as in "being mindful of others"). This is essentially how we live by being conscientious and intentional in our actions. In each of these three ways, a mindful therapist brings an awakened mind to focus on things as they are with care and concern, to literally be present in awareness with what is happening right now. It is in this broad and diverse sense of being mindful that we will examine the presence that emerges in ourselves that is so vital in shaping how we connect with our patients in healing relationships.

Being present fully enables us to be effective in our roles as professionals in helping others heal from illness and trauma, supporting their journeys toward lasting growth and well-being.

In this book, I hope the opportunity for a direct engagement between me and you can unfold in our "conversation" so that I can be present with you as we look deeply into our lives—into our ways of being—to support us in becoming better at what we do in helping others grow and heal. "Better" means more effective in how we can help others transform their lives toward resilience, meaning, and health. This will be the clinical focus of our discussion. Better also means how we can care for ourselves along the path to helping others develop well.

As they say at the beginning of a flight, we need to put our own oxygen mask on first before we can help those around us. For this reason, this book is filled with exercises to develop your own self-understanding and self-compassion in your personal and professional life. Naturally, as we deepen our own insights and self-soothing, we become better prepared to offer empathic understanding and specific skill training that can support the growth of others in their own journeys within psychotherapy.

GETTING READY

In teaching this material for many years, I have found that seminar members who are at the beginning of their education, those just starting out in their clinical work, or even individuals who have had decades of practice in psychotherapy, medicine, or education have all benefited from this approach. This is a work designed with professionals who help others grow and develop in mind. It is filled with science, in-depth explorations of the mind and brain, and a progressively more elaborated integration of the subjective internal work for you as a professional and the application of these experiences and ideas for the process of being a therapist.

The science that serves as the background knowledge for this more direct, subjective immersion of *The Mindful Therapist* as an internal clinical education is available as a collection of published works that offers an in-depth exploration of the research underlying the ideas and suggestions we'll be discussing. You don't need to have read or studied any of those texts for this book to be accessible and useful to you. However, I do invite you to consider using those resources as an important framework for further in-depth scientific and clinical exploration that would give you the freedom to explore any area we'll encounter in the pages ahead. These published books and audiovisual programs are translations of the vast array of sciences that have been synthesized into the interpersonal neurobiology field's professional library, which is the basis of this approach. Those textbooks can help you dive more deeply into the applications of science in the practice of psychotherapy and clinical care. For your benefit, a list of these educational opportunities and resources can be found in the References and Suggested Reading. Rather than embedding extensive references parenthetically in the flow of this text or even as numerous notes placed at the end, the References and Suggested Reading serve as both a reference list and a bibliography for further study.

Let me mention a few particularly relevant publications that can be specifically drawn upon as a backdrop to the conversation of this book. First, the Norton Series on Interpersonal Neurobiology, of which this book is a part, offers an in-depth library, now with over 15 texts, which provides a broad view into this perspective for clinicians. As the founding series editor, I am proud to have worked side by side with our editor, Deborah Malmud, and the series' authors in creating this professional resource.

I have also directly authored a few books that address specific areas we'll be covering. The idea of this scientific synthesis was born out of the academic text, *The Developing Mind: Toward a Neurobiology of Interpersonal Experience* (Siegel, 1999), which proposed the notion and the name of the field as well as some basic principles of development, integration, relationships, the brain, the mind, and mental health. Practical applications for parents to help them make sense of their lives and develop a coherent narrative of their early life history were then woven into *Parenting From the Inside Out: How a Deeper Understanding Can Help You Raise Children Who Thrive* (Siegel & Hartzell, 2003). An exploration of these ideas in the world of mental training and awareness can be found in *The Mindful Brain: Reflection and Attunement in the Cultivation of Well-Being* (Siegel, 2007a). That book will be especially useful for those interested in the scientific explorations of an interpersonal neurobiology perspective on mindfulness as a form of internal attunement that promotes neural integration. Finally, for those interested in the application of interpersonal neurobiology in clinical practice as revealed in the comprehensive stories of how people change within psychotherapy, accessible for the general reader as well as the clinician, information is available in *Mindsight: The New Science of Personal Transformation* (Siegel, 2010). That book explores the "domains of integration" in detail to illuminate for the reader the process by which the focus of the mind can transform the brain, relationships, and the mind itself toward health.

Here, in *The Mindful Therapist: A Clinician's Guide to Mindsight and Neural Integration*, I will be exploring for the professional relevant aspects of brain function and mental skill training pertaining primarily to the relational role of the therapist as an individual. This book is intended to be a clinician's literary "internal companion," a guide to how the therapist as person can develop a more mindful way of being as a healer. This is a book organized, as you'll soon see, by an inside view of the essential steps of the therapeutic process. Rather than repeat what has been extensively explored in the texts mentioned above, this book will intentionally focus on the internal world of the therapist. Here we will explore what is so rarely available for the professional: an inner education that integrates important, cutting-edge scientific principles and first-person immersion in direct experience with the specific purpose of developing the clinician's own self-understanding, personal growth, and clinical effectiveness from the inside out.

In this book my goal is to have a direct dialogue and invite you to immerse yourself in the subjective experience of your own mind. This will be a relational writing format, different from most other texts, which has the aim of directly addressing your own experience. There's plenty of science here as well—and so we'll be taking on the important and exciting challenge of weaving science with subjectivity. My hope is to have the experience of reading this book expand the way you embrace science and also awaken the ways you experience your own internal world. Ultimately, such a deeper self-knowing will enable you to cultivate your presence further, make therapy more effective, and offer tools to teach such ways of deepening mindfulness and self-understanding to your clients. This tapestry will invite us to integrate research findings with the important first-person experience that is so often left out of our clinical training and writing—yet crucial for our own sense of presence and essential for our clients' and our own well-being.

OUR APPROACH

The title, *The Mindful Therapist*, suggests that this book focuses on the clinician as person and professional more than it does on the specific techniques or actions of doing mindful psychotherapy. This book is more like an in-depth manual of the mind for professionals who help people's minds grow. It's designed to be like an intense conversation we might have during a (very) long walk on the beach together, discussing what it means to be a therapist, not so much what to specifically do as a therapist.

Our conversation will be structured through the 15 chapters that follow. Often less is more, and I've tried my best to make the text as useful and as straight to the point as I could. This is not a comprehensive textbook of science or a review of various fields of knowledge. It is not intended to be a compilation of case histories or a prescriptive text on what to do as a therapist. There are many fascinating books addressing the issue of doing—this one is about the objective science and subjective art of mindful being.

For those who know me—through prior writings, audio programs, or in-person seminars—you may have come to discover that I love acronyms as a way of remembering complex interrelated material. But we each hold onto our experiences best within memory in different ways. Some people share this style of learning and enjoy using mnemonics like SNAG or FACES, COHERENCE or SOCK (these are each defined in the appendix of *The Mindful Brain*)—I certainly do; yet others find these words irritating and actually difficult to remember. Some of the most urgent e-mails I've gotten have been from readers asking that I refrain from using "so many nicknames" for things. I respect those requests and rather than taking the chance of distracting even some small percentage of readers who might not benefit from using these kinds of terms, in this book I'll try to forego my acronym addiction. (I've tried my best but some have snuck in when useful.) Instead I'll just use one basic acronym to organize the structure of the entire book. Most of the concepts embedded in those previously established terms, without their abbreviations unless essential for the ease of reading, will be found in abundance here as well.

Recently I was wondering what the most important part of therapy was—what essential part a therapist plays in helping support the growth of another person. The word *part* floated in my acronym neural association centers, and then suddenly out came yet another mnemonic. I use this word, PART, to organize the chapters of this book. PART stands for the following elements of the essential part we play in helping others grow and develop:

- Chapter 1, Presence: The way in which we are grounded in ourselves, open to others, and participate fully in the life of the mind are important aspects of our presence at the heart of relationships that help others grow. This inside-out view helps us see what we need to do inside ourselves as professionals to develop this essential receptive starting place for all clinical endeavors. This first chapter will invite you to consider a new visual metaphor for mindfulness, presence, and the intersection of subjective mental experience with objective neural firing.

- Chapter 2, Attunement: As signals are sent from one person to another, we have the opportunity to tune in to those incoming streams of information and attend fully to what is being sent rather than becoming swayed by our own preconceived ideas or perceptual biases. When we attune to others—even in the urgency of an emergency visit—we offer a crucial open mind to listen deeply to what the patient needs to let us know. Without attunement, vital information can be lost—sometimes with dire consequences. This chapter explores how attunement enables the healing relationship to begin.

- Chapter 3, Resonance: In this chapter we'll discuss how the physiological result of presence and attunement is the alignment of two autonomous beings into an interdependent and functional whole as each person influences the internal state of the other. With resonance we come to "feel felt" by the other. This joining has profound transformative effects on both people. Resonance is what our human nervous system is built to require for a sense of connection to others early in life. This experience of connection brings with it a feeling of security, of being seen, and of feeling safe. The need for such intimate and vulnerable connection persists throughout our lives.

Now here come the dozen TR elements (words that start with *tr*) of the book:

- Chapter 4, Trust: When we feel resonance with someone, we open the doorway to a sense of feeling safe and seen, comforted and connected. The brain's response to such attuned connection is to create a state of openness and trust—the basic ingredients that can promote brain stimulation and growth. In this chapter we'll see how we actually have neural pathways that govern this sense of openness and permit us to activate a social engagement system.

- Chapter 5, Truth: As we open ourselves to others and to ourselves, the true nature of our internal world of memory, perception, longing, and desire emerges into awareness. It is this grounding in things-as-they-truly-are that permits deep and lasting change to begin. We'll dive deeply into these important issues in this chapter and see how knowing the ways our own narratives may be imprisoning us is a first step toward awakening the mind and stirring us from the slumber of automatic pilot. Facing realities openly rather than automatically attempting to move them in our desired but impossible direction is how truth becomes the friend of clinician and patient alike.

- Chapter 6, Tripod: This chapter illustrates the way we stabilize our mind's lens to see the internal world. Sometimes the emergence of neural representations of things as they are into our awareness can be jumpy and confusing as we experience them as fleeting images or intense sensations that flood our mind's eye. The tripod is a visual metaphor for a three-legged support of the lens of the mental camera we use to view the mind itself—the important capacity called *mindsight*. Our mindsight lens is supported by the tripod of openness, objectivity, and observation and enables us to see the mind with more clarity and depth, and to move our lives toward well-being and health.

Each of these three legs of the tripod can be strengthened with specific mental practices we'll explore.

- Chapter 7, Triception: Ultimately the ability to use mindsight to see the internal world with more clarity and to transform the mind with more power relies upon our capacity to perceive a triangle of well-being. This perceptual ability is called *triception* and enables us to sense the flow of energy and information within three interdependent aspects of human life: relationships, mind, and brain. Relationships are how we share energy and information flow; mind can be defined in part as how we regulate that flow; and brain is a term we can use to refer to the mechanism of energy and information flow in the extended nervous system distributed throughout the entire body. In this chapter we'll see how a clinician's triception is a key to being present and catalyzing therapeutic change.

- Chapter 8, Tracking: Within the therapeutic relationship we establish with our patients and with our clients (I'll be using these two clinical terms interchangeably as they each have benefits and drawbacks in our various therapeutic fields), the natural drive of the nervous system to move toward health can be released through a process of tracking energy and information flow within and between people. Ultimately this tracking is a way of placing into awareness the energy and information flow of the triangle of well-being that can then release an innate push toward something called *neural integration*. This chapter will illuminate how integration entails the linkage of differentiated parts of a system. When we are integrated, we live in harmony. Out of integration, we move toward rigidity, chaos, or both. As we'll see, integration can be viewed as the underlying mechanism of well-being and overall mental health.

- Chapter 9, Traits: Psychotherapy can offer tremendous opportunities for growth. Yet we are born with enduring and genetically influenced traits seen in our earliest months of life as temperament. In this chapter, we'll explore a synthetic view of adult personality that proposes a mechanism whereby child-hood temperament goes from an externally observable set of characteristics to an internally organizing pattern of structuring tendencies of attention and meaning.

- Chapter 10, Trauma: Overwhelming events can be seen to flood an individual's capacity to adapt flexibly to an experience. When we remain with unresolved trauma of large and small *t* sorts—of life-threatening events or significant but non-life-threatening betrayals—we can see how the layers of memory have remained in a nonintegrated form. In this chapter we'll explore trauma from the inside out and sense how the layers of implicit memory with their representations of perception, emotion, bodily sensation, and behavior may remain jumbled and dominate our internal mind-scape. The pathway toward resolving trauma can be seen to involve the integration of these disconnected elements of implicit memory.

- Chapter 11, Transition: When people first come for therapy, they often are mired in life patterns filled with chaos or rigidity. When neural integration is freely occurring, we live with the ease of well-being. When regions do not become differentiated, or if they are blocked from becoming linked, integration will be impaired. The outcome of such blocked integration is chaos or rigidity. As clinicians we can take the "pulse of integration" by sensing these movements of life's flow and feel the internal sense of these transitions toward chaotic intrusions or rigid depletions.

- Chapter 12, Training: The mind is like a muscle. We need to tone our musculoskeletal system regularly or it will not function optimally as we age. Naturally there is no actual muscle tissue in our mental life—but the need to offer specific ways to harness our regulatory capacities is real. We keep our mental acuity, our brain's synaptic webs, and our interconnections within relationships well honed by mental training. In this chapter we'll see how ultimately this training supports the way we develop mindsight skills, likely harnessing the power of deep forms of practice to stimulate the growth of myelin sheaths that make our neural networks more efficient.

- Chapter 13, Transformation: As clinicians we can feel the pulse of integration and when chaos or rigidity are present we can then strategically place a spotlight of attention on the various domains that are blocking the linkage of differentiated aspects of a person's life. *Neuroplasticity*—the process of change in the structural connections in the brain in response to experience— is promoted with such focused awareness and serves to activate specific neural groups simultaneously. This chapter reviews the nine domains of integration and how these can be seen as the transformative integrative process that shapes the overall functioning of our mind, brain, and relationships.

- Chapter 14, Tranquility: Neural integration promotes a coherence of our minds and we feel *c*onnected, *o*pen, *h*armonious, *e*ngaged, *r*eceptive, *e*mergent (things feeling fresh and alive), *n*oetic (having a sense of deep nonconceptual knowing), *c*ompassionate, and *e*mpathic. The systems view of integration reveals that this flexible and adaptive state has a sense of emotional equanimity and meaning embedded in it—what some would call a state of tranquility. This chapter will explore how developing this form of what the ancient Greeks termed *eudaimonia*—of living a life of meaning, compassion, equanimity, and connection—offers us a path to helping others develop tranquility from the inside out.

- Chapter 15, Transpiration: The human brain is constructed in such a way that it gives us tendencies not only to emphasize the negative, but also to feel isolated and apart from one another. Transpiration is a term that signifies "breathing across" and is intended to signify the ways in which breathing across all the various domains of integration we'll be exploring in ourselves and others actually can dissolve the top-down influences that make us believe we are isolated beings. This chapter will offer a way of seeing how transpiration is a state of awareness that inspires us to rewire our brains toward the reality that we are all a part of a living whole. Integration reminds us that this whole is more than the sum of its parts: We retain our individual identities while fully joining as a "we." In the healing arts we focus on *healing* and *health* and *holistic*, each derived from the word *whole*. Coming to the full realization that we are in fact part of an interdependent whole, an interconnected web of the flow of living beings across time, enables us to see the powerful role we can play in helping others as we strive to heal the planet, beginning with ourselves and working one relationship at a time to make this a kinder and more compassionate world.

THE "MINDFUL" OF BEING A MINDFUL THERAPIST

As we become open to all these PARTs of being a mindful therapist, we can see the centrality of mindsight and neural integration in moving us toward health. *Mindful* is a term that evokes many meanings. In plain language, its synonyms include alert, astute, attentive, aware, careful, heedful, thoughtful, wary, watchful, wideawake, and wise (see Rodale, 1978). In educational terms it signifies being open minded and avoiding premature closure of possibilities, as in its use in mindful education, studied by Ellen Langer (1989, 1997). In contemplative usage, mindfulness involves being aware, on purpose and nonjudgmentally, of what is happening as it is happening in the present moment (see Kabat-Zinn, 2005; Germer, Siegel, & Fulton, 2004; Kaiser-Greenland, 2010, Shapiro & Carlson, 2009; Smalley & Winston, 2010). Here in *The Mindful Therapist* we will be using all three of these connotations of what it means to be mindful. What I hope you'll come to see is that being a mindful therapist involves all these interpretations of what being mindful entails: the conscientious, creative, and contemplative aspects of consciousness. At the heart of each of these meanings of mindful awareness and being mindful are the processes of mindsight and neural integration. For this reason, this book is intended as a clinician's guide to these mechanisms that I believe are beneath what being mindful truly means in its broadest scope of interpretation.

Our discussion will unfold through the lens and language of interpersonal neurobiology. This interdisciplinary approach attempts to be integrative in the literal sense that we don't separate the biological from the psychological from the social, but rather weave

Figure I.1 River of integration. The river of integration represents the movement of a system across time. When the system is integrated, it is adaptive and harmonious in its functioning. When linkage of the differentiated elements (integration) does not occur, then the system moves to rigidity, chaos, or some combination of both.

them into a coherent whole. These are each aspects of the flow of energy and information. This is also an integrative approach in that each of the three elements of brain, mind, and relationships retain their sovereignty—they are not reducible to one another. They are fundamentals of human reality that mutually influence one another as the arrows of influence point in all directions connecting the three. Brain is the extended nervous system distributed throughout the whole body that is the physical mechanism of energy and information flow; mind is, in part, the way that this flow is regulated; relationships are the way energy and information flow is shared. Interpersonal neurobiology is integrative in yet a third sense: Seeing and shaping the internal world with mindsight permits us to track energy and information flow and promote linkage of differentiated elements as we move our relationships and our brains toward integration. This is how we monitor and modify energy and information flow so that we detect chaos and rigidity and move the system toward harmony. Our Figure I.1 reveals the river of integration in which the flexible and harmonious flow of integration is bounded on either side by rigidity and chaos.

Being a mindful therapist invites us to bring such integration and harmony into our own lives as we devote ourselves to helping others. This is our overall approach and the outline of where we can go together as we explore these important dimensions of our lives and of our work as clinicians in helping others heal and develop toward health.

THE MINDFUL THERAPIST

Chapter 1

PRESENCE

Being mindful in our lives is a skill that can be cultivated with specific mental practices we'll explore throughout this book. In every sense of the term *mindful*—being conscientious and intentional in what we do, being open and creative with possibilities, or being aware of the present moment without grasping onto judgments—being mindful is a state of awareness that enables us to be flexible and receptive and to have presence.

Being fully present through mindful awareness training has been demonstrated to be a crucial factor in giving us resilience to face challenges that arise in our daily lives. With such practice, we move toward an "approach" state of neural firing and move toward, rather than away from, difficult situations (see Davidson, et al., 2003). Rather than being consumed by worries about the future or preoccupations with the past, living fully in the present is an art form that liberates the mind to relieve mental suffering. These are the ways we develop presence in our own lives. Being present can also be seen as the most important element of helping others heal.

We are filled with potential. Health in many ways can be seen as bathing in a wide-open pool of possibility. Unhealth can be viewed as various rigid and chaotic ways we become unable to be present with this broad freedom. As human beings, we have an amazing set of possibilities, verging on the infinite, which our intricate brains are capable of whipping up into a life full of creative discovery. Yet too many of us live in physical or mental conditions that limit our options. At a minimum, we need food, clothing, shelter, a safe environment with clean water to drink, and clean air to breathe. It is a vital pursuit to attempt to ensure these crucial physical necessities of life for our living planet, this world so full of ever-increasing numbers of people and a dwindling variety of other species that share this earth with us (see Goleman, 2009). Being present in our lives enables us to be present for our planet. Not only does the effort to reach out and help one another bring relief to our suffering, but studies now reveal what wisdom traditions have long known: Working on behalf of others' well-being brings joy and purpose to our own lives (see Gilbert, 2010). We are built to nurture and to connect with one another (see Keltner, 2009). Yet finding this meaning in life in the service of others can take its toll if we are not prepared. Without ways to strengthen the mind—to build the resilience that comes with being present, with being mindful—we are at risk of becoming overwhelmed in the moment, and of burning out in the long run.

How we bring a full and receptive self into engagement with others, how we are present in life, can help in everything we do including the challenging pursuit of helping others and preserving and improving our physical world. If this is your passion, then cultivating presence and being mindful can provide you with the resourcefulness that can help you do your life's calling with more resilience and more efficacy. No matter your specific professional focus for reaching out to help, the inner dimension of what it means to be present is an important place to begin your training and your work. When we say that we are clinicians, therapists, or social and environmental activists, we are following the pursuit of bringing healing to others and our world. Whether you are fighting malaria or malnutrition, working to alleviate global warming and ecological destruction, practicing surgery, or focusing on intensive psychotherapy, there is always your own inner life that needs attending to in order for you to do your job well. *Well* means not only bringing presence to your work, but bringing resilience to your life. If you are practicing psychotherapy itself, the lessons we'll explore about being mindful are directly applicable to the growth of others. But even if you are in other forms of clinical or social intervention, the discussions and experiential immersions in these chapters may be useful in your work and in your personal life. In many ways, being present helps all around: We develop focus, resourcefulness, and perspective that support us as individuals and aid in helping others as well.

Caring for your self, bringing support and healing to your own efforts to help others and the larger worlds in which we live, is an essential daily practice—not a luxury, not some form of self-indulgence. But you may have heard people say that self-reflection is only for the selfish, that we need to "get out of our lives" to really find meaning. Then why would we spend even a moment looking inward? Why has research demonstrated that self-awareness is a starting point for emotional and social intelligence? (see Goleman, 1996 and 2007). Because no matter the challenges we confront, from famine and disease to environmental assaults, from psychological torture and escaping cultural genocide to the familial betrayal of childhood trauma, we come to our efforts to heal as human beings with a subjective inner life. There is no escaping this reality, no matter what others, or we, try to say about it. If we don't care for ourselves, we'll become limited in how we can care for others. It is that simple. And it is that important—for you, for others, and for our planet.

For these reasons, in this book we will be focusing primarily on the important starting place for all endeavors to help: the inner side of human life. We can call this the inner subjective world, the mental sea inside. This book is a professional's manual for growing from the inside out. It is this often-quiet subjective inner starting place that usually gets lost in the noise and tumult of outrageous acts of trauma, hidden beneath the clanging of external worlds in conflict.

But it is this inner sea that is the source of all healing—an internal life that provides the sustenance for quieting the clamor, of negotiating between nations at war, of soothing cross-generational tensions and liberating people to live freely and in the present.

THE REALITY OF SUBJECTIVE EXPERIENCE AND PHYSICAL EVENTS

This emerging discussion is not a conversation for those looking for quick fixes or easy answers. We are going to look reality head-on, weaving the internal subjective world of our lives with the external objective findings from modern science. For those new to this effort to weave a tapestry of the subjective and the objective into one integrated fabric, welcome to the world of interdisciplinary thinking. I know it would be easier to just put out exercises and overarching statements, but such an attempt would leave you, as a professional, without the necessary knowledge to be ready to approach your important work in helping others. In science we say, "Chance favors the prepared mind." My hope is that this unfolding conversation of science and subjectivity will prepare you to create the life and work that you want.

Let's begin with a framework that can help set the stage for how we approach synthesizing the quantitative rigor of scientific discoveries with the subtlety of our subjective lives. When we take a step back from the bustle of daily life, we come to one view in which reality can be divided into at least two fundamental aspects, two sides of one reality of our existence. In front of our eyes we see the visible side—the physical arrangement of things in the material, physical world. For example, if you raise your arm in front of your eyes, you can see your hand moving. You can also notice a flower growing in a garden, smell its aroma, touch the softness of its petals. These are all elements of the spatial side of our physical world. Yet equally real is the side of our one reality that is in the experiential aspect—the subjective sense of the red of the rose, the wafting sensations of its aroma in your inner experience, the memories of all flowers you've ever seen. We can also peer into the eyes of other people, soak in their facial expressions, and sense what their inner subjective world might be like. We receive input from the outer physical world of flowers or faces through our first five senses and then simultaneously experience subjective sensations enabling us to perceive that external world or that internal subjective world. Moving closer in, we can sense the input from the body—brought in through a sixth somatic sense. These are ways we take in the data from the physical world—of our body and of the external landscape in which we live. This is "how" we create subjective perceptions of the physical side of reality. There are quotes around the word *how* because no one on this planet actually knows the real "how" of how the physical property of neurons firing, for example, "creates" the subjective experience of seeing a rose. No one knows how we move from seeing a person crying to knowing the person is feeling sad. No one. And no one knows how thinking of a rose in your subjective experience gets the brain to fire in a particular pattern. And for this reason, some people say that turning to the physical world and trying to relate it to the inner subjective world is a useless task. Some have even said that it is destructive: that trying to weave the world of science with the world of subjectivity destroys the importance of our inner mental life. I hope you'll see that weaving a view of how the physical objective world coexists with the inner subjective world, if done with humility and openness, is actually quite empowering. We can look at this fundamental starting place in all discussions of mind and brain and find a new way of looking at this old question.

It is possible to perceive our inner sea—one that is distinct from this spatial, physical world of body and external objects. When you become aware of the rose as experienced in your sensory world and the images and emotions that the word *rose* evokes within your experience in time, you could say that you are sensing brain firing patterns. But do you mean by this that your sense of the rose is actually a sense of electrical conduction and synaptic linkages becoming active inside your skull? Or are you saying that these are correlated with one another—that at the time you have the subjective sense of seeing the rose, you know from your readings of research that the back of the brain—the occipital cortex—is becoming active? To look at this problem from a different angle, it is helpful to clarify some basic ideas.

The experiential, subjective side of reality is non-objective in that you couldn't weigh it, hold it in your hand, or capture the subjective nature of such inner experiences with a camera—not even with a functional brain-imaging scanner. This inner world, the subjective essence of our mental life, is not the same as brain activity. We may ascertain that in the moment of time when we sense fear we can also capture on a computerized scan an assembled technical image that the amygdala is becoming active in the limbic region of our brain. But notice how in truth we can only say that the physical firing and the subjective experience occur virtually at the same time: The amgydala firing is not the same as feeling fear. We need to keep an open mind about the direction of causal influences: Imagining fear may induce the amygdala to become active as much as the amygdala becoming active "gives us" the feeling of fear. How can we reconcile this important two-directional influence of mind (subjectivity and the mental, internal side of reality) and brain (the objective physical aspect of reality)?

Before we go too far, let me note that we need this question to be addressed right from the start if we are to have a deep, science-rich, subjectivity-illuminating discussion of what being mindful truly means. Here are some fundamental notions that will guide our journey.

Subjective experience does not exist in a physical location but it does exist in time. Think about "where" your feeling of fear or your sense of awe at the aroma of the rose is located in space. Right now, what do you feel inside yourself? What images arise in your mind's eye? While you may not be able to quantify the spatial dimensions of height, width, and depth that the feeling or image has—you can't actually put a physical ruler on it to measure the image in your mind—you know that your experience is real right now. But where is it in space? If you say "in my brain," you are equating neural firing with mental experience. The truth of our experiential, subjective side of reality is that it can coexist in time with the material, "objective" side of reality that does exist in space and can be measured in physical dimensions. Time is what these two sides of our one reality share. We can feel love now and simultaneously reveal activation in specific neural circuits of the brain. What they share in common is a co-occurrence in time—and so we say that they are correlated. Yet often the question arises of which came first—and then we're left struggling for answers.

If the answer to the issue of brain and mind were as unidirectional as the common statement, "the mind is just the activity of the brain," then there wouldn't be much more to talk about. Your brain will take care of everything. The natural implication would be that we are slaves to our brain. But findings from science now confirm the notion that the mind can activate the brain's circuitry in ways that change the brain's structural connections. In other words, you can use the subjective inner aspect of reality to alter the objective physical structure of the brain.

This issue is not just some academic discussion or debate about intellectual issues. If we can awaken our minds to move our brains in a certain direction of growth, we can then build the neural circuitry of resilience and compassion. We can use the mind to transform our brains and our lives. Not bad for a mind that is often disregarded in modern life, basically ignored in contemporary education, and invisible to the physical eye.

As we move forward in our discussions of what being present means—of how we become a mindful therapist—these fundamental notions of reality are actually deeply relevant though they may initially seem somewhat abstract. If these considerations are new and you are feeling a little out there in the ether, please bear with me. Soon we'll see that the subjectivity of mental experience and the objectivity of neural firing can be happily synthesized into one framework that helps to prepare your mind to take on challenges and understand mysteries that before may have seemed impossible to master.

GETTING DOWN TO BASICS: PRIMES AND POSSIBILITY

The experiential and physical sides of reality can be considered *primes*. Prime is a term denoting that something is a basic, grounded element that cannot be further dissected, further reduced. A prime is solid ground—and we can consider the experiential and physical sides of reality as primes. Spending a week with a range of scientists and contemplative practitioners exploring the topic of science and spirituality led to some fascinating discussions in which we wrestled with these issues of subjectivity and neural firing. With one physicist-physician-philosopher, Michel Bitbol, I had a deeply rewarding discussion of the nature of reality and this view of primes. What emerged from this discussion was the idea that the experience of a sensation like love may correlate in time with the firing of specific brain areas in physical space, but both are primes and "coarise" together. The feeling of love and the activation of neural circuits share the time dimension—one is experiential, the other physical. It is fair to say the neural firing can create the feeling of love; and it is equally fair to say that the feeling of love can create neural firing. We do not need to give dominance or superiority to one side or another. They are two sides of one coin. Would you fight with someone over whether one coin consisted of either heads or tails in its wholeness? We can look forward to the likelihood that as time progresses, more scientific and philosophical explorations of this question of mind and matter will yield new insights into the nature of reality. But for now, we can have the working position that the wholeness of one reality has at least two aspects that co-occur in time: the physical and the mental sides of reality.

So this is our working framework of reality on which our synthesis of science and subjectivity will be based. After that conference on science and spirituality, I was riding the train back to Florence with several students from the week-long gathering. We had been immersed in experiential mornings of tai chi, qigong, dance, and singing, followed by intellectual discussions of the nature of reality and human experience, and then afternoons of more discussions, experiential immersions, and time for private reflection and informal gatherings. During the evenings we continued with the same. It was quite a week that taught me the lesson of how important experiential practice is to balance the lure of abstract conceptual discussions. On the train, a mother from Wisconsin picking her daughter up from a year abroad listened in on our discussion of how to reconcile these issues of reality. I took out my journal and wrote out a figure to try to illustrate visually this notion of two sides of one reality. Listening to our discussion, the mother leaned over to me when we were getting ready to leave the train and said, "Please send me the conference directors' address as I feel like I need to send them a tuition check. This was so interesting—and useful!" I hope it will be for you, too. In Figure 1.1 you'll find a visual image of this way of viewing reality.

Imagine that reality is shaped by probabilities—a view supported by quantum mechanics (which we discussed at length throughout our week). Within a singular plane of reality, picture the sense of completely open possibility. Nothing is determined; anything is possible. Then as events happen through time (along the x-axis toward the right), sometimes our position with respect to this open *plane of possibility* moves outward, away from the plane, and we move toward a state of probability. If I say "fruit," you've moved from anything-is-equally-likely to becoming more likely to think of a fruit. This shift from possibility to probability is visually depicted as moving from the plane to an elevated *valenced plateau of probability* on each side of the plane—the physical and the subjective. If I then say "tomato" you may go straight up to the tomato image that

Subjective Experience

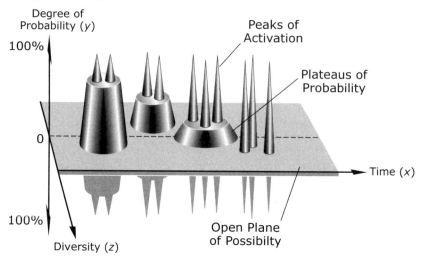

Neural Firing

Figure 1.1 The plane of possibility. This is a visual metaphor for embracing several dimensions of human experience. (1) We can envision that our primes of neural firing (below the plane) and mental subjective experience (above the plane) reflect one another—and sometimes one leads the other, as the brain drives subjective experience or the focus of attention drives neural firing across time (represented on the x-axis). (2) Based on degrees of probability, the y-axis (vertically above and below the plane) graphs when open possibility exists in the plane (as in open mindful awareness), or certainty manifests at a peak of activation (a particular thought, feeling, memory—and their parallel in neural firing). (3) The diversity of mental experience or neural firing possible is symbolized along the z-axis (away and toward you out of the page) so that the wider the zone along this axis, the more variety of neural firing/mental experience is possible. The plane is wide open; the plateau is broad or narrow, but limited in its diversity; a peak of activation is singular in its array of mental experience or neural firing. (4) A peak represents a specific activation of mind or brain instantiated in that instant—activations that are committed to manifest as that particular activity in that moment of time. A plateau represents a state of mind or profile of neural firing that may have various shapes and degrees of height and broadness: Lower means less certainty of which firings might be possible and wider signifies more variety, a wider set of propensities; higher indicates a greater probability of firing of those options that are primed or made more likely to occur in that state or profile, and narrower indicates a more restricted set of choices of which peaks might arise from that particular plateau. The open plane of possibility reveals a zero probability that any particular peak or plateau will arise and thus represents an open state of mindful awareness and a receptive neural profile at that moment.

would be revealed as a *peak of activation*. You've moved from open possibility to probability to activation of an actual committed event at that instant in time. To capture this movement, we can picture a point that is either on the plane of possibility, on the valenced plateau of probability, or the peak of activation.

As each of us have tendencies derived from both our temperament and our accumulated experiences, we may also have a set of proclivities in how we live in the world as well. This aspect of both our subjective mental experience and our neural firing patterns is revealed as distinctive shapes, perimeters, and heights of our plateaus that we call personality, as we'll discuss in Chapter 11.

A key to this figure is that this movement away from the plane of possibility (along the y-axis, up and down) happens in two directions virtually simultaneously. At the very time we experience the mental image of the tomato on the subjective side, we also move outward to the neural firing pattern within the brain that correlates with the image of the tomato. These are peaks of activation. The sense of fruit may be beneath direct conscious access—or it may just be revealed as a hunger for a snack—but the neural priming, the brain's getting ready to fire off images of all sorts of fruit, would be manifest in synaptic linkages becoming more likely to fire off in the future. These valenced states are depicted as plateaus of increased probability.

In the open plane of possibility, a nearly infinite number of combinations of neural firing and subjective experiences are available. As we move through time, our personality expresses itself as tendencies of neural firing and the subjective focus of our attention and emotional responses in the shape of our various plateaus across time. As we continue to narrow our patterns of experience and firing, we move from spaciousness of possibility and clusters of predispositions in our set of plateaus toward a *particular plateau* as some firing patterns or subjective experiences become more likely to occur. This, for example, might happen if you ready yourself to play tennis—your brain moves toward firing patterns preparing you to compete; your mental sea activates a sense of excitement and memories of prior games. When you take your racket and make specific actions, your physical side of reality moves toward a peak of activation in that instant as your neural firing patterns activate specific motor pathways. On the mental side of reality, this peak involves feeling a certain rush as you sense the movement of your body and the thrill of competition. If you were to imagine yourself playing a game, the subjective experience of creating detailed images of a tennis match might drive neural firing patterns—just as the actual playing of the game might make the neural activity drive your subjective experience.

This visual metaphor of the connection between the two fundamental primes of the physical/neural side and mental/subjective side of our one reality enables us to go back and forth between these two sides of the single domain of existence. We are not creating a dualism here—but rather accepting the stance that the physical and mental sides of reality are equally real and mutually influence each other. For some, like Descartes, these were two independent worlds. Modern philosophers (see Wallace, 2008) also see combining the physical and mental worlds into one as a philosophical error. Yet modern neuroscience sometimes goes to the other extreme, making the brain supreme and the mind a slave— just an outcome of neural firing patterns. I'm sure there will be a host of objections to seeing mental and neural each as different primes that coarise, but for now let's go with this model, as it helps us envision one very important issue: Sometimes the brain leads the mind, pulling it along, as it is the driving force of our experience. But other times, as this model reveals, the mind leads the way and uses the brain to create itself. Studies now reveal that mental activity can get the brain to fire off in specific patterns—and ultimately change the brain's structure (see Doidge, 2007). One example of such study is the research into the impact of mental imagery as a form of practice. Musicians and athletes who imagine practicing their instruments or sports not only attain excellent results in terms of maintaining and advancing their physical skills, but they have demonstrated alterations in brain growth as a result of this mental activity.

This framework for viewing reality also enables us to explore more deeply what being present may really mean. Presence may require that we move both our neural and our mental sides of experience flexibly toward the open plane of possibility. Rather than being rigidly stuck in repeating patterns of peaks, blindly influenced by our moods in plateaus of probability, or being a slave to our particular personality predilections in rigidly confined plateau patterns, we can move freely to the plane and create fresh approaches to old problems. Such a view permits us to put words to the notion that being receptive makes us available to shift into an open internal place and enable unpredictable states to be created so that we may resonate with others. This is a way of seeing how we can intentionally cultivate creativity and presence in our lives.

This metaphor of the plane also helps us see how our brain's firing patterns will change just as our subjective inner sea will be altered in response to the signals from someone else. If we have preconceived ideas, if we are taken over by judgments, our plateaus of probability or our peaks of activation will block us from being truly open, from having open presence. Presence happens when we can freely move in and out of the open plane of possibility. Learning to monitor these neural and subjective aspects of reality and then to modify them toward the open plane of possibility is a visual image of what it means to be mindful. Learning to develop the skill of moving into the open plane of possibility can cultivate presence in our lives and in our relationships.

We can say that being present with others involves the experience of openness to whatever arises in reality. Presence means being open, now, to whatever is. We come to acknowledge our own proclivities and in that awareness, free ourselves to move from peak to plateau to plane with ease and will.

This model links our subjective core with our neural reality in a way that is unifying rather than divisive. But we can only be open to seeing how this unfolds. I used to think like this back in high school, and believe me, it didn't make me many friends in the locker room or the school yard. So you can understand how I might feel reluctant to go full throttle with this view right from the get-go. But I think it may work—and teaching this in seminars has proven very rewarding, so here we are.

Naturally we often try with words in sentences and paragraphs to get the gist of something out from inside of us to connect with others. Or we can communicate using pictures, drawings, or photographs, or with music, dance, or touch. But whatever way I try to get my inner subjective experience out into the world to connect with you, the truth is that my inner world can never be fully communicated. We can only do our best in this setting. My heart is into sharing this view with you, so I hope you'll continue even further along this journey. All any of us can do is try our best, humbly knowing that it is never complete. Any map of a territory is just that: a guide, not a prison. If the metaphor is useful to illuminate the way and to facilitate communication, then perhaps it will serve a helpful function for us. Let's see how that goes.

And so we've imagined a visual image of "reality" as including a plane of possibility and the axes of time, diversity, and probability. As we move from open possibility toward probability and activation, we move out in the two directions above and below the plane toward our two aspects of the physical and mental sides of reality. Perhaps you've thought of more aspects besides the physical in three-dimensional space and the mental in subjective experience, the "space of the mind," if you will. For now, let's stick with these two sides of reality and see where we can go with this view. Let's return again with a general example to illustrate how this model of reality works in real time. As we move from the level of this two-dimensional plane outward, into the third dimension above or below the plane itself, we've moved from open possibility within the plane to instantiated actuality beyond the plane. Within the plane, possibility is wide open, or what some might prefer to call infinite or undefined. For example, you can think of anything you'd like at this moment. You are in the plane and the possibilities of mental experience or brain activity are open, undefined, virtually infinite. When you read "Eiffel Tower," your physical brain response might be to activate specific neural firing patterns that have encoded the tower in the past while your experiential side may involve seeing the tower in your mind's eye. With seeing or hearing the name "Eiffel Tower," you went from open possibility within the plane to lived actuality as a peak beyond the plane. At this moment in time you've moved outward on one side with the experience of seeing the tower, and you've moved outward on the other side of neuronal activity. These are the ways subjective experience is correlated with the physical component of neural firing. It's as if a probability cone was stretched outward in two directions away from the plane, above and below the plane's level. This bidirectional movement of the cone is symmetric on either side of the plane as subjective and physical mirror one another. As the cone moves away from the plane, on each side, the infinite width within the plane narrows at the plateau and comes to a point of the cone at the peak. Now that you've seen or heard "Eiffel Tower" and the image subsides and neural firing ceases, you return moving down from peak to a slice of the cone lower down called the valenced plateau of probability. This is the plateau that makes it more likely you'll think of crepes than of tacos. As time involves this stretching, first we move toward increased probabilities (of wanting a crepe). Then events may occur and the further away from the plane we move, the more restricted the probabilities become until we are actually thinking of that crepe. This is the tip of the cone, our peak of activation. We've narrowed from open possibility (within the plane) to increased probability (in the plateau) to specific actuality (at the peak). As you move back toward the plane, first you return to a plateau of probability, and then back to the nearly infinite set of possible firing patterns (physically) or to experiences (mentally) that are wide open and you've now returned to the open plane of possibility.

Presence can be viewed as the flexible motion back and forth from within the plane to plateaus and peaks as we move from possibility to probability to activation, and back again down to possibility. Presence is this open and flexible movement through time.

Presence involves the flexible movement in and out of these layers of experience so that we are not locked into some biasing propensity of restricting probability, or fixed patterns of activation. We fluidly and freely move from a specific thought or feeling (in experience) or a particular firing pattern in the brain or overt behavior (in space) toward the more flexible probability, and ultimately back into open possibility. The capacity to move in and out of this set of transitions is what we are going to define as *presence*. And presence is a learnable skill. This is the key: We can learn to loosen the grip of habit and engrained aspects of what we call personality to become more mindful. We can learn to monitor our internal world—in mind and brain—and then modify it so that we can cultivate presence as not only an intentionally created state, but as an enduring trait in our lives.

What a way to begin our conversation. My own experience at this moment in time is filled with worry that you'll find this all too abstract. A worry tunnels through my experiential mind: "I hope you don't slam the book shut!" A part of me wants to delete this whole bit regarding the notion of two sides of one reality, of the plane of possibility, the plateaus, the peaks. Why can't we just make this some straightforward book on the research into mindfulness? Why can't we just have a salad or a sandwich in the courtyard and talk about the homecoming game next week? My plateaus are primed for rejection and isolation. But maybe, just maybe, this time will be different . . . and of course, our whole field of helping others, especially within psychotherapy, requires that we dive deeply into the nature of our subjective mental lives. My peaks of conviction of rejection move back to some plateaus of concern . . . and now, with a few breaths at the center of my awareness, resting back into a familiar but less restrictive plateau of merely doubt and vigilance. I follow my breath, in and out, now letting myself move back to an open plane of possibility. Sometimes we need to name it to tame it, to look head-on into the plateaus and peaks of life and loosen their rigid hold as we soften the peaks, broaden our plateaus and relax back into the open plane of possibility. This is where we all begin, indeed it is a place we all share, and it is a great place in which we can find clarity when we return. This is how we move back to presence.

By starting with the grounding in this view, we'll be able to fluidly move back and forth from discussions of the brain (in physical space) to explorations of internal life (in the mental sea inside), which is crucial to all that we'll be doing. If we don't start with these basics, it may be difficult to develop an in-depth understanding of these important issues about healing. We could be then at risk of unhelpful and simplistic statements like, "the mind is just the activity of the brain" or "knowing about the brain has no place in psychotherapy because therapy is a subjective and intersubjective experience." But being prepared also involves making these ideas about reality and healing accessible to everyday life. Let's bring this important initial conceptual framework into a story revealing its practical application.

THE PLANE IN ACTION AND THE VITAL IMPORTANCE OF PRESENCE

If I am seeing a patient and she comes in with a headache, I may review in my mind all of the possible causes of her pain. This, by the way, is a true story of such an encounter when I was a trainee in pediatrics over a quarter of a century ago. As this 15-year-old, Maria, tells me her story, I become concerned that she is suffering because of the stress of homework and the conflicts she is having with her friends. But as her story unfolds, something grabs my attention in the way she points to her head and tells me that only when she sleeps on her right side does her head really hurt in the morning. Those words, "really hurt," echo in my mind. I look at the back of Maria's eyes and find that the retina looks a bit cloudy—a sign of increased cranial pressure. I bring in my supervising doctor (I am just an intern in pediatrics) who tells me the patient's eyes look fine. But that doesn't sit well with me, so I have a neurologist come in to consult and check her eyes as well. He also concurs that Maria's eyes look fine. At my request, the consulting infectious disease expert comes in too, agrees with the others, and tells me that Maria needs a spinal tap. It's 5 o'clock, so I need to take her down to the emergency room to continue with the evaluation.

As I am preparing to carry out this procedure, cleaning Maria's back, getting my instruments ready, a huge wave of "No!" arises from my belly and into my head (we can view this now with our new framework as neural firing rising up from networks in my gut and heart, through an area called Lamina 1 in the spinal cord and then registering in the midline areas of my prefrontal region, including the insula and the anterior cingulate cortices—areas we'll discuss in great detail soon). Then my subjective side of reality picks up a sensation that enters my awareness. I experience a sudden sense of panic. I tell the patient and her mother, and the medical student who is studying with me, that we cannot go forward. Even though it will cost thousands of dollars, I insist that they get a CT scan to rule out anything that might be raising her cerebrospinal fluid's pressure. If that pressure is indeed elevated, the brain would push downward as the spinal tap was initiated and the patient would die almost immediately.

The mother pleads with me to "just do the tap" as the infectious disease professor had recommended. But my body says no. After the mother borrows money from her employer—rather than having Maria transferred to the county hospital—the brain scan is done. I go about seeing other patients in the ER awaiting her results. Then I receive a call from the radiologist; Maria has been found to have massively elevated pressure due to parasites growing in her brain. (They are growing at the exit of her spinal fluid down into her spine, and they likely moved to further block the exit of this pressure-raising fluid whenever she laid her head to the right—causing the increased pain in her head.) I relate this story to you now to illustrate the notion that being present with someone can save a life. Though my teachers—all three of them—were likely viewing the physical exam findings accurately, my whole being was involved in sensing what might truly be going on with Maria. The professors did the best they could with their unavoidably limited amount and forms of data. I was the clinician being with Maria. Being present with her literally means being open to all that emerges from that "being with." Presence is vital in our clinical work. Nothing substitutes for presence.

With Maria, I needed to be open to many possibilities. My initial idea that Maria was just stressed had to be released so that I could be receptive to consider other notions, other feelings, other sensations. I needed to allow myself to move back toward the plane of possibility from those naturally created considerations—those plateaus and peaks of thought and analysis. I had to be open to the possibility that my teacher was wrong, and that the other two consultants were wrong, so that I could trust another possibility. Others' opinions and reactions move us from the plane into plateau as we consider their point of view. That is necessary and important. Life cannot be lived in a vacuum in which we sit cross-legged in the plane all the time. We need to brush our teeth, pay our taxes, and make actual decisions. Each of these requires careful consideration and action within the plateaus and peaks of life. Presence involves the fluid movement from plane to plateau to peak and back down again to the plane in an ever-opening movement across time. What intellect and consultation did not provide, my own body's signals offered up as a gut instinct that helped me know what to do—or in this case, not to do. Our gut feelings are in no way always accurate, but they often provide an important source of knowing. Being open to the many ways of knowing may be crucial as we make our way through life. Being open involves receiving the input from throughout our experience, from the body to memory, from intellect and sensation, and then assessing its validity. In this case, it saved Maria's life. I was just being present and doing my job.

In all these ways, we can see that instantiated peaks marched through time—as "facts" shared in Maria's clinical evaluation, as opinions offered by reliable consultants, as clinical decisions that had to be considered and interventions planned. But presence enabled my physical and subjective sides of reality to move back to the open plane of possibility. Perhaps my plateau of learning to constantly question authority and never take anything for granted was helpful in moving my way through the barrage of recommendations that would have ended Maria's life. I had made a point early in my education to not assume that people's conviction of something being true was necessarily related to the accuracy of their statements. That, as my friends know all too well, is just my personality. No one knows all the factors at play in an experience and I try to keep an open mind as best I can about the nature of reality. That's my propensity, my general baseline starting place. Yet the fact is, we do need to come to firm views of things, to take a stance, to move in a specific direction of treatment. We do need to listen to our older, wiser elders. But simultaneously we need to get continual feedback about how our clinical evaluation and interventions are going and be open to letting go of considered specifics, of moving back from the peaks of activation and plateaus of probability into the plane of possibility. Such feedback is a key element of effective psychotherapy of all sorts (see Norcross, 2002). Presence enables us to seek such feedback and helps us to move in and out of the flow from possible to probable to actual and back and forth again with ease. The key is to be aware of where we are in that movement—in the plane of open possibility, resting in our familiar plateaus, stretching out to the bias of our state of mind as a raised plateau limiting our options, or instantiating in that instant on a particular actuality as we commit to a particular peak of activation. With this awareness of where we are in these *conal movements* to the two sides of reality, we have the freedom of choice, moving flexibly in and out of the plane of possibility with the open fluidity of presence.

BRAIN BASICS

As we move through these chapters, we'll embed direct discussions of relevant aspects of the brain. We could draw on a wide array of sciences, as other books in this series do wonderfully. But here we'll stick primarily to neuroscience to focus in on this boundary between the subjective and the objective in the creation of mindful presence.

Presence depends upon a sense of safety. The brain continually monitors the external and internal environment for signs of danger in a process called *neuroception*, a term coined by Steven Porges (see Porges, 2009). When danger is assessed, we go on high alert and activate the fight-flight-freeze response. Neuroceptive evaluation involves prefrontal, limbic, and brainstem processes and is shaped by ongoing appraisal of the significance of an event and the reference to historical events of a similar type from the past. For example, if I raise my hand and you've never been hurt by another person before, you may interpret this to mean that I'll be asking a question or hailing a cab. On the other hand, if you've been traumatized earlier in your life, you may interpret the intention of my raising a hand with a sense that I'm about to strike you. Same action—yet coupled with a different interpretation that is driven by a past-biased assessment of safety or danger. Our past experiences, especially of unresolved trauma, restrict our plateaus and create valenced states that bias how we'll be able to openly assess various situations. It's hard to be present when you think you're about to be hit. These plateaus make us filter input in a particular way and then make a specific action or interpretation more likely to occur. From our particular plateaus we move up to one of a set of specific peaks. With a history of trauma, your system moves from open possibility to proclivity and probability, and then to activation in fast succession, making you vulnerable to being driven away from the state of presence. Knowing your own tendencies of neuroceptive evaluation is an important first step in creating presence as a therapist. Teaching such inner ways of sensing the world can be profoundly important for clients, as we'll see in future chapters. When we see things as threatening, we have left the open state of receptive presence and entered the reactive state of fight-flight-or-freeze.

The feeling of fight may emerge as a tensing of the muscles, an increase in our heart rate and breathing, a clenching of the jaws, and a rising feeling of anger or rage. Flight may also be activating as well, as the accelerator-like sympathetic branch of the autonomic nervous system is also engaged, but this time we are driven to run rather than to attack. You may have an impulse to bolt, to avoid a topic, to turn your eye gaze away from me. Fight or flight narrows our focus of attention on strategies of attack or routes of escape. This narrowing of attention shuts off the openness of presence as we become filled with biased probabilities or fixed activations.

With freeze, we do not engage the sympathetic nervous system, but rather the dorsal branch of the brake-like parasympathetic system. Now we've activated the slowly responding unmyelinated part of the vagal nerve that slows our heart rate and respiration, drops our blood pressure, and can even move us to faint. This is the "dorsal dive." The benefit of these responses is to get us to lay flat to keep blood moving to our head—or to look dead in case a predator is about to devour us. Carnivores prefer to eat living prey rather than the possibly decaying carcasses that would make them ill. The dorsal dive can save your life out on the savanna.

Naturally a feeling of helplessness that can evoke the freeze reaction also pervades our whole system and limits our options for response and thinking. We become frozen, stuck in a state of terror, and shut down our sense of possibility as we isolate ourselves from involvement with others, and even with ourselves. Here the plateaus and peaks are on survival mode and drive our inner experience and neural firing patterns in engrained and limiting ways.

With the sense of danger, we cannot activate what Porges calls the *social engagement system*. And we don't access what I've called a *self-engagement system* either (see Siegel, 2007a). Instead of being present with mindfulness, we become removed, alone, and paralyzed. This is how we move from being receptive to being reactive.

In these ways, a sense of danger and its subsequent activation of the fight-flight-freeze response obscure a therapist's or a client's presence. With patients we then disengage, shut down, and find ourselves removed. Notice how this is not the same as not being able to find the words to speak or just feeling unclear about how to proceed. Perceived danger removes us, shuts down our options, and limits presence. And for our patients, becoming reactive restricts their capacity to be open to our own presence and therapeutic interventions.

Being open to whatever arises can sometimes create a state of wonder, when no words easily come, but we remain open to others, and to ourselves. In this way, too, presence requires a tolerance for both uncertainty and vulnerability. It is these very features that enable us to offer help to others who struggle with their own guardedness and drives for certainty.

If I had become a prisoner to this fear of danger in dealing with Maria, her mother, or my professors, I might have pushed on with the spinal tap, fearing my professors' response to my not doing what they had recommended. Fortunately I didn't ask them about the CT scan so that they may have talked me out of it. I just "knew" what I had to do. Being present to the importance of the signal of "No" as a sign of danger was ironically crucial: I had to be present for the emerging sense of becoming reactive to doing the spinal tap. And so the key is to be aware and flexible as we allow our own internal responses to inform us rather than entrap us. Being present doesn't mean that anything goes or that we cannot make decisions and take action. Presence is not the same as being passive. Presence means we can become open to the truth rather than clouded by our own or others' erroneous and fixed judgments. Presence is an actively receptive state.

As therapists it is essential that we monitor our internal world for neuroceptive signs of the assessment of danger. When we detect a fight-flight-freeze response in our own body as tension or deflation, as an internal sense of anger, fear, or helplessness, we need to do the internal work necessary to bring ourselves out of such distress so that we can return to a state of presence. This is how we can sense peaks and plateaus in our inner life and intentionally move ourselves, when it is right to do so, back toward the open plane of possibility.

MINDSIGHT SKILLS

As we move through our chapters, we'll also dive deeply into practical exercises to develop our perceptual abilities to track energy and information in the triangle of well-being. This *triception* (perception of the triangle) is what mindsight permits as we sense the interconnected nature of the mind, the brain, and our relationships with one another. These are the mindsight skills that we'll explore in this chapter to support our ability to be present.

After nearly two decades of working with a view of the mind derived from an interdisciplinary study group of scientists, it has been profoundly rewarding to have a working definition of a core aspect of the mind that provides useful applications to help reduce suffering. The vast majority of mental health practitioners have not been offered any definition of the mind. I've found that of over 85,000 therapists in a wide array of disciplines on four different continents, less than 5% have ever had even one lecture defining the mind. Amazing, don't you think? But as surprising as that may be, it turns out even many mind scientists and philosophers of mind suggest that defining the mind is not possible or that it should not be done—and they also do not have a definition of the mind. Here we'll explore a definition of aspects of the mind that have been of great benefit in helping people in clinical settings—but be well informed that this is not a common or necessarily scientifically or philosophically sanctioned move to define the mind.

The mind can be defined, in part, as an embodied and relational process that regulates the flow of energy and information. As one important feature of the mind is a regulatory process, the mind has at least two essential aspects: monitoring and modifying. When we drive a car, we need to monitor where we're going and then modify our direction and speed. Mindsight enables us to see the flow of energy and information more clearly and in depth and then to shape that flow in a desired positive direction—often toward an integrated state that we'll be exploring throughout this book.

To monitor energy and information flow with more depth and power, we'll be exploring specific mindsight skill training exercises throughout the book. These sections can serve as a mental gym, a time to pause from the ideas and conceptual framework, to take a break from the brain science, and dive into experiential exercises aimed at building the strength and agility of your own mind. With our working definition of one aspect of the mind as a regulatory process, we can build these two components of regulation as we cultivate the mind. We can strengthen monitoring skills and we can build modifying skills. These are the two components comprising what we'll be doing in these skill-training sections of each chapter.

As a start, let me introduce you to a monitoring exercise. Notice how you feel when you read or hear these words:

No.

No.

No.

No.

No.

No.

No.

Now sense how you feel when you read or hear these words:

Yes.

Yes.

Yes.

Yes.

Yes.

Yes.

Yes.

What did you notice?

Some people feel a tightening with "No," a constriction, a shutting-down, sometimes even anger at me for saying the words.

With "Yes," what did you feel? Some find this uplifting, energizing, freeing, opening, giving a sense of relief and release. There is no right or wrong response; whatever you feel is the reality of your subjective side.

The physical side of those experiences for many of us may be that with "No" we enter a reactive state—perhaps with elements of fight, flight, or freeze. With "Yes" we may create a receptive state. These two basic aspects of our internal experience, being reactive or receptive, are crucial elements with which we can become familiar.

When we are reactive, presence is shut off. When we are receptive, presence can be created.

This was just a small monitoring exercise to begin the focused attention skill of looking inward. Doing this with patients enables them to experience, firsthand, the difference between being receptive and being reactive. With couples I've found that doing this "no-yes" exercise is invaluable in teaching the skill of sensing these reactive states and then asking for a break to help move them back to receptivity. No helpful communication can generally emerge from a reactive state.

Now here is a modifying exercise: Try finding a quiet place where you'll not be disturbed by people or technological intrusions for at least 5 minutes. Once there, I invite you to try (what may be familiar to some) the widespread practice of focusing on the breath. This universal and basic exercise goes like this:

If sitting up, place both feet on the ground, legs unfolded. If sitting on the floor, you can cross your legs or lie flat. (Try not to sleep, at least not yet. This will require that you monitor your state of alertness, something we'll explore more later on.) Now let your eyes focus on the middle of the room. Now focus on the far wall (or the ceiling if you're lying flat on your back). Bring the focus of attention back to the middle of the room, and then to about book-reading distance. Notice how you can determine where your attention goes.

Now let your eyes close, if you feel comfortable with that, and let your attention find your breath. (You'll need to read this whole entry first if you're not listening to this out loud.) You may notice the gentle sensations of air flowing in and out of your nostrils. Just spend a few moments sensing the breath there, in and out. Now, notice how your attention can move down to the level of your chest and sense the movement in and out of the chest as the air moves in and out of your lungs. Just ride the waves of the breath, focusing on the sensation of your chest rising and falling with each breath.

Now notice how you can let your attention move down to the level of your abdomen as you sense the inward and outward movement of your belly. (You may find putting your hand over your abdomen helpful if you find it difficult to sense your belly's movement at first.) As air moves into your lungs, the diaphragm pulls downward and pushes your abdomen outward; as air moves out of your lungs, your belly moves inward. Just sense the breath in and out, riding the waves of the breath as you focus on the sensation of your abdomen moving in and out. (Abdominal breathing is more relaxing than chest-breathing, and it may be helpful to practice this belly-focus on your own to cultivate this more calming breathing).

For this initial exercise, just let your awareness rest on the sensation of the breath wherever you notice it most readily—the abdomen, the chest, the nostrils, or perhaps the sensation of the whole body breathing. Just let your attention ride the sensations of the breath, in and out.

After a few minutes of this exercise, how do you feel? For some, sensing the breath is difficult. For others, sensing the breath is deeply soothing. If focusing on the breath is not helpful for you now, it may help to continue to try a few more times. But after a while, you may want to find another focus of attention to begin with, such as the bottoms of your feet as you walk slowly for a dozen paces back and forth, or find another initial practice such as yoga or tai chi or centering prayer. Others prefer focusing on a peaceful place—an image from memory or imagination such as a beach or a park. The breath for some does not turn out to be a source of comfort while other objects of attention do. Each of us is different and finding the particular basic focus that brings you to an open, receptive place will be important.

Whatever the focus of attention, each of these mindful awareness practices involves an aiming of our awareness on two basic dimensions: *Awareness of awareness* and *attention to intention*. Such mindfulness practices may activate the receptive state of a self- and social-engagement system and bring a deep sense of clarity. As the majority of people find the breath soothing, we'll focus there, but if for you another focus is preferred, please substitute that for our breath awareness practices in the pages ahead.

Studies reveal that with mindful awareness practice, we come to approach rather than withdraw from challenges. This subjective finding is correlated with the physical changes of a "left shift," in which the electrical activity of the left frontal area of the cortex increases after mindfulness meditation training (see Urry et al., 2004). This left shift is thought to reflect a shift toward the approach state of the left hemisphere—in contrast to the tendency of right frontal activation to be associated with withdrawal from novelty or challenge. For this reason alone, formal mindfulness training is thought to promote resilience, the ability to approach rather than withdraw from difficult issues. In these ways of creating receptivity and an approach state, mindful awareness practices can be considered the basic training of the mind for any therapist.

Beyond focusing on the breath (or body part or image or candle or stone if those are what your target is), here is the next modifying aspect of this practice. When your focus of attention becomes distracted, when you notice you are no longer aware of the sensations of the breath, lovingly and gently bring your attention back to the breath (or body part or image). Getting distracted is just what our minds do. As we've seen, if you think of this mindfulness training as being similar to toning a muscle, we need to have both the contraction and the relaxation to achieve muscle growth. Contraction is our concentration—the activation of the muscle of the mind's attention—while relaxation is our becoming distracted as attention is deactivated. We activate intentionally, deactivate unintentionally—inadvertently, unavoidably and repeatedly—and then reactivate the directing of attention to refocus on our chosen subject of attention. See if you can let go of your frustration, letting it float off as just a feeling arising in your field of awareness, and then return your focus to the breath. Refocusing attention and letting go of feelings of impatience or irritation, attending to your intention to focus on the breath and be kind to yourself, and being aware of your awareness are all aspects of strengthening the monitoring and modifying aspects of your mind.

If you can find a mindfulness practice that you can do every day—even if just for 5 or 10 minutes a day, perhaps building up to 20 minutes a day—I hope you'll discover like so many people that you can develop a new capacity to both monitor and modify your internal world. Whatever your focus—the breath in mindfulness meditation, your postures in yoga, your movements in tai chi, the sense of motion of energy in qigong, your words in centering prayer, your feet in walking meditation, the body in a body-scan, images in single-pointed imagery of a peaceful place—the idea is similar: When you get distracted, lovingly and gently return the focus of your attention back to its aim.

Over 100 years ago, the father of modern psychology, William James (1890/1981), said that such a practice of returning a wandering attention back to its target again and again would be the "education par excellence." He also stated that the trouble was that we didn't know how to accomplish this. The truth is, we actually do. Such mindfulness practice is akin to keeping your brain healthy and fit. We keep the health of our bodies well by keeping physically active with regular exercise. Mindfulness exercises are daily *brain fitness practices* that study after study suggest keep our brain healthy and our mind resilient. This is the way we can keep our selves well: with regular exercising of our attunement to ourselves through mindfulness practices.

In other publications, I've proposed that integration is at the heart of well-being (Siegel, 1995, 1999, 2001) and I have highlighted nine specific domains of integration that can be cultivated (Siegel, 2006, 2007a, 2010). In many ways, integration forms the foundation for our explorations of interpersonal neurobiology (also see Cozolino, 2002, 2010; Badenoch, 2008). Here we'll be referring to these various domains of integration as they fit into our larger framework of the PART of therapy that works (PARTr 12).

Mindfulness is one aspect of the first domain of the *integration of consciousness*. For ourselves as therapists, doing a mindfulness training exercise creates an intentionally established state of mindful awareness. We are open to what is, noticing feelings and thoughts come and go, and yet keeping our mind's eye on our state of awareness and our intention. With the repeated creation of an intentional state, soon the brain responds by strengthening the neural connections activated at the time, and we can develop mindfulness as a trait. Here is a good example of how we can use the focus of our attention with our minds to stimulate the neuronal activation and growth of specific circuits of the brain. (I'll reintroduce the term

SNAG, stimulate neuronal activation and growth, here as it is so useful for encapsulating what we do in therapy.)

These traits involve a set of nine middle prefrontal functions that include regulating our bodies, attuning to others, having emotional balance, calming fear, pausing before acting, having insight and empathy, being moral in our thinking and our actions, and having more access to intuition. Put another way, it is possible (but not proven as yet) that with mindfulness practice we may become more nonjudgmental, develop equanimity, be more aware of what is going on as it is happening, and develop the capacity to label and describe with words our internal world. We may even develop the ability to have more self-observation. These five features are the mindfulness traits that Ruth Baer and her colleagues (2006) have described in their assessment research as independent dimensions of being a mindful person. Future work will tell if mindfulness practices systematically develop these described traits.

THE ROLE OF INTEGRATION IN PRESENCE

Putting all of these practices and concepts together, what presence may essentially be is the ability to create an integrated state of being that becomes a trait in our lives. We've stated that integration is the linkage of differentiated parts. When a system becomes integrated, it is the most flexible, adaptive, coherent, energized, and stable. (Okay, here's our second acronym, FACES. I just think these are very useful . . . we'll limit them to just a few). This flow of energy and information that links separate elements together has the subjective experience of harmony. Like a choir singing "Amazing Grace," each singer retains his or her own individual voice while simultaneously linking together with intervals that drive the flow of the whole song. The sensation of harmony is the subjective side of the physical state of integration.

With integration we have openness of possibility, a fluidity of movement in and out of propensity, probability, and activation, and back again to undefined, open possibility. This is the harmonious flow of a receptive state where we feel joined with others, and ourselves. Integration is at the heart of presence.

Throughout this book, integration is a central theme that organizes our approach. We'll see how we can learn to monitor integration more deeply, examining those banks outside the river of integration in which we become chaotic or rigid, or both. And we'll learn techniques for moving from these nonintegrated states toward integration. Such a practice is helpful for ourselves as therapists, and is essential for supporting such integration in our patients. By sensing when aspects of physical reality are not differentiated and/or not linked, we can then use the focus of our attention to stimulate these unrealized dimensions into actualization. We can cultivate specific domains to support differentiation and promote linkage. This process of integration can happen within ourselves and within our clients. In these physical ways, we can then find the correlated changes as we move from tendencies of chaos and rigidity to begin transforming our lives and the lives of our patients toward harmony. In other words, we can move from reactive to receptive states by promoting integration.

Our work with mindfulness will always have these two sides of a focus on our own integration and a focus on that of our clients. Indirect effects of our own mindful presence can include these many deep ways in which we can support the growth of others toward integration. Direct effects would be the teaching of our patients many of the mindsight skill exercises that we'll be exploring here for you as a person. This direct teaching of mindsight—offering mindfulness training, lessons in brain function, explorations of relationships—supports the clients' own capacity to sense and shape the flow of energy and information within the triangle of well-being. When that flow can be monitored well, patterns of chaos and rigidity can be detected and then a particular domain in need of work can be identified. This is the client's growth edge. Searching for aspects of that domain that do not have differentiation and/or linkage is then the work of therapy. Promoting these basic elements then catalyzes integration. This is the direct way in which a client can be taught to modify the flow of energy and information toward integration.

As we'll see in the next chapter, with presence we are ready to link our differentiated self with another entity. This is how we become attuned with one another, the interactive dimension of being present.

Chapter 2

ATTUNEMENT

Presence is our openness to the unfolding of possibilities. Attunement is how we focus our attention on others and take their essence into our own inner world. We can be attuned to nature, focusing in on the ways the breeze brushes the upper limbs of the trees surrounding a glimmering pond at the beginning of spring. We can attune to a barren hillside strewn with glacier-tossed stones, soaking in the mystery of time and the magic of the land. Being in nature and attuning to its important embrace is crucial for our well-being. Here we'll focus on the person-to-person aspect of attunement, the ways we take in the internal worlds of other people and allow them to shape who we are in that moment. The physical side of interpersonal attunement involves the perception of signals from others that reveal their internal world: noticing not just their words but also their nonverbal patterns of energy and information flow. These signals are the familiar primarily right-hemisphere sent and received elements of eye contact, facial expression, and tone of voice, posture, gesture, and the timing and intensity of response. The subjective side of attunement is the authentic sense of connection, of seeing someone deeply, of taking in the essence of another person in that moment. When others sense our attunement with them, they experience "feeling felt" by us.

Attunement sounds simple. Yet so often we can become transfixed by our own internal notions of what should be rather than remaining open to what is. In other words, our own preoccupations can limit how we truly take in another. As we'll see, the brain is an anticipation machine that shapes ongoing perception by what it automatically expects based on prior experience. While it is true that there is no such thing as immaculate perception, attunement requires that our perceptual array be as open to incoming sensation as possible—rather than being markedly biased by similar experiences and our ensuing restrictive expectations that are born from that earlier learning. That is how top-down constraints imprison us from experiencing the bottom-up flow of incoming data. To be truly open to another person's signals, we need to transcend our own prisons of memory and move toward an open state of presence. To attune freely we need to be fully receptive.

You may be wondering about what the difference between attunement and presence might be. *Presence* we're defining as a state of being open. *Attunement* requires presence but is a process of focused attention and clear perception. We use presence (which we can have even when we're alone) and move it into the social sphere of taking in another's internal state for interpersonal attunement. As we've seen, attuning with nature is important and vital in our lives as well, soaking in the natural environment that sustains our lives on this planet—an "eco-attunement." We'll even explore the notion that reflective practice of being open to oneself generates internal attunement, as the observing self takes in the experiencing self with receptivity and acceptance.

Here let's first look at the physical side of interpersonal attunement through the lens of the brain.

BRAIN BASICS

We have evolved with a great deal of neural circuitry devoted to tuning in to the internal state of another person. Research on infant-parent interactions reveals that from the very beginning of life, our social worlds are filled with caregivers tuning in to the external expression of internal states of the baby. These attunements have been found to serve as a basis for the development of secure attachment between child and parent. Personal experience and scientific observation each confirm the importance of interpersonal attunement for our sense of well-being—and our growth toward resilience. While the definitive neural correlates with attunement are yet to be elucidated, the discovery of *mirror neurons* at the end of the last century offers us new insights into a possible path of energy and information flow that may occur with attunement. Keep in mind that the mirror neuron story is only one possible view—one that needs further validation—but it offers us a place to begin with an exploration of attunement and the potential correlates of these fascinating findings.

When we perceive an action that has intention behind it—one that has a predictable sequence of behavioral motions—a set of neurons in our cortex responds by getting us ready to act in a similar fashion. These mirror neurons are called this because they function as a bridge between sensory input and motor output that allows us to mirror the behavior we see someone else enact. Recall that perception of the outer world is generally mediated in the back of the cortex (in the occipital, temporal, and parietal lobes toward the back), but the motor and motor planning areas are located in the frontal lobe of the cortex. What this anatomical separation means is that single neurons link these two regions so that when we see a particular action—like someone drinking from a cup of water—this set of mirror neurons becomes activated, meaning they fire off electrical currents called an action potential. Here's the fascinating finding: If we were to drink from a cup, these specific neurons that were firing when we saw someone else drinking would also become activated. We see a behavior and get ready to imitate it.

Our brain appears to be hard-wired to scan the social world for behaviors with intention—motions with predictable sequences that can be followed and the outcome of the behavior anticipated. We then create in ourselves the follow-through of that action—getting ready to drink the cup of water when we see someone else slurping down a cold beverage on a hot day. As the brain is an anticipation machine, it is natural that pattern detection would involve the creation of neural representations that get us ready for the next moment in an observed sequence of motions (see Freyd, 1987). In many ways we can view mirror neurons as a specialized component of this pattern-detecting machinery that links perception and action. While it is an important finding, it isn't really shocking: The brain anticipates and the brain integrates. Mirror neurons do both as they note the sensory implications of motor actions and then link the differentiated areas of perception (pattern detection) and motor action (imitating the behavior).

Some researchers, like Marco Iacoboni (2008), suggest that our mirror neurons are also essential for how we attune to others' internal states. While this is certainly an exciting speculation, more research needs to be done to confirm this particular role of the mirror neurons in our social lives. This hypothesis suggests that beyond imitating behaviors, we use these cortical mirror neurons to detect and then simulate the internal state of another person.

Our mirror neurons interact with neurons in the superior temporal cortex to create a map of the sensory implications of motor actions, what I call SIMA. This mapping lets us know what is happening next in the pattern of predictable behavioral sequences. These are motor actions of others that have intention driving them forward. We have signals from this mirror neuron–temporal cortex conglomerate directly sent to the premotor area and then to the motor area in the frontal lobe to imitate external behaviors we see. This crucial SIMA function of our mirror neuron/superior temporal area also links its firing patterns to a part of the middle prefrontal area called the *anterior insula*. Information in the form of specific neural firing patterns from mirror neurons is relayed downward through the insula to areas beneath the cortex. These subcortical regions include the limbic area, and ultimately flow downward also to the brainstem and body proper that will respond and mirror, or resonate with, another person as we attune to their internal state. As this mirroring is never actually a true replica, we could even dub this a "sponge system" as we soak up what we see in others and actually make it uniquely our own. This is a form of *internal simulation.*

We'll explore the joining process of resonance that emerges from attunement in the next chapter, so here let's stay focused on the internal perceptual component, the tuning in to others. With attunement, we focus on signals from others and embed this flow of energy and information from their internal state deeply into our nervous system. The key issue is that the antennae of how we perceive are not limited to the five senses we use to see the physical world, correlated with the posterior cortical areas we utilize to see, hear, taste, and touch. Instead, taking in the inner world of another person is a process that drives information downward, beneath our cortex, beneath initial awareness, and its outcome is embedded subcortically. We literally soak in what we sense inside another to shape our own internal world. However this sponge-circuit works, mirror neurons or not, it seems apparent that we move rapidly from cortical perception to subcortical response.

As our body simulates an internal state of another, we have a shift in our subcortical firing patterns. Our body proper—muscles and viscera, such as our heart, lungs, and intestines—interact with the brainstem and limbic areas to instantiate our present state of being. The signals we perceive from our own body, brainstem, and limbic zones, these subcortical areas, are the access we have to "know" another's internal world. If the sponge (mirror) neurons are our receiver, then our subcortical areas are the amplifier. These subcortical shifts are what changes in us when we attune to someone else.

Notice that the act of attunement is not necessarily intentional. At times we may automatically soak in the internal states of others as we pick up their signals and have internal shifts in our own state. We can also purposefully direct our focus of attention to another's nonverbal signals in an effort to "know where they are coming from." Even with such active efforts to attune with this effortful focus of attention on someone else, if we fail to be open to our own subcortical communication from inside ourselves we'll miss out on being aware of the outcome of attunement. We would have focused attention externally to take in the nonverbal data, but would not have been able to be open to our own internal states that would be required to feel another's feelings.

The first phase of attunement is the focus of attention on the signals from another. This hypothesis suggests that our mirror neuron complex initiates a set of firing patterns relayed downward through the insula to stimulate changes in our subcortical limbic, brainstem, and bodily areas. This is the first phase of *simulation*. Next, these shifts in our subcortical states can be relayed upward, ultimately passing in the opposite direction back up the insula to be deposited in the middle aspect of the prefrontal cortex. This is the second phase of *interoception*, the way we have a perception of the interior. From the body itself, interior data of the networks of neurons surrounding our heart and lungs, the state of tension in our muscles, our facial expressions, and feelings of pain pass up the spinal cord through a layer called Lamina 1. Lamina 1 flow moves upward, sending signals to the brainstem and the limbic region's hypothalamus (what some would call a subregion of the diencephalon). At this point, bodily data shapes our state of reactivity or receptivity via brainstem mechanisms and alters our hormonal milieu via the hypothalamus. But the insula in primates takes bodily information and moves it even further upward, now in the *posterior insula* that registers bodily states in the cortex, but not in the prefrontal areas. For some researchers, this posterior firing of maps of the body represents a primary cortical representation and may involve the parietal lobe—a region that may turn out to play an important role in self-awareness and a sense of identity (for further discussion of these circuits, see Craig, 2009). This basic neural firing pattern enables us to have a cortical sense of the body's state—a primary map of the body—but this is not yet related to consciousness. Uniquely in humans, this posterior insula firing is transmitted forward to the anterior insula. It is the anterior insula that is invariably activated when people have awareness of the internal state of their body—the important process of our sixth sense, called *interoception*. Because of this secondary movement forward to the anterior insula, some researchers suggest that we have a secondary representation, a representation of the posterior representation, that uniquely gives us some "distance" from the neural maps of our bodily state. This metarepresentation of the body permits us to have more regulatory oversight of bodily function that can involve conscious processes.

The anterior insula cortex also is one of the few areas that appears to have special cells, the von Economo or spindle cell, which is a wide-bored neuron capable of extremely fast electrical transmission. These spindle cells are thought to connect the anterior insula (which some authors formally place as a part of the ventrolateral prefrontal cortex, a fundamental part of our middle prefrontal area) to the somewhat distant anterior cingulate cortex (which is more toward the middle-center, and also a part of what we are calling the middle prefrontal cortex—see Siegel, 2007a). This rapid communication between the anterior insula and the anterior cingulate may be important in relaying bodily states (the metainsular maps) to the important functions of attentional allocation, social relatedness and emotion regulation (via the anterior cingulate's role in these self-organizational processes). To state this more succinctly, awareness of the body's state influences how we organize our lives. Knowing your body strengthens your mind.

This discussion is important because as we attune to another person, we focus on his signals, shape our internal state through a downward flow subcortically, and then these subcortical shifts move upward to the posterior insula where the primary cortical body map is created—especially on the right side of the brain. Next, the anterior insula (also on the right) receives this primary data and it makes a secondary representation—a map of the map of the body. This "metamap" capacity, enabling us to be one step removed from the direct sense of the body, seems to be associated with an awareness of the self. This statement emerges from research findings that correlate the density of spindle cells with the experience of self-awareness. Lamina I data deposits itself ultimately in the anterior insula and the anterior cingulate—the two regions that uniquely share spindle cells. When self-awareness involves the larger sense of a body in physical and social space, we may combine the anterior insula and anterior cingulate's activity to create a sense of who we are. Researchers studying disorders of self-awareness, such as eating disorders, might explore the possible role of these regions in the development of such conditions. Related to this notion is the discovery that those animals with spindle cells have self-awareness in proportion to the density of these unique cells. In this way, adult and then young humans, followed by apes, and then even whales and elephants, all share the ability to have forms of self-awareness and the presence of spindle cells.

When we attune to someone else, we need to tune in to our own internal shifts. But if we were to just have this be the end of the story, you would be at risk of confusing who is you and who is the other with whom you are attuning. Though the jury is far from decided on this question of "knowing me, knowing you," some scientists suggest that we have different degrees of involvement of various regions—special supervisory or "super mirror neurons," as Marco Iacoboni (2008) has proposed, and different degrees of bodily input—that may help me know when I feel sad because I see you crying or because I myself am the locus of the feeling. In attunement to another person, we may have a sequence that Iacoboni suggests may go like this: We take in someone else's signals, shift our own subcortical states, and bring those states back up through the posterior and then anterior insula, examine those insular maps with our medial prefrontal and anterior cingulate regions, and then have a third phase, prefrontally mediated, in which we *attribute* these shifts to what we've seen in the other person. Naturally, such a complex pathway can be bogged down by rigid valenced plateaus of probability, which skew accurate interpretations of the meaning of sensations.

As we've seen in the last chapter, if I raise my hand in a discussion with you and you've spent a life in a classroom, you'll interpret my gesture perhaps as my intention to ask a question. If you are from New York, you might think I am flagging a cab. But if you were abused as a child, you might sense that I am going to strike you. You will have attributed your internal state of fear as being generated by my intention to hurt you. Here we see that trauma would have created a valenced plateau biasing your perception of my actions toward "likely to hurt me" and you've moved rapidly to an instantiated peak of "he is about to hit me." Mirror neurons learn from experience so that they interpret the predicted sequences from initial data in unique ways based on prior experience. With unresolved trauma, we can propose, the sensory implications of motor actions are skewed toward vigilance for danger and assault. Our past experiences create patterns of plateaus through which we filter ongoing sensory input to bias our perception. At that moment, you are far from receptive, even though I may have just been waving hello to a friend.

Initial perception, subcortical shifts, interoception, and attribution are the fundamental steps of attunement in Iacoboni's model. This is the physical side of reality from the brain perspective. To attune with accuracy and achieve this sequence with clarity we need to let go of expectations and rest in the uncertainty of being awash in our own internal subcortical shifts. To be truly receptive to the other's internal state, we need to be willing to relinquish control of our own and identify when reactive states are clouding our vision and preventing us from attuning to another. Such a perception of our own internal state would then be dependent upon attuning to our selves, of being mindful of how our layers of plateaus and peaks may be blocking our being open to the true experience of another person.

True attunement is risky business. It is "easier," for example, to perform a physical exam on a patient and simply look for specific clinical diseases to rule out as you would click off the boxes on a checklist. No, no, no. Yes, no. Okay, exam done. Attunement is quite different from bulldozing your way through a questionnaire. We are open to the patient, not certain of what is happening within the subjective side of the interior of this person. We must be willing to go on a journey of discovery to find out what is really happening, being attuned to ourselves in the process, letting go of a feeling that we know everything or that we are in control of outcomes. Being open in this way may take us in directions we cannot predict, into areas that may require more time than we may think we have, into realms that make us feel uncomfortable, out of control, incompetent. At this point, some new to this work may want to choose another profession, or at least a specialty that is less filled with the necessary uncertainty embedded in perceiving the extremely important subjective side of reality. But hold on—there is an art and skill set to attuning to yourself and others that is, I'll invite you to consider, worth the journey. There's a gold mine of internal education in learning the art of self-awareness and inter- and intrapersonal attunement.

The key to clinical presence is to be open. The key to clinical attunement is to be willing to say "I don't know" and "tell me more." Your intention to help, a neural stance of positive regard likely involving the social engagement system and having a desire to connect and to assist, is woven together with an interest in supporting another with kindness and compassion. These are the internal states we need in order to attune to another.

MINDSIGHT SKILLS

Interoception is the skill of perceiving the interior of our body. As we use our cortical awareness to focus a spotlight of attention on this internal world of our bodily states, we draw upon the sensations of our muscles, the signals from our heart and intestines, the overall feeling inside of ourselves. Interoception is a crucial aspect of the monitoring function of the mind that opens the gateway to attunement with others. I invite you now to just take a brief 5- or 10-minute period to let your sense of the body—the sixth sense—fill your awareness. To achieve this it is helpful to find a quiet place where you can lie flat on a surface such as a floor, couch, or bed. Tapes of body scans are available in which the speaker gently takes you through each of the areas of the body, region by region. If your attention wanders, then gently and lovingly return your focus to the area of the body being focused upon at that moment. With the reading of a book, experiencing such a scan is hard to achieve, as you'll be scanning these words and not just being aware of the nonworded world of sensations. So here I'll offer you just an outline of what an audio body scan would provide.

Let the body find its natural state resting on a flat surface. You may just let the sounds in the room fill your awareness at first. Now just notice the sensations of your back, arms, and legs against the floor or couch. Let your breath find its natural rhythm. You may want to just ride the wave of the breath for a few moments and then we'll begin the body scan. Let your awareness take in the sensations of your feet as you notice the feelings of the heels against the ground or couch. Take in the sensations of how the heels connect with the arch of your feet, reaching upward to the balls and toes of each foot. Now see if you can let the feeling of both feet, heel to toe, fill your awareness.

As your awareness moves upward, you may sense the ankle joint linking your foot to your lower leg. And sense how this lower leg feels in the back, and now the front—at the shin. Let your awareness move to the knees, sensing the open space in the back . . . and now the knee cap at the front. This amazing joint connects your lower legs to your upper legs, which you may notice in the back . . . and now the front of your thighs. Moving upward, your attention can go to your hip joints, connecting the legs to your pelvis. As your awareness moves to the back, you may notice the sensations of your buttocks against the floor or couch . . . and notice your awareness moving forward to your groin and your genital region.

As your awareness moves upward, you may feel the movement of your breath at the level of the abdomen. Let your attention move inward, into your intestines, and just notice if you sense any feelings or images arise as you focus on your gut. . . . Now let your attention move to your lower back, resting against the floor or couch. As you move up your spine and your back, sense the feeling of energy that might emerge in your backbone, connecting your whole body up and down. . . . And notice your shoulder blades and how they connect to your shoulders. Now let your awareness move to your chest, where you may sense a movement with each breath.

Letting your attention move inward, see if you can invite your lungs to come into the focus of your awareness. Sensing the breath, feeling the air moving in and out of your lungs, just ride the waves of the breath, in and out. Notice how you can also invite the sensations of the heart into your awareness. Let whatever sensations or images arise fill your awareness right now. . . .

As you let your attention move upward, into your neck, you may be able to sense air moving in and out of your trachea. Now let your attention move outward and feel your neck leaning against the floor or the couch. Let your attention come to the back of your head, and now up to the top. As your awareness moves to the forehead, notice the sensations as you feel the muscles of the face. You can let your awareness now move to your eyes, your nose, your cheekbones. Notice how you can let your mouth enter your awareness, moving down to your chin, then around to your jawbone and your ears.

As you let the fullness of your whole face fill your awareness, see if you can let your entire head fill your internal sensations. We'll now take in the sensations of the whole body, beginning first with the outer layer of muscles and bone from head to toe. Just letting these sensations fill your awareness. Now let the interior of the body—your vital organs of the lungs, heart, and intestines—again fill your awareness. As we get ready to close this sensing exercise, let the whole of your body, interior and exterior, fill your awareness. Now just rest in the sensations that arise as you let the body just rest in its natural state, the breath in its natural rhythm, letting the earth support you, sensing the power of the awareness of just letting things be as they are.

To develop monitoring skills, it may be helpful to regularly perform a similar body scan exercise like this to keep your connection of the insula's input into your consciousness-creating cortex fully honed. Studies by Sara Lazar and colleagues (2005) even suggest that with regular mindfulness meditation, the right anterior insula and other aspects of the middle prefrontal region remain thicker—that is, they do not show the usual diminishment with aging. This preservation may be due to the growth of neural connections in areas that are repeatedly activated. The saying in neuroscience is that "neurons which fire together, wire together." This is the way we stimulate neuronal activation and growth—how we SNAG the brain toward a more vertically integrated state as we connect body to cortex with interoception. The more we focus our attention toward bodily sensations within our subjective experience in awareness, the more we activate the physical correlate of insula activation and subsequent growth. As we'll see, the more interoception and insula activation, the more capacity we'll have for attuning to others and being empathic toward their experience.

Let me just emphasize this last point: the focus of attention activates specific neural firing patterns. It is here where we can use the subjective side of focused attention to drive the physical side of neuronal firing. We can focus the mind to SNAG the brain and create a more integrated nervous system. To open ourselves to compassionate connection with others, we can actively cultivate a compassionate attunement to ourselves.

The second mindsight skill exercise we'll explore next moves us from monitoring to modifying the internal flow of energy and information. Remember, these are all exercises you can do yourself first for your own development. But each of these exercises, once mastered, can be used to directly teach mindsight skills to your clients.

The following exercise of mindsight training focuses on times when you may not have had the benefit of harnessing relationships with others to use interpersonal communication to help regulate your internal state. These missed opportunities to connect in our past may have shadows on the capacity for us to light up our communication with others in the present.

Find some time to have 15 minutes on your own with a personal journal and a pen—or with your computer, now free from intrusions from the Internet. Write down what you feel your greatest fears may be of connecting with another person. You may find it helpful to write down times in your life, recent or in the distant past, when communication with another person in your personal life was challenging. What was going on for you then? What signals from the other did you find most distressing? How did this difficult connection make you feel?

Now consider a time in your life when someone had significant difficulty attuning to you. What was that time like—what led to it and what was the outcome like for you? What did it feel like to be ignored, dismissed, chastised, or misunderstood? What did you notice were the possible reasons the other person was unable to attune to your internal state of mind?

For some individuals, the feeling of needing connection but not receiving such attunement from another creates a state of shame. Shame often has the internal sense that something is defective about the self and is accompanied with an internal impulse to turn one's eyes away from contact with others, a heaviness in the chest, and a nauseous feeling in the belly. Shame can also have elements similar to the "No" feeling of the earlier No-Yes exercise—a shutting down with a feeling of withdrawal. The intensity of shame can go underground, its pain driving its connection to our daily life beneath the radar of our awareness. As clinicians, it is crucial to know about the role shame has played in our own lives so that we know when we may be vulnerable to becoming reactive and so that we do not have a blind spot for the experience of shame in others.

As clinicians, we are in such a profound relationship with those who come to us seeking help. In interacting with patients there is often an intense sense of vulnerability, on both our parts. In these moments of heightened need to connect—with our negative, frightened states as well as with moments of joy and elation—we are in a tender moment of needing to be listened to, to be understood, to be cared about. It is at these times that shame is at most risk for arising in our lives. With an increased need to connect, missed moments of joining can quickly turn from misunderstandings to painful withdrawal into a shame state. While this is possible for anyone, those of us with difficult early histories filled with shame may be at highest risk of feeling the pain of missed connection and amplifying our reactions.

For this mindsight exercise, we can look inward at our own history first to assess when shame may have been a painful reality of our past. Learning about these moments, what do you notice now about how you felt then? See if you can bring up any bodily sensations that come along with visual or auditory images (pictures or conversations) of those times in the past. Now see if you can locate where in your body this feeling of shame may also reside: sensations in your chest, a welling of tears in your eyes, a nauseous feeling in your belly? Now take these images, sensations, feelings, and recollections of this past time and put them aside for a moment. Some imagine a file cabinet in their mind that is locked in a closet that only they have the key to open. Put your file of this memory in its drawer and close it for now.

In the front of your mind, see if you can imagine a peaceful scene—a park, the ocean, a meadow, a forest, your room at home, anywhere that brings you a sense of safety and perhaps tranquility. Now let this peaceful image intensify in your mind's eye. You may find it helpful to focus your awareness on a few waves of your breath as you let the images increase. Notice the sensations in your body. If the image is working well for you, you may sense that you feel at ease with a feeling of calm and clarity. Perhaps you notice that your arms feel relaxed, your breathing easy, your heart slow and steady. This is your home base, a deep, grounded place of tranquility that is always available to you. For some, just noticing their breath or imaging their peaceful place brings this tranquil state into awareness. This is a place that is all yours, a place of calm deep in your mental sea beneath the surface waves or even storms crashing above. This is a place of strength that can be a powerful resource in your life.

Knowing that you are able to build this internal source of strength, you can practice just sensing your breath or imaging your peaceful place each day. For this exercise today, let's return to the file locked in your mind's memory cabinet. Bringing the images of a time you felt shamed by a disconnection with someone back into the front of your mind, see if you can let the bodily sensations, emotional feelings, and any other associated elements of that time return to the forefront of awareness. With this memory now reinstated, see if you can find the most distressful aspect of that experience. What was the meaning of that dimension of your interaction? Was there fallout from what happened? Notice what bodily sensations and emotional feelings arise. As they become more intense, see if you can "breathe into them." This means that instead of running from this uncomfortable state, you actually focus on perhaps some more intentional and deeper breaths as you stay present with whatever arises. If the feelings and sensations become too intense and you feel that you cannot stay present with them, you can then draw on your peaceful place imagery.

For this exercise, even if the recollection does not feel overwhelming, bring your peaceful place into the front of your mind. Notice how this breathing-into activation (focusing on the breath and peaceful imagery) may enable your sensations of the memory to shift. For some, this change involves remaining open and moving away from a reactive place of withdrawal. This is the key: You can sense your level of distress and then shift your state into more balance. This is the essence of learning to monitor and then modify your internal state.

When applying these skill-training practices with clients, it may be helpful to introduce the peaceful-place imagery first, before working on exploring painful issues from the past. Coupling the relaxation and sense of safety associated with that imagery with the sensations of the body can ground a person in the visceral reality of tranquility and clarity. It is this grounded place that can serve as a vital resource of safety and strength during the explorations ahead.

WINDOWS OF TOLERANCE AND NEURAL INTEGRATION

A concept that enables us to dive deeply into our therapeutic work is the notion of a "window of tolerance" (Siegel, 1999). In Figure 2.1 you can visualize this essentially as a band of arousal in which we function well. Outside the window we become dysfunctional. We move to the edge of the window on one end and we've come closer to chaos; at the other edge we are nearing rigidity. You may notice that this resembles our river of integration—and moving outside the river is like moving beyond the window. The river is a metaphor that flows across time, while the window refers to a given state in that moment. We may have a wide window for some situations or feelings, yet a very narrow and easily ruptured window for other conditions. In whatever situation, when we are inte-

CHAOS

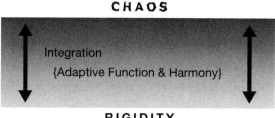

RIGIDITY

Figure 2.1 Window of tolerance. Our mental experience and our neural firing patterns for particular emotions or situations appear to have a span of tolerance in which we can function optimally. Within that span, within the window, we do well; outside the window, we push beyond tolerable levels of arousal and move to either chaos or rigidity and lose our adaptive and harmonious functioning.

grated, we are flexible and adaptive and function well within the window. When we're moving beyond the window's boundaries—into chaos or rigidity—we've lost integration and moved out of balance and harmonious functioning.

I may have a very narrow window of tolerance in a state of anger. In this example, as my blood begins to boil when I feel slighted, I may shut down rapidly in rigidity or I may move to the other edge and explode in chaotic rage. In this case, I've lost the harmony of functioning well within the window. I may be able to function better with sadness, tolerating a wide range of intensities of this emotion in myself, or in others. Knowing our windows, and especially noting which ones are particularly narrow and restricting our ability to be present and attuned with others' emotions, is a vital aspect of attunement and being a mindful therapist. Knowing when we're nearing the edge of the window and leaving a receptive presence will enable us to track when we're no longer able to attune to others.

If a client has moved beyond the window of tolerance, using the inner resource of a peaceful place image and the associated bodily sensations of safety can be an essential modifying technique to empower the client to move back toward an integrated state. Our job with clients is to feel the movement toward the window's boundaries and work at this "safe but not too safe" zone of treatment where change becomes possible. Sticking only within the center of the window, we do not enable the contained disorganization and reorganization necessary for the system of the person to change. Sensing these edges, moving with the client in and out of these precarious transition zones, but ending the session within the window are movements that make therapy both tolerable and empowering.

The physical correlate of the subjective sense of shutting down would be that we've moved into inflexible neural firing patterns. Far from the open plane of possibility, our physical side has stretched into plateaus of probability and activated peaks that are far from a receptive mode. We cannot take in data in an open and accepting manner, and are not able to move flexibly from peak to plateau and to plane. On the subjective side, the feelings may include a sense of constriction and reactivity—revealing the rigidity and chaos of a nonintegrated state.

As we attempt to tune in to one another, knowing our windows of tolerance for particular issues is crucial. You may have had a relative with a terrifying drug addiction that made you feel helpless and upset, and perhaps still shapes your life. If you have not spent time resolving the continuing stress that such a painful situation created, your window of tolerance for hearing clients speak about experimenting with street drugs may be extremely narrow. This situation may make attuning to someone in an evaluation or in the treatment phase of your clinical work especially challenging around issues of drug use and abuse. You will likely not be open to the internal state of your patient, shutting off presence, and making attunement unlikely. You'll feel such a shutting down, and certainly your client will too.

Knowing ourselves is the first place to start as we try to widen our windows of tolerance for a broad variety of states in ourselves. We need to learn the art of monitoring our internal world so that we can sense when we're moving inflexibly far from the plane of possibility. Without such refined awareness on our part, we may project a feeling of impending chaos or rigidity onto our clients, inappropriately try to move them to their safe place in an attempt to keep them in the window, and directly give them the sense that they, too, are unable to tolerate whatever feeling or memory is emerging at the time. This is how our own internal state of distress can influence our clients' states.

We also need to develop the practice of not only sensing this movement beyond the window, but being able to intervene and modify our state toward receptivity. This is the practice of attuning to ourselves and integrating our brains so that we're moving in subjective and physical ways toward the open plane of possibility. Learning to become receptive in this way and being and remaining within the window of tolerance empowers us to attune to others so that we can resonate with their internal states.

Chapter 3

RESONANCE

Presence permits us to be open to others, and to ourselves. Attunement is the act of focusing on another person (or ourselves) to bring into our awareness the internal state of the other in interpersonal attunement (or the self, in intrapersonal attunement). Resonance is the coupling of two autonomous entities into a functional whole. A and B are in resonance as each attunes to the other, and both are changed as they take the internal state of one another into themselves. When such resonance is enacted with positive regard, a deep feeling of coherence emerges with the subjective sensation of harmony. When two strings of an instrument resonate, for example, each is changed by the impact of the other. Naturally, as A is changed because of B, B then is changed further as A's changes induce further changes in B. This is the dynamic and interactive state of resonance. Two literally become linked as one. The whole is larger than the sum of the individual parts.

In many ways we feel "close" or "heard" or "seen" by another person when we can detect that he has attuned to us and has taken us inside of his own mind. When we ourselves register this attunement, either consciously or not, our own state can change. The observed takes in the observer having taken her in, and the two become joined. This is resonance. Beginning with a genuine sense of care and interest by the focus of the other's careful attention, resonance extends this positive interaction into a fuller dimension of the other being changed because of who we are. This is how we feel "felt," and this is how two individuals become a "we."

In this way resonance moves us beyond understanding and into engagement. Understanding others is extremely important: the interest in and intention to grasp another's point of view is a crucial element in healing relationships. When another person perceives our genuine curiosity, openness, and acceptance, there is a sense of professional caring, what we might be so bold as to call a "healing form of love." It's tricky, naturally, to risk confusing the romantic sense of "love" within the context of psychotherapy and this healing stance. But the feeling of compassionate concern, of genuine interest and engagement, of the mutual influence that each person has on the other (mutual, but not symmetrical in therapy), are all components of a powerful sensation that certainly evokes the private sense of "love." Even with its asymmetry, I can freely say that my patients have changed me. I am who I am because of them.

There are many forms of love, of course—love for a sexual partner, a companion in life, a child, a friend, a neighbor, humanity. Each of these forms of love seems to have the fundamental elements of curiosity, openness, and acceptance that equal love—which fortunately can be easily recalled with the acronym COAL. COAL is the essence of what it means to be in a mindful state. When we have a COAL state with ourselves, we can call this self-compassion, which certainly is a form of nonnarcissistic self-love. One way around the ethical issues about confusing professional feelings of concern and care with the personal forms of love would be to use the mindfulness term *loving-kindness*. The essential issues are the same: We bring a COAL state of being present, attuning, and resonating with the person in question.

Resonance makes two a part of one system, at least temporarily. Attuning to ourselves within mindful states, we have the observing and experiencing self in resonance. Attuning to others, we open ourselves to the profound adventure of linking two as part of one interactive whole. This joining is an intimate communion of the essence of who we are as individuals yet truly interconnected with one another. It is hard to put into words, but resonance reveals the deep reality that we are a part of a larger whole, that we need one another, and, in some ways, that we are created by the ongoing dance within, between, and among us.

Resonance requires vulnerability and humility. We don't know where an interaction will take us and we cannot control its outcome. Resonance immerses us in the unknown and brings us face to face with uncertainty. These existential realities may be uncomfortable for those clinicians who strive to know and to be certain and to be able to control. Naturally each of us would like to have the important aspects of knowledge at our fingertips so that we would be able to predict outcomes and to help others. This drive is why many of us have entered the healing arts. And working hard in our training, we strive to be certain about the skills we've acquired, the facts we've learned, the approach we've been taught, the strategy we've come to believe in. Yet controlling outcomes or knowledge in certain ways is counter to what the clinical encounter entails. Ironically, sometimes the most powerful statements we can make are an authentic "I don't know" or "I'm not sure."

My favorite graduation present at the end of my clinical training was from a supervising psychiatrist who gave each of us a button that I still have hanging over my computer screen: It reads, "Don't be too sure."

We come with the relational role of being a guide, perhaps, or a teacher, and in some ways an attachment figure—someone who provides a safe haven where the other can be deeply seen and feel safe and secure. At other times we are the expert on the mind, and perhaps on the brain and relationships too, and on the notion of health and unhealth, ease and disease. Yet our patients are also experts in their own right, deeply knowledgeable in other domains. Our patients are certainly expert in being themselves. No one else shares this distinctive skill base. Even without self-awareness, the people who are your clients are still the best "them" that they can be.

So we come as individuals, each with our own expertise, to find one another in this journey across time. Our job is not to be the one who knows everything, but the one who is present, attuned, and open for resonance with what is. As we join in this moment in the physical realm—making appointments to be in the same space at a given interval of the clock—our nervous systems align their firing patterns as two sets of electrochemical entities phase shift into resonant couplings. What this means is that at times our heart rates align, breathing becomes in-sync, nonverbal signals emerge in waves that parallel each other, and in some cases shifts in EEG findings (electroencephalograms) and heart rate variability co-occur. The functions of our autonomic nervous system, balancing brake and accelerator in the coordination of heart and brain, become aligned as we resonate with each other. These changes represent concrete physical and quantifiable ways in which two states become as one.

On the subjective side of reality, resonance can be detected internally as we look to the other and recognize evidence that the other is changed because of our own internal world. We see a tear forming at the edge of the other's eyes as we have just told a sad story. We see the outrage in a person's demeanor after we've described unfair and harsh treatment we have undergone. Letting our patients know that we feel their feelings enables them to "feel felt." Sometimes our clients may be so distracted by their own state that it is helpful to gently open our own internal world to them so that what we genuinely feel inside is brought out in its expression. For example, if I am deeply moved by the recounting of some recent painful event, I may feel the weight of that experience inside but show it outwardly by placing my hand on my heart. It is crucial not to pretend to be present and resonant in this way, but rather to be sure that your presence is communicated—often nonverbally—through your attunement and your true resonance. Bringing the inside out is a fundamental part of our connection with one another.

BRAIN BASICS

When the sperm and egg first join, we are formed through the universal union in which two become one. This philosophical and cytological origin of the self as being fundamentally social is also revealed in the developmental pathway in which the outer layer of cells becomes the neural tissue in our body. If you place your fingers together and have your fingertips meet each other, this hand image can represent the large collection of cells that formed when the single conceptus from the egg and sperm's union became 2, 4, 8, 16, 32, 64, and 128 cells. On and on we grew until we became so large that an outer layer and inner set of cells were parts of our makeup. Now let your fingernails roll inward toward the palm, with your knuckles kissing each other as the fingertips move inward. This is how the outer layer—the ectoderm—invaginated inward to become the neural tube. The importance here is that the origins of our nervous system as the outer layer of cells reveals how our neurons were originally organized on the boundary between the inner and the outer—and their functions continue to include linking these two realms.

Resonance in the brain is a natural state in our development that illuminates how we're hard-wired to connect with one another, bringing the inside of the "outer" person, the other, into our own inner world. We saw in the last chapter that the mirror neurons and related areas enable us to take in the signals from others and move this perceptual data downward to various regions below the perceiving cortex. Subcortical shifts include alterations in our limbic area, our brainstem, and our body proper. We have changes in our heart rate, breathing, and intestinal functions, along with engagement of our muscles and endocrine system, and changes in our facial expression and tone of voice. These subcortical shifts take place as part of the "resonance circuitry" (see Siegel, 2007a, Appendix IIIC) that then moves these data up the insula. We've reviewed how this flow is first deposited in the posterior insula where we are "not yet aware" but do have a cortical representation of the body—especially on the right side of the brain. We then move that data forward to the right anterior insula where we connect with the other parts of the middle prefrontal cortex (the anterior cingulate and medial prefrontal regions) to enable us to have interoceptive awareness. This, as we've explored earlier, is a secondary representation that enables us to gain some neural distance and have awareness of our bodily state, not just have the body's state influence us. This step-away of a metarepresentation of the body gives us more flexible capacities of regulation: When we monitor with more clarity, openly attending to the waves of bodily sensations and not just being bombarded by them, we can modify our internal state with more strength and agility.

These middle prefrontal shifts of the anterior insula and cingulate circuits likely influence a part of the medial prefrontal region's assessment of our internal state: "What am I feeling now? What does this mean to me?" These aspects of self-awareness can then enable the attribution of self-states to the other. "And what might these internal feelings in me indicate about you?" These are the fundamental ways prefrontal registration of subcortical resonance emerges into awareness as a feeling for another person and empathic insight into the other's psychological frame of mind. In other words, we take in all the nonconceptual data of the body, brainstem, and limbic areas and then cortically assess this input to get a conceptual sense of how we feel and how the other may be feeling. Resonance enables us to feel others' feelings, but we don't need to become the other.

The dyadic component (a pair interacting) of this resonance process may not require awareness—depending instead on physiological coupling that occurs subcortically. If I start to cry as you tell me a sad story of your childhood, you may become aware of my tears before I myself am aware of my own sadness. This would certainly be resonance—but without my own cortical awareness of this subcortical shift involved as yet.

And so the resonance circuits permit our joining perhaps long before self-awareness is initiated. This latter step in the process that involves conscious experience appears to rely on medial prefrontal aspects of the middle prefrontal region—the areas just beneath the forehead, in the middle. In this way, we can say that the sequence from mirror neurons to insula first enables an initial interpersonal perceptual process of attunement to begin. The insula then drives that data subcortically and it is here where resonance is initiated. The insula (first posterior and then anterior) as well as the anterior cingulate and perhaps other aspects of the middle prefrontal cortex then take in these subcortical shifts to ultimately enable awareness of how we are feeling and create images of what we imagine is the internal world of another. The key is that the joining of resonance occurs beneath awareness—with correlates in the subjective and physical sides of the experience.

Letting this resonance circuitry do its magic is like getting out of the way of nature. For most of us, resonance just happens. If our motivation is present and our mirror neurons are developed to soak in the internal state of another, we'll resonate. This is the *neurobiology of we*. But if we have a narrow window of tolerance, if we tend to become reactive instead of remaining receptive, presence is shut down, attunement cannot happen, and resonance does not occur. For any of us, such a shutting off of joining may occur beyond our control and even beneath our awareness. As therapists, knowing the triggers that shut off our resonance circuitry is essential in maintaining the presence, attunement, and resonance needed for our work. Teaching clients to detect these states in themselves offers a pathway by which together you can help them identify sources of isolation and disconnection. Patterns of interpersonal rupture can often result from learned strategies to ward off resonance. Developing the capacities to monitor and then modify such shut-off states is essential for remaining open to others.

Often the feeling of isolation comes along with a drive to be

Left Mode of Processing	Right Mode of Processing
Later to Develop	Earlier to Develop
Linear	Holistic
Linguistic	Non-Verbal
Logical	Visual/Spatial Imagery
Literal	Metaphors
Lists	Stress Reduction
Factual/Semantic Memory	Autobiographical Memory
Digital: Yes/No Up/Down	Integrated Map of Body

Figure 3.1 Modes of processing. Each mode, left and right, may be quite distinct in each of us and have a predominant activation on one side of the brain or the other. Our neural functions often involve widespread activations throughout both sides of the brain, but these "modes" seem to be dominant asymmetrically and their functional clustering, whatever their particular anatomical distributions, appears to be quite differentiated and therefore capable of being linked to promote more complex and adaptive functioning as a whole. We call them *modes* to embrace their modalities of clustering and the reality of their widely distributed neural activities.

certain of the outcome of interactions, to guarantee the results of communication. We can understand the tension between a drive to know and a willingness to accept whatever arises perhaps more deeply when we examine the differences between our two hemispheres. Figure 3.1 offers a brief outline of the dominant features of the right and the left hemispheres. Ideally we can find a way to harness the power of both—and to cultivate an integrated state in which they work together as a functional whole. Notice that one useful strategy dominant in the left hemisphere is to focus on the logical and linear sequence of events in the world. The "digital processing" mode of the left, searching for yes-no, right-wrong, up-down dichotomies, offers us a clue as to where people might seek refuge if longing for certainty dominates their lives and removes them from resonance. We can find strategies of joining that eliminate the more vulnerable and unpredictable right hemisphere, bathed as it is in the dominance for autobiographical memories, integrated body maps, and raw spontaneous affective input from the subcortical regions.

Sometimes we resonate left to left and find connection in intellectual pursuits. Such a joining has the power of ideas and the containment of language and linearity. Yet in bolder times we may additionally join right to right with others, finding a more integrated way to also nonlinearly resonate with bodily sensations in dance, music, or the spontaneous unfolding of intimate conversation. With our patients, too, we may find different combinations of joining, sometimes, left to left, or right to right. With deep integration, I believe, a right-left to right-left state of full resonance can be achieved. In clinical work, this may occur when we have gone deeply into explorations of right-hemisphere-dominant bodily awareness and coupled these with narrative explorations that weave a deep, visceral way of making sense of the past, present, and anticipated future. Here we may find that connecting in this way is an integrated left-right process in ourselves and in our clients that may inspire the collaboration of the two hemispheres to work in concert with one another.

MINDSIGHT SKILLS

Being a "we" often begins in our infancy. Yet over one third of us have had a history of insecure attachment and did not have a reliable experience of joining in which we were respected as individuals who were worthy of being a part of a linked and vibrant whole. Knowing our attachment history can be an essential starting point as a clinician—or a parent—so that we can offer our presence, attunement, and resonance as the first PART of the nurturing relationship. For this reason, in this section we will outline relevant aspects of attachment research and how they can inform and transform your own understanding of what your childhood history may have been and what that means for your capacity for resonance.

Research reveals that the best predictor of a child's attachment is actually how a parent has made sense of his or her own early life history. Even foster or adoptive parents with a coherent narrative revealing how they've made sense of their life histories have their nongenetically related children develop secure relationships with them (see Dozier, Stovall, Albus, & Bates, 2001). With security children develop emotional balance, the capacity for healthy social relationships, and their intellectual potential. If parents make sense of their lives, their children do better than those children raised by parents who have not made sense of their perhaps painful pasts.

Though the research into this area is still unfolding, we can use the findings of the Adult Attachment Interview (AAI) (see Main, 2000) to explore how therapists might best make sense of their own childhood history to create a coherent narrative, to have what is called a secure adult state of mind with respect to attachment in their own lives. The great news is that parents, and therapists, can "earn" their security by making sense of their lives if they did not have healthy, secure attachment in their youth. The brain remains open to change throughout the life span: Making sense of our history integrates the brain.

For this mindsight skill training exercise we'll be exploring the fundamental elements of this important research instrument. (For an overview and synthesis with neuroscience, please see Siegel, 1999. For an in-depth practical application of that interpersonal neurobiology approach for increasing coherence in your own narrative, please see Siegel & Hartzell, 2003. To see the direct application of the AAI in various clinical settings, please see Siegel, 2010.)

Memory emerges in two layers. The first is called *implicit memory* and involves our behavioral learning, emotional reactions, perceptions of the outer world, and likely also includes our bodily sensations. We can also generalize across experiences, summating elements of lived moments into schema or mental models of events. Further, we have as a part of implicit memory the readying ourselves for action or feeling called *priming*.

Many researchers believe that by around 18 months of age, the maturation of the dentate gyrus portion of the hippocampus occurs and allows the second layer called *explicit memory* to begin to develop. Consisting of two basic elements—factual memory and memory for oneself in an episode of time called episodic or autobiographical memory—explicit memory requires the focus of attention and the participation of the hippocampus for encoding. Explicit memory is more flexible and gives us the factual scaffold of our understanding of the world as well as weaving a set of autobiographical puzzle piece assemblies. In other words, implicit memory provides the pieces; explicit memory assembles them into fuller pictures of the whole. Whether as factual or as autobiographical assemblies, explicit memory involves a flexible capacity to sort through a range of recollections. We can, for example, remember one birthday, or we can gather all birthdays we've had into a set of related experiences. We can also bring up a sense of our senior year in high school, happy vacations, or painful relationships. Explicit memory enables us to have an internal search engine that can flexibly explore various dimensions of our lived experience.

We can also look to the past to understand how resonance played a role—or not—in our lives. For many of us, explicit memory is not available in any continuous way for the time before we were about 5 years of age—or even 3, or a year and a half. Given that a lot of time during which we were in connection, or not in connection, with our early caregivers occurs during these first years of life, it may be difficult to access explicit memories from this early period. This is called normal childhood amnesia and is a function of the primarily genetically determined timing of the development of areas such as the hippocampus. So what do we do if we are looking back toward our earliest years and the natural state of childhood amnesia blocks us from explicitly recalling that time of our lives? We learn to sense the internal world of implicit sensations and explore their potential effects on our lives now.

By the time we are 2 years of age, the prefrontal area responsible for the telling and understanding of stories begins to develop. Maturing well into our 20s, and perhaps throughout our lives in more subtle ways, the prefrontal cortex enables autonoetic consciousness, or self-knowing awareness. This is how we create what Endel Tulving (1993) has called "mental time travel" in which we link the past, the present, and the future. The narrative that emerges from such prefrontal activity also contains a narrator, a function in which we can speak of ourselves from the third person: "Dan is working too hard. He should take a break and relax more." Now who said that? In my own head, I can narrate my own existence even as I am experiencing my life directly. This reveals the many-layered tracks we have of neuronal firing and subjective experience. We have many channels of information flow, and narrative lifts us out of the present moment to reflect on patterns of our own feelings, behaviors, and expectations.

To monitor your own life narrative, it may be helpful to write down your responses to the basic questions of adult reflection inspired by the AAI: What was growing up like in your family? Who was in your home with you? Think of five words that reflect your earliest recollection of your childhood relationship with your mother. Then think of an example for each word that illustrates a memory or experience that supports the word. Now do the same exercise for your father, and for anyone else who was an attachment figure for you in your life (a grandparent, nanny, neighbor, older sibling). Who were you closest to and why? What was it like the first time you were separated from your parents or other caregivers? What was it like for you, and for them during this separation? What would you do when you were upset? If you were sick, injured, or emotionally distressed, what would happen? Were you ever terrified of your caregivers? How did your relationship with them change over the years? Did anyone ever die in your childhood or more recently? Did anyone you were close to leave your life? How were those losses for you, and how did they impact the family? Are you close with your caregivers now? Why do you think they acted as they did? How did all of these things we've been exploring in these questions influence your growth as an adult? How do you think these things influenced your decision to become a clinician? How do you think they have affected your work and studies to be in clinical work? What are the main things you've learned from being parented by your parents? If you have or anticipate ever having children, what would you want them to say that they learned from being parented by you? What would you want for them in the future? How do you feel all of these issues of your attachment history may impact your ability to be open, to attune, and to resonate with others—in your personal or your professional life?

Take a good amount of time to reflect upon and write down your responses to these questions. Don't be surprised if this sequence of inquiries tires you out—in my experience of administering the AAI in research protocols, many people have said in effect that this 90-minute interview (these questions are offered orally) was the "best therapy session" they'd ever had. And this with my being as neutral as I could be. So be kind to yourself as you go through these questions. On the surface they seem straightforward. But the brilliant researchers who designed the AAI created a sequence of questions that often go deeply into the recesses of a person's mind and evoke significant emotional revelations and reorganizations. It is for these reasons, too, that learning the AAI and applying it in clinical evaluations and treatments is a useful approach. (Please see Steele & Steele, 2008; Wallin, 2007). For therapists, we can suggest that the AAI-inspired questions for self-reflection ought to be a basic self-development tool that each of us uses to prepare ourselves to make sense of our lives and make ourselves available to be fully present with others. Making sense integrates our brains and makes our minds move toward the plane of possibility and open receptivity. This is crucial for ourselves, and our patients.

After writing down your self-reflections, how do you feel? What do you see as your way of making sense of your childhood? After such reflection, the following brief overview may make more sense and feel more useful in your own self-reflective journey.

About 65% of the nonclinical population has a secure AAI. These individuals can draw on details of their past to communicate both the negative and the positive aspects of their own early life experiences. "Early" means the earliest they can remember—especially focusing on experiences with others in close relationships. It is important to recall that it is never too late to make sense of your life and earn a secure adult attachment status. That's the great news about neuroplasticity and the power of the reflective mind to change the brain—to move it toward integration.

In contrast, about 20% of the population has a dismissing AAI in which joining and resonance were generally likely to have been absent from the majority of their experiences with their primary caregiver. Finding a way to live with autonomy as their way of surviving, of being a "little adult" while still a young child, was the best they could do given the emotional desert in which they were growing. In the brain of such individuals it may be that integration between the two hemispheres is blocked. In my own clinical experience of performing the AAI in clinical practice over the last 20 years, there seems to be prominent excess in left mode dominance, a diminished right mode development, and an absence in the use of mindsight in social situations. Seeing the mind as the internal subjective center of gravity in another's life—or sometimes even in their own—is often missing. To understand the physical side of this mental finding of a lack of autobiographical detail typical of the AAI findings, we can turn toward the hypothesis that these individuals lacked the nonverbal communication to promote much right hemisphere stimulation and subsequent growth and development of the right mode of processing. Recall that it is the right hemisphere that is the main repository of autobiographical memory. Yet it is the left side of the brain that appears to have the drive to tell a story. With the dismissing stance in an adult who likely had an avoidant attachment as a child, it feels as if the left hemisphere is just making up stories, yet the client insists, "I just don't remember my childhood." Even when asked to give five words reflecting their relationships as a child, dismissing individuals bring up personality traits of the parents—not aspects of their connection. Clearly if this is your pattern, the relational aspect of your interactions with your patients may take a back seat to diagnostic categories and more methodical strategies of intervention. Given the research findings that it is the empathic, attuned relationship between clinician and client that is the most robust predictor of how change unfolds (see Norcross, 2002), being firmly rooted in a dismissing stance may not be readily helpful to the therapeutic relationship.

The great, great news is that these attachment categories are changeable. With the focus of attention often coupled with attuned relationships with a caring other—with a partner or a therapist—people can move from an insecure AAI to an earned secure AAI. Studies reveal that those with earned security have children who are securely attached and grow to be resilient and thriving adults.

In about 10–15% of the general population, the AAI finding reveals preoccupation, in which attempts to simply focus on the past are intruded upon by concerns about the present and the future. In my own personal and informal assessment, this is the category of many colleagues and students at the time they begin their therapeutic training. This preoccupation reveals how the parents may have been inconsistent and intrusive in the child's life. The result is not a disconnected self as in the dismissing grouping, but here it is more a confused self. Where you begin and I stop can be a blurry boundary in this situation, revealing how interactions were not integrative—the caregivers were intermittently available, sometimes there and sometimes not. These relationships are marked by occasional but repeating intrusions in which caregivers flood the child with their own leftover garbage. If this is your history, then resonance with your clients may be fraught with concerns about losing your own autonomy. Your own sense of who you are and who your patient is may become blurred and you may misinterpret your confusion as empathic understanding, which it may or may not be. As we'll see, the steps toward earning security are parallel to developing mindfulness traits. Indeed, an informal review I engaged in with Mary Main and Erik Hesse of the characteristics of the details for coding an AAI as secure revealed striking consistency with both mindful traits in the interviewee and being in a mindful state during the interview itself. This impression has preliminary empirical support by the dissertation research of Amy DiNoble (2009).

A fourth AAI category is that of the disorganized/disoriented grouping in which the narrative reveals elements of unresolved trauma or loss. Here the narrator becomes confused or disoriented at times of discussing frightening events or the death of people or important attachment-figure pets in their lives. The mind seems to lose its otherwise coherent way of telling the story of its life history—and the person temporarily becomes disoriented and disorganized. For many, the clinical tendency to dissociate under stress may be a recurring experience. Dissociation involves various elements along a spectrum including a sense of being unreal, feeling numb or disconnected from one's body, feeling depersonalization or a kind of distance from being grounded in oneself, and outright amnesia for events in one's ongoing life. Disorganized states in this attachment grouping are felt to be due to the conflictual situation in which caregivers were a source of terror in a young child's life. There is no solution to such fear—one part of the child's brain has the drive to escape the source of terror, the parent; while another circuit drives the child to seek comfort and security—but from the same person, the parent who is terrifying the child. There is no resolution to this biological paradox, and the child fragments. This is "fear without solution" (See Main, Hesse, Yost-Abrams, & Rifkin, 2003). This fragmentation can continue into the adult's life, shaping the response to emotionally challenging interactions and leading to the inability to rely on one's own internal resources. Narrow windows of tolerance are plentiful for a range of emotions and interpersonal situations. This is the legacy of terrifying childhood experiences—of abuse, yes, but also of more subtle ways in which parents look terrified, were intoxicated, or in other ways massively withdrew and frightened their children (see Dutra, Bianchi, Siegel, & Lyons-Ruth, 2009).

Many of us may have some elements of each of these four patterns of adaptation to our childhood experiences. The important lesson from the clinical application of these research findings is that deeply seeing the ways we've come to live in the world in response to our life history can transform us. As therapists, we are confronted each day with the need to be present with our patients. To move from presence to attunement and resonance requires that we be deeply familiar with the ways in which we ourselves may not have had these elements of connection in our lives. Once equipped with this inner knowledge, we can become empowered to alter our ways of being, with ourselves, and with others.

Mindsight involves not only sensing the present, but deeply knowing the past so that we are not imprisoned by unexamined elements of our experience that restrict us in the future. Making sense of our past frees us to be present in our lives and to become the creative and active author of our own unfolding life story.

Offering the AAI to patients is an excellent exercise in exploring the past in an organized and research-established way that can illuminate patterns of adaptation. The interview itself is a master skill-training session for systematically exploring the nature of attachment, memory, and narrative. Even without its formal coding into specific categories, the AAI is an important element of clinical assessment relevant for most people coming for evaluation and treatment. These elements of knowledge can then become the starting place for you to work with your clients in helping them make sense of their lives. To achieve this fully, it is crucial that you as a therapist explore your attachment history first and make sense of how your past has influenced your own development.

MAKING SENSE AND INTEGRATION

Developing a personal understanding of memory and narrative processes enables you to change how you make sense of your life. In this way, reflecting on your attachment history is a fundamental way to monitor the internal architecture of your mind and then to modify it toward security. As you can see this process evokes several domains of integration. Interoceptive awareness involves vertical integration, and linking the differentiated right and left hemispheres and their unique modes of processing is a part of bilateral integration. Focusing attention on the implicit layer of memory and harnessing the power of the master puzzle piece assembler, the hippocampus, is a form of memory integration. Developing your ability to narrate the themes of your life in an open and flexible manner—to move from a cohesive, restrictive autobiographical story to a coherent one—is a form of narrative integration. With integration as a focus of your own internal work, the experience of resonance becomes more readily available to you to engage in with your clients. In many ways, becoming more attuned to yourself is the first step toward earning security—and developing mindfulness as a way of being.

These exercises to monitor one's own memory system and attachment narratives invite you to become an expert on your own personal history. Cultivating the various domains of integration supports the many ways people can move from insecure to secure attachment in their adulthood. There is a great deal of support for the notion that each of these insecure AAI findings is a result of impaired integration. With the proper focus of attention you can bring your attachment stance from incoherence to coherence. You can make sense of your life—no matter what happened to you in your childhood. And this is true across the life span.

But we do know, also from attachment research, that those with difficult childhoods are likely to repeat those patterns of adaptations to sub-optimal experiences with their own children if they don't take the time or have the opportunity to make sense of their lives. We can imagine the implications of this research for the actions of therapists: If someone has an insecure adult attachment status, their own patients will likely be treated in ways that reflect that insecure history. It is essential for all people in the healing arts to care for themselves—which includes creating a coherent narrative of their own lives.

Sometimes the things we may have missed in our early life—attuned relationships or consistent parenting—may have led to avoidant or ambivalent attachment adaptations. But with events that overwhelmed us, having experiences in response to which we could not develop an organized approach, we are left with a potential for fragmentation. We literally—on the physical side of reality—fragment as we devolve from an integrated state. This is the course of trauma.

Trauma in many ways is like a dog bite. We all have the instinctive impulse to pull away from the bite. But as we pull away, the dog digs his teeth even deeper into our fingers and we sustain serious wounds. Instead, if we push our hand more deeply down the dog's throat, he'll gag and release our hand with only minor and more quickly healing puncture wounds. Doing the AAI is an invitation to focus your attention down the throat of attachment traumas. You can learn to make sense of times when resonance was not there, when attunement to you when you needed it most was absent, and when your caregiver's lack of presence made you live a life of isolation, intrusion, or disorganization. And you can also look straight into overwhelming events and pull together the unassembled pieces of implicit memory that may be fragmenting your life and preventing you from living fully—especially under stressful conditions.

As you do this important modifying work of taking in what you've monitored in these reflective exercises, you will see that memory retrieval can be a memory modifier. With reflection and active exploration, what was a painful reality in the past can become a teacher for you in the present. Science shows that you do not need to be a prisoner of the past. You can make sense of your life and free yourself from the early adaptations that helped you to survive—but that are now in need of updating. Now you can thrive, not just survive. You can take off that winter coat of defensive adaptation and free yourself to live fully in the present and create your own future. This is how you can connect to yourself, from the inside out. And this is how you can free yourself to be present, attune, and resonate in your journey as a clinician.

Chapter 4

TRUST

When we have the experience of sitting with someone who is present and attunes to our inner state, we are invited to become a part of resonance in which a "we" is created as two become woven into one interacting whole. As a form of integration—not homogenization—each individual retains elements of uniqueness and identity. The first time we experience such joining after our birth is as our parents attune to us and we become joined as infant and caregiver. The vulnerable position of a baby, dependent on the other person for her very survival and fraught with potential fear and anxiety, is made safe by the attuned presence of the attachment figure. This tender moment is repeated in a young child's life as she learns to trust that all will be well. This trust is a letting go, a willingness to rely on others for connection, comfort, and protection. Trust is a state of receptivity akin to Porges's (2009) notion of love without fear. This receptive state is created by the evaluative circuits of the brain and opens us to the world around and within us. Shaped by experience and enacted with ongoing needs for being safe, this neuroceptive evaluation seeks attunement to activate the social engagement system. If I am sad and you see my pain and comfort me, I can feel held and secure. I feel felt by you; I can come to trust you, to trust our relationship, to feel at ease with our interaction, to trust our connection.

Being vulnerable is also a starting place in most clinical encounters. For our clients in psychotherapy or our patients in medical practice, something is not right in their lives and they seek our counsel to make things better. Sometimes that improvement is an evaluation that clarifies confusion; in other situations, interventions can remedy a wrong, heal a wound, or promote growth where there has been stagnation in development. In all of these clinical encounters, people come to us with the request, "Please help me."

Presence, attunement, and resonance are the way we clinically create the essential condition of trust. As our patients feel this healing love without fear, as they come to the neuroceptive evaluation of safety, trust is created within their subjective experience.

Even recent studies of teaching mindfulness practice to physicians have demonstrated that clinician burnout can be significantly reduced if these professionals are taught to attune to themselves and reduce their stress (see Krasner, et al., 2009). One way of interpreting these findings is that the physiological state of stress was reduced by the mental practice of mindful awareness. Here is a wonderful example of how learning to trust your own inner life, to become vulnerable to what is and accept one's own inner world with openness, objectivity, and observation, has a profound influence on maintaining a positive attitude toward clinical work. Trust is not a luxury. With this openness, too, we can only imagine how the patients working with these fortunate physicians may also have benefited from the physicians' continuing presence in their lives.

And so trust emerges from the attunement we feel with ourselves so that we can remain open to others. This presence-attunement-resonance sequence sets the stage for all the "TRs" (our words beginning with *tr*) to come. The physical side of this trusting state can help us see how trust creates the conditions for change.

BRAIN BASICS

We are hard-wired to connect with one another. From the very beginning of extrauterine life, our brains seek positive forms of *contingent communication* in which we send a signal that is hopefully received, made sense of, and responded to in a timely and effective manner. Across all cultures studied, contingent communication is at the heart of healthy parent–child relationships throughout the world.

As our social brains send and receive signals, they also evaluate the safety or danger of our current environment. As patterns of contingent communication unfold, the baby creates repeated internal neural firing patterns of safety: I am seen, I am understood, I am cared for. Relaxing into a state of receptivity, the vulnerable young child's developing brain encodes these patterns of interaction and accompanying internal response so that the child develops a secure attachment with that caregiver. We can also imagine the parallel finding with self-attunement in mindfulness practice: We develop a secure attachment with ourselves. We come to trust that we can rely on ourselves for comfort and connection. We decrease stress, and, as we've seen, inhibit burnout.

Feeling trust is a state-dependent process in which the interactions with a specific other person engender a feeling that being vulnerable—of depending on the other for support—is a safe way to be. It is okay to let down our guard. These patterns of on-guard defense and then release into connection are embedded in synaptic linkages that build the architecture of implicit memory. We feel the emotions, sense our body's state, perceive the other's face, and enact behaviors from our earliest days on the planet. Implicit memory also creates summations of repeated episodes of experience as mental models or schema of specific types of interactions. We ready ourselves to respond with priming that sets the stage for making some reactions more likely than others.

Each of these elements of implicit memory—our emotions,

bodily sensations, perceptual biases, and behavioral responses as well as our mental models and priming—directly influence how we come to trust another person. If you have had repeated experiences of being unseen or mistreated or betrayed, you are more likely to be vigilant for these examples of misattunement, perhaps seeing them more readily, or even imagining them when they in fact are not really occurring. Understanding your own history as a clinician is crucial so that you are aware of how trust and mistrust have played important roles in your life. Our review in the last few chapters of self-reflection will have provided an important starting place from which to continue to explore the ways the past has shaped your ongoing readiness for connection.

Moments when a miscommunication leads to abrupt shifts within a clinical encounter may reveal aspects of our own personal histories. Such inevitable misunderstandings or confusions and our patients' subtle or intense responses to them may also evoke in us a drive to deny our responsibility for such ruptures in our connections, or to blame their origins on others. The rapidly shifting dynamic circle of interactions—of two people joining in the clinical encounter—is filled with vulnerabilities on both individuals' parts. The key as a clinician is to be open to the meaning of these missed connections, for you and for your client. Readily sensing the importance of such disconnection and honoring the rupture with a statement, "I'm sorry for what happened," and then exploring the deeper meanings of such ruptures, is crucial in re-creating and maintaining therapeutic trust.

As we've stated, research on the essential ingredients of effective therapy reveals that our therapeutic relationship is one of the most important factors responsible for the positive impact of psychotherapy. In 1998, Henry (page 128) concluded a panel on therapy outcomes with these words: "As a general trend across studies, the largest chunk of outcome variance not attributable to preexisting patient characteristics involves individual therapist differences and the emergent therapeutic relationship between patient and therapist, regardless of technique or school of therapy." Building on this finding, Norcross identifies the alliance, empathy, and goal consensus and collaboration as being key ingredients to the psychotherapy relationship. Here alliance is described as the quality and strength of the collaborative sense of the relationship. Empathy—the most robust factor—is defined as the therapist's sensitive ability to understand the client's feelings, thoughts, and struggles from the client's point of view. Goal consensus and collaboration was attained via the collecting of feedback regarding the client's impressions, efficacy of interventions, and satisfaction with the therapy relationship itself. Norcross suggests that the relationship be customized so that the therapist is able to create a new therapy for each patient and tailor the relationship to the specifics of each case, but find guidance in the general technique principles derived from research evidence. Now that is a great description of what being mindful as a therapist entails.

Patients come to therapy at differing stages of change—and the therapist can tailor ways of being for each stage. For example, therapists can take on the role of nurturing parent, interactive teacher, coach, or consultant depending on the stage of change of the client. Norcross further recommends "making the creating and cultivation of the therapeutic relationship a primary aim" of therapy. Being a mindful therapist who engenders trust with the patient can be seen to offer the open presence that each of these key features of effective therapy requires.

An essential component of that relationship is the openness of the therapist to seeking and receiving feedback from the client. In many ways, these findings support the notion that mindful traits of the therapist are at the heart of effective therapeutic relationships. With trust, the gateway can be opened to activating the love without fear state of the social engagement system. This is a receptive state—one in which we can propose that positive neuroplastic changes can be initiated and maintained. We are all human, we all have social brains, and finding a way to acknowledge and respect each other's inner world of vulnerability with curiosity, openness, acceptance, and love enables us to demonstrate our belief that trust is a basic neurological need.

MINDSIGHT SKILLS

Similar to our No and Yes exercise in Chapter 1, the feeling of trust is a receptive state—a Yes mode—in which we welcome input from others and may even acknowledge our own needs for connection. Being open is a state of being that is receptive rather than reactive. To achieve alliance, empathy, and goal consensus and collaboration, trust is essential.

Yet most of us have had some experiences in our pasts, whether in childhood, adolescence, or adulthood, in which being vulnerable was not a sacred state respected by others. In this situation, we may have adapted by becoming reactive rather than remaining receptive. Such an adaptive state can involve the classic defensive strategies of denying our own feelings, cutting ourselves off from bodily sensations that fuel those feelings, rationalizing why what happened didn't matter, or withdrawing from others with the stance that we don't need to depend on others for our own wellbeing. With repeated occurrences, violations in our trust in another can lead to adaptations that become woven into our flexible repertoire of responses or even become more inflexible aspects of our personality traits.

In ourselves as clinicians and in our clients as well, looking for historically created and presently enacted adaptive strategies in response to mistrust is an important inner exploration that can illuminate how vulnerability and trust are unfolding now. These are aspects of an inner narrative that can be explored in journal writing or walks in nature: What were the patterns that you adopted to deal with betrayals of your trust? How did you respond to being ignored, intruded upon, or terrified? In what ways did your development since childhood become influenced by times when others let you down? What role does vulnerability play in your life now?

In many ways, we can perceive this adaptive strategy as the enduring proclivities that shape our valenced plateaus of probability and the
patterns of our peaks of activation. As we move away from the open
plane of possibility, that ground of being in which we all began life—
open to whatever is and ready to accept the world as it unfolds—we
eventually become constrained by biases that filter our perception
and shape our behaviors. Moving away from the plane, we are shaped
by synaptic linkages of adaptation and subjective patterns of habit that
form and continue to mold the parallel unfolding of neural firing and
mental life. It is in this movement into the worlds of probability and
activation, of shifting from open possibility to lived actuality, that we
see the constricted adaptations in need of liberation.

These are the ways restrictive patterns pull us away from the
plane of possibility and keep us imprisoned in repeating thoughts,
feelings, and behaviors. It is these subtle or not-so-subtle habits of
mind away from receptivity that can block us from creating the
trust our clients need to feel when in our presence. The good news
is that you can learn to find your way to releasing those constricting plateaus and incessant peaks of repeating mental activities and
neural events. You can learn to relax into the open space of the
plane of possibility. This is a practice for yourself that we'll explore
in the chapters ahead. And this skill is one that can then be taught
to your clients directly.

From the receiving end, when we encounter another person
whose constrictions are so inflexible as to distort how he or she
can take us in, we feel this limitation and trust does not emerge
in our inner experience. Instead of feeling felt, we feel misunderstood, ignored, judged. Learning to sense your own constraints in
the physical and subjective sides of reality will enable you to see
where restrictions exist and do something to free yourself from
their grip on your life. Such constrictions bring us toward rigidity or make us prone to chaotic outbursts. The idea is to find these
constrictions—these impairments to integration, as we'll see—and
free them up so that we can live in harmony and at ease.

As you monitor your internal world, you may find that coming back to the classic division of the receptive versus the reactive state may be a helpful reminder as to how our constrictive adaptations feel and how they may continue to imprison us. We react rather than receive when we are on the autopilot protective mode of hiding our vulnerability.

To develop the trust-related mindsight skill of monitoring and modifying the internal world, we'll start first with monitoring your narrative history of times when trust was not present in your life. Then we'll dive into a basic reflection exercise to promote a sense of safety and trust.

Imagine a time in your life when depending on others didn't turn out so well, when you were let down, disappointed, ignored. What happened? How did that one experience possibly get repeated in the future? In what ways did you learn a new pattern of adapting to that hurt? How has that adaptation influenced your long-term development? Are there specific situations in which you find being open and vulnerable more natural, while others are extremely challenging? Writing down your reflections on these issues can begin to lay a foundation of understanding how vulnerability and trust play a role in your life. Don't edit what you write: Just take journal and pen in hand (or computer if you're going digital) and write, write, write. Editing is a later process possibly needed when something is moving toward public consumption. This is writing to reveal only to you, if you prefer, what lays hidden in your narrative structures and bound in swirls of memory deep within your mind. Journal writing is good not only for your immune system and sense of well-being (see Pennebaker, 2000; see also Goldberg, 1986). This grounding in self-understanding can also make your insights into your clients' reactions more open. By knowing yourself deeply you can deeply open yourself to knowing others. Such understanding can bring you to more presence as you let go of old adaptations to social pains from the past. Making sense of your life is an integrative process that frees you internally and interpersonally.

Modifying our old patterns enables us to be attuned to others in a more open and contingent way. Knowing when you are becoming reactive, you can apply your inner resources (a peaceful place in imagery, for example) and focus on your breath to bring you back to receptivity. Right now I invite you to create an internal place of clarity and calm. Returning to the breath-awareness practice we developed in Chapter 1, let yourself find the breath and sense the rhythm of your breathing, in and out, as you let awareness ride the waves of the breath. As attention becomes distracted from the breath, just let your awareness lovingly and gently take note of that distraction and then redirect your attention to the breath.

Now I invite you to imagine a place, from memory or imagination, which fills you with a sense of safety and security. This may be the image of somewhere that brings a deep sense of calm and tranquility that we developed in chapter 1, or a new image that emerges that has a sense of being grounded and clear. As you further develop this inner safe place, let the rhythm of your breath fill your awareness too, sensing the movement in and out of that life-giving force. You may notice the peaceful sense in your limbs, a calmness in your chest, the relaxation of your facial muscles. Knowing that this place is always there for you, let the rise and fall of the breath encircle you as you imagine this safe place in your mind. This is a tranquility that is always available to you. This inner attunement is an invitation to initiate presence, to be brave in the face of your own vulnerability. In many ways, this is learning to come to trust within yourself the open plane of possibility that we all share. This is the place where we begin that often gets buried under the barrage of adaptations we necessarily enact to survive in this imperfect world. The courage to connect with others is also an open door for your client to be present in the therapeutic relationship as well, seeing you be open, extending your hand to theirs on this mutually created journey to trust. This is the way open minds meet together in the shared plane of possibility.

May (I, he, or she) be happy and live with a joyful heart;
May (I, he, or she) be healthy and have a body that gives (me, him, her) energy;
May (I, he, or she) be safe and protected from harm;

and

May (I, he, or she) live with the ease that comes from well-being.

Offered to self, mentor, friend, and neutral acquaintance.
    Now giving and asking for forgiveness from someone with whom you have a conflict.
    Then offering phrases to the whole world of living beings, and then again to yourself.

Figure 4.1 Loving-kindness phrases. These phrases can evoke internal states of clarity, compassion, and likely integration as they facilitate the neural firing of our resonance circuits, which enable us to be attuned to others and ourselves. With practice, these intentionally created states of kindness can become long-term traits of compassion and caring concern.

For the next part of this practice now focusing on modifying, we'll do another exercise as we explore the classic loving-kindness meditation (see Kornfield, 2008) that I believe helps further activate both the social- and the self-engagement systems. When we harness the social circuits of compassion and kindness, we create a state of other-directed and of self-compassion that, with practice, can become a readily accessible internal stance and trait in our lives. Figure 4.1 has the basic outline of this practice.

Letting your eyes go closed, focus on your breath. Now let the breath go into the background and let these words fill your awareness. Please repeat in your mind each phrase. First, we'll direct these wishes toward your self. Then we'll in turn offer abbreviated statements for a mentor, a friend, and a neutral acquaintance. Next we'll identify someone with whom you have a conflict, some tension still unresolved in your relationship with one another. We'll offer them forgiveness, then ask for it in return—and then offer them loving-kindness wishes. We'll next offer these wishes to the whole world of living creatures before returning to the place we began and offering these wishes to ourselves. In Figure 4.1 you'll see the four phrases. Some prefer to offer the full phrases at the start and finish. The abbreviated phrases would be: May [you] be happy; May [you] be healthy; May [you] be safe; and May [you] live with well-being.

Some people feel awkward trying this out—and even feel like they are being brainwashed. This is a great exercise for you to do, but applying it to patients early on in their work may feel too intimidating. It should be introduced cautiously and at the right timing in your work together. Stimulating specific circuits of the brain with intention is indeed an act of mind training, a way to harness specific areas of the brain. But here we're building on the reality that we can stimulate the neuronal activation and growth (SNAG) of the circuitry of compassion. I've found that this dimension of mental focus can stimulate feelings of compassion and has the sense that we are activating important social circuits in the brain. In fact, studies of expert meditators focusing on nonreferential compassion—compassion without a specific target in mind—actually had the largest amount of gamma waves ever recorded (see Lutz et al., 2004). These EEG findings are consistent with massive neural synchrony, an outcome of an integrated brain. A host of new studies suggests that developing a compassionate mind is a win-win-win situation as we promote better physiological health, improved psychological well-being, and enhanced interpersonal relationships (see Gilbert, 2010). Kristin Neff (2009) suggests that self-compassion includes a sense of kindness toward the self, a feeling that one's experiences are a part of a common humanity, and mindful acceptance of our thoughts and feelings without becoming identified by them.

Interweaving loving-kindness exercises with breath awareness and the body scan we've already introduced is a natural blend of attunement-focused mind skills. When we attune to ourselves, we harness the neural circuitry of self-awareness, opening ourselves to the very neural capacities that enable us to tune in to others.

Our present state of scientific knowledge suggests that we can solidly affirm that kindness and compassion are to the brain what the breath is to life.

TRUST AND INTEGRATION

Imagine our plane of possibility as a state of being open to whatever arises. Now consider the view that as complex systems we have a natural tendency to move toward maximizing complexity as we self-organize across time. As separate elements of a system specialize, the conditions are set for the innate self-organizational process of flexible adaptation to link those differentiated elements together to form a more complex state. This is how integration can be seen to be the fundamental process that maximizes complexity in dynamic systems. This movement is inherently dynamic, creating more flexible, adaptive, coherent, energized, and stable states across time. In this way, we can say that the linkage of differentiated elements creates a FACES flow—the vital outcome of integration. This is the way we become open to what is within us, and open to what is inside of others.

This is why kindness and compassion are good for you and everyone else: they are profoundly integrative. Trust emerges with our sense of being open and connected to ourselves, others, and the larger world in which we all live.

With trust, we move into the plane of possibility and release restrictions to our innate capacity for moving toward integrated states. We can let our defenses down, soften our peaks, broaden our plateaus, and move fluidly between possibility and activation without fear. This is the spontaneity of trust. We can be ourselves in the presence of another. In contrast, when our adaptations constrain such movement, we move away from the harmony of integration and toward the banks of chaos or rigidity. We have feelings that flood us, or habits that imprison us. When we free ourselves from those eruptions and prisons, when we relax out of the repeating peaks and inflexible plateaus, we return to the plane of possibility. Trust frees us to move naturally toward this open state in which our system's natural drive toward a harmonious flow of integration can be realized.

Now let's imagine in a bit more detail that we're moving away from the plane of possibility, with the patterns of energy and information flow between the reciprocal mental and physical sides now being restrictive. As our physical neuronal firing is constrained by past synaptic learning that limits movement toward an open, integrated state, we may find that we have repeated behaviors, engrained emotional responses, or recurrent thoughts that rigidly shape how we live. This may be true of ourselves as clinicians as much as it is true of our clients. Likewise, both therapist and client may experience blocked ways in which integration does not occur and rather than rigidity, we find that we have impulsive behaviors, a flood of unpredictable and disruptive emotions, or irrational and random thoughts that plague our lives, confuse our reasoning, disrupt our relationships. Whether we are constrained or confused, blocked integration impairs our life. In such a state, we are far from the ease of well-being and live in a subjective world that often lacks trust in others, and even in ourselves.

Trust and integration go hand in hand. We might say that our innate drive as complex systems to move toward the complexity of integration is something to be released, rather than created. Kindness and compassion engender trust and can be seen as our natural state. There is a vulnerability we enter—of not controlling but permitting—that trust and being kind and open entail. Our job as therapists then is akin to Michelangelo's statement that he did not create the figure but liberated it from the stone. So, too, can we align ourselves with the natural drive to heal: This is the self-organizational movement toward harmony. The key is to feel the pulse of integration as revealed within states of rigidity or chaos and then dive deeply into that domain to sense how differentiation and/or linkage may be impaired. Here we see that trust is a starting place to engage more fully in the experience of change.

Ultimately we as clinicians are companions along the road of life with our patients. Trust emerges when we realize that the false separation created by the cloak of professional identity is just an illusion. Each of us, therapist and client alike, is doing the best we can. Naturally we bring our ethical and therapeutic role to the relationship: We honor boundaries and confidentiality and keep the clinical goal of the patient's healing front and center in all encounters. But even with these caveats, we still are fellow travelers along the path of discovery. Our most powerful therapeutic tool is trust—and this can only happen with authentic presence as we move forward, together, with kindness and compassion to face whatever arises in the journey to heal.

Chapter 5

TRUTH

While trust is an ever-emerging state of being in which we are willing to be open and connect with kindness and compassion, truth is related to a grounded reality of the essence of things as they are. Truth, as we'll use this term here, refers to an integrated coherence, of how something flexibly connects many layers of facts and experiences into one interwoven whole. Naturally, philosophers, physicists, and attorneys have different applications and connotations of the notion of truth. For our purposes, we'll be exploring the way in which the authentic emergence of some fact, concept, or interaction unfolds over time in a way that is free of restrictive constraints that are cobwebs from the past, distortions in the present, or fears that limit our experience of the future.

The effective use of mere words may be especially challenging here, but let's try to see if we can let the truth about truth emerge within these linguistic packets on a page. Here is the basic notion: Systems function with the flow across time of energy and information in patterns that we can perceive (we'll explore these, especially in Chapters 6 and 7 coming up). These patterns have a grounded quality to them—a prime state—in which their "true characteristics" emerge. These characteristics, when explored, fit into a set of conditions that settle into a natural order, a way in which the pieces of a puzzle create a cohesive whole. This is a snapshot in time, one slice of reality now, a cross-sectional view of what is. When it is cohesive, it fits together, sticks together, and has lasting holding power. But cohesion by itself does not reveal the notion of truth. In fact, many a personal narrative is cohesive in ways that protect us from knowing the truth. With truth, coherence emerges over time as the larger frame of "what is" has space for the various disparate elements to come together as an integrated whole as unfolding across time. We sense coherence in the fourth dimension of time, linking patterns of then with observations of now as we anticipate the emergence of next. Cohesion holds things together now; coherence reveals the interlaced web of reality across past, present, and future.

I know that you may be wondering, "What is this abstract notion of truth all about?" Here is the essential feeling: Across time, things cohere together in a way that weaves a tapestry of reality that surrounds us with "making sense" reflections on the past, authenticity in the present, and accurate predictive value for the future. Sensing the truth is a four-dimensional job as we see across the past, present, and future—along the fourth dimension of time—to sense the "yesness" of interwoven fabric of the whole. I know that may sound odd, but bear with me and I hope you'll see the practical implications for your own life and work.

Let me offer you an example from clinical practice. As a trainee trying to make sense of the flashback phenomena of posttraumatic stress disorder, I once took care of a woman who feared that she would "fall flat on her face" if she tried new things. By diving deeply into the neuroscience literature, the recently emerging findings about the role of the hippocampus in assembling pieces of implicit memory together into their explicit forms met our criteria for truth. Knowing about the hippocampus allowed many clinical pieces of otherwise confusing data to become assembled into a coherent frame that not only made sense, but helped people heal. With this perspective, we could make sense of the past, see more clearly in an authentic way into the present, and predict patterns that would emerge in the future. By viewing posttraumatic stress through the lens of mind experience and brain mechanisms of impaired neural integration, past views, present encounters, and future interventions could then become woven into a coherent approach to helping understand and to resolve trauma. In this patient's situation, an early tricycle accident had left her with an implicit fear of trying new things, especially when she was filled with excitement. Her brain side of reality coupled excitement and explorations of novelty with dread, physical pain, and humiliation. The result was a life constrained by an implicit fear of trying something new. Exploring the nature of her brain and the neural mechanisms of memory opened the way for her to make sense of her implicit mental models and then release that fear from its disabling grip on her life. I learned then that teaching people about their brain could empower them to make important changes that created a deep sense of coherence in their lives. The truth allowed them to make sense of their inner world in new and powerful ways and enabled them to be more fully in the present and become the authors of their own unfolding life into the future. This is the emergence of a coherent mind.

For the woman with the tricycle accident, the experience of "falling flat on her face with the excitement of trying something new" as a toddler embedded in her own implicit memory storage a fear of trying out new things when she became a teen and a young adult. Exploring together the nature of her authentic fears and inner experiences revealed how the truth of her accident could help her create coherence in her life. With just the manifestations of and adaptations to the experience of her accident, she was imprisoned by the past and truth was far from her life. Seeing clearly, understanding the truth of how the past had fragmented her brain's ability to integrate elements of implicit memory into her ongoing life narrative, enabled her to transform her life.

Here is the key: The truth sets us free. No matter its pain, knowing the truth gives us coherent options from which to choose our path. We may elect to avoid certain dimensions of life—not trying to play basketball after a back injury, leaning toward art instead of music if we're acoustically challenged—but with truth we are given choice.

There is an old saying (which I'd love to attribute to someone if I knew where this came from) which states that we get freedom from acknowledging our limitations. As a young adolescent I remember feeling the electric charge of that paradox: Freedom from acknowledging constraints? Wow. At our meeting on science and spirituality in Italy, Stuart Kauffman was excited to discuss a notion he was playing with of "enabling constraints": that the factors that shape what we can and cannot do, the features that define our parameters, are in fact what enable us to achieve all sorts of developmental tasks. The sentiment here is that as we accept the truth, as we draw a circle around what defines our possibilities, we actually liberate ourselves from the delusion that we can do everything. Truth—even about our enabling constraints that limit us—sets us free. Within that freedom we find healing, hope, and coherence.

BRAIN BASICS

There are sets of neural firing in which patterns can coalesce and synchronize to yield representations that fit well together. This, we can propose, is the neural basis of the truth. This sense of truth embeds meaning at its core, so it is natural to wonder how the mental experience of meaning correlates with the physical manifestation of meaning within neural firing. I've proposed that the brain encodes meaning through the A, B, C, D, and E of neural processing (another memory tool). We make associations, have beliefs, generate cognitions, are influenced by developmental phases, and evoke emotions in response to our experiences. This is how we make meaning of our life's journey.

To reveal truth, meaning is created across these five dimensions so that they cohere in a flexible and adaptive way. (Notice we're not saying that they "cohese" in a certain way.) That young woman with the tricycle accident could make new associations, examine her beliefs, generate new ways of thinking in her cognition, gain insights into the developmental impact of her accident on her life, and reassess the emotional reactions to starting a new job once the truth of the accident was revealed. Meaning takes coherent shape when truth is present. Without truth, the meaning in the brain is distorted by maladaptive associations ("I'll fall flat on my face if I take that new job I am excited about"), restrictive beliefs ("I can't try something new"), rigid and inflexible cognitions ("What should I be doing with this job choice?"), outdated or distorted developmental needs (her relationships were impaired and she could not move into the next phase of her professional life), and flooding or blunted emotional reactions (with persistent worry and fear). She was stuck and needed help.

Each of these elements of moving away from the truth can be seen as an example of rigidity, chaos, or both. As these are examples of the outcome of blocked integration, we can inquire into the notion that truth and integration are overlapping processes. Wait a moment; you might think, is all of this about promoting integration? Well, the surprising finding is that integration becomes an organizing principle that, well, seems to be a coherent way of assembling our wide array of clinical experiences into a framework that is, yes, coherent. We use the power of our internal vision, of mindsight, to illuminate the inner nature of the flow of energy and information within and among us. When truth emerges, integration flourishes.

Making sense is an integrative process. Within our subjective experience, we link disparate elements of memory and ongoing life events into a flexible and open sense of what is, of what could be, and where we need to go. On the physical side, we link the neural net profiles of activation in ways that cohere together. Instead of abrupt dissociations of thought and flooding affective states that

impair neural integration, we link the A, B, C, D, and E of neural firing patterns into a coherent whole across time. As we adapt
to life's challenges with frequent distortions in how we see reality, our brain responds by rigid compensations that are blockages
to integration. We can impair linkage—as often happens in unresolved trauma—and we can impair differentiation—as may be seen
in developmental arrests. These various ways in which truth is distorted and integration impaired block vitality and keep us from living a harmonious life.

MINDSIGHT SKILLS

To know and cultivate the truth, we need to differentiate what
we are aware of from the experience of awareness itself. Making this
distinction between, say, a thought or feeling and the awareness of
the thought or feeling is a first step to moving from cohesive states
of defensive adaptation to coherent states of truth-filled living.

Here we'll explore a wheel of awareness metaphor of the mind
through an immersion in internal experience. The basic idea of the
wheel, as depicted in Figure 5.1, is essentially this: Awareness is a
subjective state of receptivity that enables us to know that the process of being aware is distinct from that which we are aware of. The
visual metaphor of a wheel is a useful map to envision this distinction with the hub as the symbol of receptive awareness, the rim as
composed of anything we can be aware of, and spokes representing the focus of our attention from the hub to any point on the
rim. That's it. Simple, but for clients—and for ourselves—it seems
to offer a shared reference point for letting go of enduring cohesive
states and receiving the re-sorting of rim elements in the pathway
toward coherence. Let's do an experiential exercise to make these
metaphoric notions grounded in your own subjective reality.

Naturally one can engage in internal reflection with a wide array
of goals. One might be to simply build the strength of attention as
we repeatedly return, again and again, our wandering mind to its

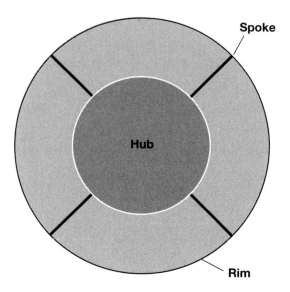

Figure 5.1 The wheel of awareness: rim, spokes, and hub. The wheel of awareness is a visual metaphor for how we can be aware (via the hub) of any element
in our inner or outer worlds (on the rim). We can focus attention (the spokes) on
any element of the rim or be open to monitoring whatever arises from the rim
in the open spaciousness of awareness in the hub.

intended target. Even this basic exercise is profound, as we need to
be aware of our awareness, and pay attention to our intention to
accomplish it. These are the two factors shared in common in all
mindfulness practices.

As our focus of attention is stabilized through the breath awareness practice we did in Chapter 1 and which we'll review just
ahead, we'll be ready to dive more deeply into an exploration of
the architecture of awareness itself. This will be the first of a series
of practices exploring the mind as we broaden and deepen our
mindsight skills. This is the wheel of awareness exercise.

First we'll extend the most basic place to begin, the breath. This
widespread practice of sensing the breath offers us the powerful place with which to harness the hub of our wheel of awareness. Let's go further, now, with the breath awareness practice and
develop this more fully in your experience.

Let's begin by just sensing the breath. Let the sensations of your breath fill your awareness as you ride the wave of your in-breath, then your out-breath. Just sensing, let awareness become filled with the waves of the breath, in and out. As you let your awareness ride the waves of the breath, let me tell you an ancient story that has been passed down across the generations.

The mind is like the ocean. Deep beneath the surface it is calm and clear. No matter what the conditions are at the surface, deep below it is stable, tranquil, serene. From this depth of the ocean, you can look upward at the surface and just notice whether it is flat or choppy, wild or in a full storm. Whatever these conditions, deep inside it is calm and stable.

It is an ancient teaching that the mind is like the ocean. Just sensing your breath brings you beneath the surface of your mental sea. From this place, you can look to the activity of the mind and just notice it from this calm and tranquil place. Sensing your breath brings you to this calm place where you can just observe the mental activity, the brain waves at the surface of your mind. These activities are the thoughts and feelings, memories and perceptions, hopes, dreams, and longings that arise and fall away. From deep in your mind, you can feel the clarity of your inner self as you just notice these sensations, images, feelings, and thoughts as they come and go in and out of your awareness. Just sensing your breath brings you to this calm and clear place in the depth of your mind.

Take a few moments to simply enjoy the serenity of this inner place of your mind. When you are ready, you might take a deeper and more intentional breath, letting your eyes come open if they're closed, and we'll continue our discussion.

In many ways, this depth of our minds within the mental sea is like the hub of the wheel of awareness. From the hub, we can look toward the rim and just notice whatever arises there.

For this exercise, let yourself just feel the visual imagery of being in the depths of the ocean or resting in the hub of the mind. These are visual metaphors that work well for many people—but you may find your own imagery that works especially well for you. Whatever the image, the idea is the same: From this inner place of clarity, just let whatever arises come into your awareness.

We'll use the wheel of awareness as our shared metaphor for this next phase of the exercise. Picture the wheel, and see if you can just let elements from the rim come into focus. For a basic breath awareness practice, the instructions are simple: The intended subject of attention is the breath. When you've noticed that your awareness is no longer on the breath, lovingly and gently redirect your attention to the breath. Remember, getting distracted is just what the mind does. Like an exercise, we contract and relax the muscle of the mind as we focus, get distracted, and then refocus the mind on its intended subject of awareness. Some like to make those quiet mental notations of the general category of rim activity that distracted awareness: thinking, remembering, feeling. Letting that distraction go, you refocus attention on the breath.

If we did this breath awareness exercise each day, we'd be building the circuitry of executive function. We're monitoring our own awareness and intention, and then modifying our focus of attention. In the wheel of awareness terms, we're strengthening the hub of our mind.

After you've done this exercise for a few weeks, or if you feel ready to try this now, there is a next layer of wheel development that can be a bit more challenging. This can be called a mind awareness exercise and it encompasses the whole of the rim as the subject of intentional focus. This will be an open monitoring exercise where rather than focusing on the breath as a target, we invite anything from the rim to come into our awareness.

Image yourself resting in the hub. You may want to just notice how thoughts and feelings first appear—is it suddenly or gradually? How do these thoughts or feelings stay present in awareness? How do they disappear from view? Just sensing your inner world, notice whatever comes into your field of awareness. Unlike the breath awareness practice, now we let the breath go into the background and our intention is to have no designated target. Just let whatever happens, happen.

Now notice the sensation if you sometimes get "lost in a thought" or "immersed in a feeling." Was there a time when you lost track of your awareness, when you moved to the surface like a cork bobbing up and down on the surface of the sea? When we become identified fully with the rim, when we are no longer resting in the clarity of the hub, we often identify with the activities of the mind as being the totality of who we are. Mindfulness enables us to separate hub from rim so that we are not swept up into mental activity—unless we choose, with intention and awareness, to become lost in that flow. Here we see that mindfulness can involve the choice to become lost in flow, but flow is not the same as mindfulness. A mindful stance embeds an attitude of kindness and compassion and the capacity for self-observation as we monitor our own awareness and intention. With flow, we wonderfully lose ourselves in the experience, becoming "at one" with the experience of the rim.

You may want to spend a few minutes now simply resting in the hub and just notice whatever arises on the rim. See if you can examine more deeply how things first appear in your mind's eye. How do they stay present within awareness? How do they fall away, disappear, become out of your focus of attention? Some like to count thoughts; others prefer to just sit back and let the movement of mental activity go by as if they were passengers on a train just noting the scenery out the window. You are now developing the vital capacity to distinguish awareness itself from the mental activity that is the object of your awareness.

This is a gentle and often helpful place to start as we begin our exploration of harnessing the hub and differentiating awareness from the objects of our attention. In future exercises we will elaborate the various elements of the wheel of awareness in great detail.

THE COHERENCE OF TRUTH

From the hub of our minds we can disentangle ourselves from the constraints of identifying with mental activities as who we are. It is this overidentification, this melding of self with the particulars of mental life on the rim, which can inadvertently limit our sense of possibilities. Consider this: The hub represents the experience of being in the open plane of possibility. The structure of personality, clinging on to a self-constructed cohesive notion of personal identity, the grip of unresolved trauma, the implicit lessons of hatred for others or of the self—these are all the ways in which movement beyond the plane may have become limiting. These are all examples of impaired integration. When we work with clients, we sense the pulse of this rigidity and chaos and from our own inner hub we stay within an open plane so as not to get swept up in the depletion or the storms. From this inner place, we can then focus with the client on SNAGging the brain—stimulating neuronal activation and growth—to promote differentiation and then linkage. At the very least, if our clients or we ourselves haven't differentiated hub from rim, we're prone to ways in which the flow of mental life persists in its differentiation without linkage in the maintenance of nonintegrated states. With a strengthened hub, it becomes possible to embrace the many mental activities and discern which are "true" and to be retained and nurtured, and to assess which are "untrue" and allowed to dissipate like ripples on a pond.

In therapy, truth is our friend. Whether as therapist or client, seeking coherence and the truth from which that integrated state comes forth is the path of healing. In this way, the guiding principle is that truth, coherence, and integration are overlapping constructs. Even in facing severe histories of trauma, integrating memory liberates a deep sense of vitality in one's life. Truth may be filled with pain, but the outcome for a person's life, dominated previously by the expenditure of enormous amounts of energy to avoid knowing the reality of what had occurred and now freed to rest in what actually happened, releases a deep sense of freedom.

In reflecting on the central hub, the open plane, and the concept of accepting things as they are, you may begin to wonder, then is the idea that we are supposed to just sit cross-legged in some nirvana state of no-action—accepting things, whatever they are, just as they appear? Is being a mindful therapist some exaggerated sense of "anything goes"? No, not at all. The idea is that when we're stuck on the surface of our mental sea and strapped to the rim of our wheel of awareness (same idea in different metaphors), we're whipped around without ballast (the sea) or spun around and ground into the pavement (a strange wheel implication, I know) without relief. Naturally we have to live and not always be in the plane of open possibility. Plateaus and peaks are necessary. As my colleague Jack Kornfield (2008) likes to say, we need to remember our Social Security number: After the ecstasy, the laundry. We have to get up and choose our meal, brush our teeth, and go to work. We need our plateaus of probability and our specific peaks. But sometimes those plateaus and peaks are filled with constricting adaptations, locking us into maladaptive patterns, keeping us from the truth. The hub of the mind offers a ground of being that is not only the essence of presence, it is the basis of resilience and clarity. When we harness the power to rest in the hub, we can see the rim more clearly and soften our peaks, broaden our plateaus, and let the coherence of truth emerge from previously cohesive but unhelpful constructs of confusion. As with any form of integration, we need to combine disparate elements: hub and rim, open plane with plateaus and peaks, depth with surface. This is how we use the integration of consciousness to free us toward living with coherence.

A clear view of truth and the experience of coherence are what emerge when we step away from being overidentified with only the rim. In this way, our wheel of awareness exercise begins a deep practice of stabilizing mindsight's lens and coming to attend to the world of our inner experience. We develop integration of consciousness as we differentiate hub from rim, awareness from that which we are aware of. The subjective side of this state of harnessing the hub is the sense of being *c*onnected, *o*pen, *h*armonious, *e*ngaged, *r*eceptive, *e*mergent, *n*oetic, *c*ompassionate, and *e*mpathic. This descriptive acronym is at the heart of the subjective feeling of coherence that emerges from the physical side of integration. The objective side of this view is derived from a mathematical analysis of coherence itself (see Thagard, 2000) and is built upon examining what emerges with integrative functioning of our complex systems. With coherence, we feel across time a deep sense of integration—the harmonious ease of well-being. Just listening to a choir sing in harmony at various intervals gives you that sense of, well, coherence.

Practicing this initial wheel of awareness exercise is just the beginning of getting in touch with this core mental experience—an inner sanctuary—that can serve to support therapist and client alike. It is also where we meet, face to face, hub to hub, in the journey toward healing, together.

Chapter 6

TRIPOD

As we venture into the mental sea to explore the world inside, our inner vision can initially be unstable, cloudy, and overwhelming. You may have felt this in the exercise in the last chapter, in which receiving input from the rim into the hub may have been jumpy and unclear. That's not surprising, as many of us have had little training of our minds to stabilize attention. Ironically, our various levels of schooling seem to want us to develop our mind, but never train the instrument we'll be developing directly: We pile facts and skills into our children's heads without first aiming an educational spotlight on the mind that is doing the learning. To view the inner world, we use what we can call our mindsight lens to enable us to peer inward so that we can know the sea inside with stability. As with any perceptual lens that is unsteady, the images we create can be blurry if our camera is not held firmly in place. Taking our metaphor of a mental camera further, we can imagine a tripod that stabilizes our mindsight lens so that what we see has more depth and clarity. Instead of a buzzing hive of confusion, strengthening the lens of mindsight makes what we see stable and clear—and in this clarity we can see subtle aspects of the mind with more fine detail, with more depth, and with a more flexible sense of equanimity.

We can picture the tripod of this lens as having three equally important legs that lend stability to our mindsight view, as illus-

trated in Figure 6.1. These are the fundamental mental approaches
of openness, observation, and objectivity. In many ways, the tripod enables us to build the strength of the hub so that awareness
becomes distinct from the object of our attention on the rim. Here
we'll review each leg of the tripod and explore ways in which
we can cultivate these aspects of our mind. This cultivation begins
with ourselves as individuals so that we can strengthen our own
mindsight lens. Then we can begin the important step of teaching these now-familiar skills to our patients for strengthening their
own mindsight abilities. As with all of these mindsight skill-training exercises, what applies to our own development can then be
adapted for the direct teaching of our clients. This is how we move
from the indirect but powerful effects of our own mindful presence in the therapeutic relationship to the direct effects of teaching mindsight skills to our patients at appropriate times if helpful.

OPENNESS

Being open means cultivating the receptive states within ourselves that rest beneath the surface layers of judgment and expectation. To reach and maintain a state of openness requires that we
monitor our internal reactivity—sensing when, for example, we
are on automatic pilot and becoming thrown by the ways in which
emotions distort our perception of others. Instead of condemn-
ing ourselves as this realization becomes clear, we are open to what
is, accept it, and then move to transform it, if we choose. This is
the modifying role of the mind. Likewise, when we are open we
can move toward accepting our own emotional reactions without making harsh criticisms or becoming swallowed up by expectations or reactions of guilt or shame. This may seem ironic—to
accept an emotional response that might be biasing our perceptions
yet at the same time to seek to be open and accepting of others—
but this is the core of the challenge. Beneath emotional reactivity,
before judgment and expectation, rests an open space of receiving

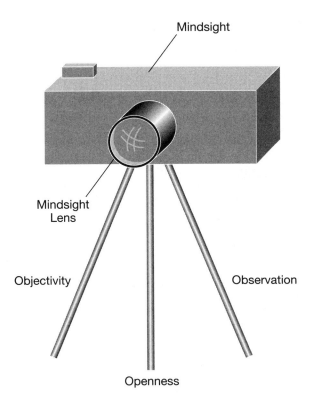

Figure 6.1 The mindsight tripod. Openness, objectivity, and observation form the three processes that stabilize the lens of mindsight to see and shape the inner world with clarity, depth, and power. With openness we accept things as they are; with objectivity we realize that what we are aware of is just one element of our experience and not the totality of our identity; with observation we have a sense of ourselves as observers witnessing the unfolding of experience as it emerges moment by moment.

things as close to they actually are as we can possibly muster. This is the open plane of possibility that began our journey, and this is the essence of presence that begins to emerge as we cultivate the openness of our mindsight tripod.

You may have noticed that what we've already been practicing helps to stabilize our mindsight lens with openness. Being present, accepting what is rather than shifting things into what we'd like them to be, and being receptive to whatever arises in the moment, are the many layers of openness that are akin to the notion of beginner's mind. We try to let go of the top-down constraints that limit our ability to receive bottom-up input from moment-to-moment experience.

BRAIN BASICS

The study of the forms of mental processing available to us reveals that we have at least two modes of representing reality. One mode is that which you are experiencing right now: the linguistic, verbal mode of expression. These words are encapsulated digital pieces of information with shared linguistic meaning. But the word is not the thing itself, and being open requires that we acknowledge the limited scope of words to capture the essence of reality. Another mode is the more direct, if you will, imagery mode in which we create non-linguistic representations, called images, of the world and of ourselves (see Kosslyn, 2005). These images can be in the visual realm but also include representations of any form of sensation—including auditory, tactile, gustatory, or olfactory. We can even have bodily images—maps of our whole body that fill our perceptual reality in the moment.

Our image maps may be a bit closer to things as they are than the more constructed and conceptual word maps of the linguistic domain. In the brain, the neural correlates of our mental images are pieces of information, something that stands for or symbolizes something other than itself. Even an olfactory image of the scent of a rose is in fact a neural firing pattern or mental sensation of a rose's scent, not the scent itself. But our imagery mode may be as close as we can get to that rose.

Recalling the six layers of the vertical columns lining the neocortex can be helpful in understanding the possible neural underpinnings of openness (see Hawkins and Blakeslee, 2004). Bottom-up data moves from layer 6 to 5 to 4 while top-down prior learning information flows from layer 1 to 2 to 3. Essentially the crashing of bottom-up with top-down at layers 4 and 3 correlates with our awareness of the present moment. One notion of a mindful brain is that we practice the skill of disarming the predominance

A Schematic of the Six-Layered Cortical Column and the Bottom-Up and Top-Down Flow of Information

Layer	Top-Down	Top-Down Dominance	Top-Down
1	⇓	⇓⇓⇓	⇓
2	⇓	⇓⇓⇓	⇓
3	⇓	⇓⇓⇓	⇓
AWARENESS	⇒→⇒→	→⇒⇒⇒	⇒→→→→→
4	↑	↑	↑↑↑↑↑
5	↑	↑	↑↑↑↑↑
6	↑	↑	↑↑↑↑↑
	Bottom-Up	Bottom-Up	Bottom-Up Dominance

Figure 6.2 Information from sensation flows "bottom-up" from the lower layers of the column streaming from layers 6 to 5 to 4. Information from prior learning, called "top-down," streams from layers 1 to 2 to 3. Awareness is thought to emerge by the co-mingling of these two streams. In the first condition, bottom-up and top-down are balanced and the resultant awareness blends the two streams. In the second condition, top-down input is dominant and prior expectations and categorizations overshadow incoming sensory streams within awareness. In the third condition, sensory input in the here-and-now is dominant and awareness reflects a predominance of input from this sensory flow. Mindfulness may enable layers 3 and 4 to be disentangled by at first practicing enhancement of the bottom-up flow of present sensory experience.

of top-down flow so that we can sense the primacy of bottom-up with more clarity. Some even suggest that being mindful is akin to becoming immersed in sensation rather than thought. I think about mindfulness a bit differently—that mindfulness enables us to differentiate different streams of awareness from one another—and then link them. Being mindful is profoundly integrative. In this view the stream of sensation (as opposed to observation or thought or non-conceptual knowing) is an important element to ground us in the present moment. In many ways, direct sensory streams ground us in bottom-up in the here-and-now. Our other streams of observing, constructing concepts, and knowing can be in the present moment but are about issues from across time, and hence are more a blend of bottom-up with top-down to various degrees.

If mindfulness is about being open to what is, then embracing all of these streams of awareness is an important place to start. Let's look at words and images as a way of understanding the mechanisms beneath this awareness.

If a word is a digital representation (on–off, yes–no, right–left) derived primarily from the neural firing of the left hemisphere, then images can be seen as the analogical representations (meaning they contain an array of features representing the spectrum of aspects of the thing itself). Such analogical representations may have right hemisphere dominance. When we move outward from our plane of possibility toward the subjective realm in imagery, we move simultaneously toward the physical realm in neural firing patterns. The notion of the preverbal is that it is at least a bit closer to the thing as it is, and therefore a vital part of the tripod leg of openness. The take-home message here is that being open may require we let go of the tendency of words and other top-down constructions to dominate our present awareness.

Here let me offer some fascinating findings that emerged from a meeting on comparative neuroanatomy. Professor Katerina Semendeferi from the University of California, San Diego, was presenting a talk on the "Neuroanatomical Perspectives on the Evolution of Mind" (UCLA, November 2009). She was discussing the areas of the brain that had become markedly different from our great ape cousins in the evolution of our human brain. Three aspects were very different: 1) The human brain had developed much more isolation of the two hemispheres from each other; 2) Within a given hemisphere, there were more interneurons linking separate regions to one another; and, 3) in layer 3 of the frontal rostral (forward) most part of the prefrontal cortex, there was a significantly increased amount of neuropil—the axonal fibers that link cells to one another in contrast to the other layers which were dominated by just the cell bodies. What these findings suggest is that we do indeed have quite separate hemispheric anatomic isolation yet increased interconnectivity within a hemisphere. It also suggests, by implication of the expanded layer three area, that this increased neuropil might reveal how we have more information flowing at this level than our primate cousins. In fact, one view of our human heritage—especially after we enter adolescence—is that we become dominated by top-down cortical flow that blocks us from living fully and freely in the here-and-now.

Layer three contributes to how bottom-up meets top-down. We can imagine that having more axonal fibers in this area implies that more information processing may occur at this important juncture between these two streams of data. This finding is intriguing in light of the notion of mindfulness as an intentional practice that helps us become free from top-down enslavements that are the burden of having inherited such a conceptually constructive complex of our creative cortex. Perhaps our human legacy enables us to work at this Layer 3 level to disentangle our streams of information input to make sense of our experience. This is both the opportunity and the burden of our intricate brain—and a reason we may require mental training to free us from the cortical contraptions that enslave us and make living in the moment so challenging as we leave our childhood days and enter the internal chatter of adult preoccupations.

I know for myself I would begin to seek refuge in dance and music to find some relief from the busy life of my own cortical bombardments. Moving my body to the flow of music was a liberation I cherished. We'd learn much later that music in fact is profoundly integrative: The melody links widely separated areas together in the cortex while the rhythm links body proper to skull-based brain (see Levitin, 2008).

Music may be the closest neural language we have to a direct expression of what is inside us. The neural symphony in our skulls and the mentalese in our subjective life find outer expression in the ebbs and flows of energy within the experience of music. I recall having wonderfully animated discussions with my dear friend, the late poet-philosopher John O'Donohue, about this nature of the limitations of words to express things "just right." A lover of music

and a walking poem himself, John agreed with the general limitations of words in prose, but he affirmed quite vigorously the
unique use of words in poetry. There, he told me, words in poetry
did not stand for something other than themselves—they were just
what they were. Nothing more, nothing less. Even if we are not
poets ourselves, we can listen deeply to poetry and each of us can
appreciate the direct sensory experience evoked with the power of
poems. John and I had been working on a project to explore how
integrative poetry is, in the brain itself and in the "space between
us" that is the bridge linking one another.

John used to say that he'd love to live like a river and be carried by the surprise of his own unfolding. Sometimes I recite those
words in my head, sometimes aloud. Perhaps because John has
passed away now, and perhaps because he was such a good friend,
those words fold around their linkages in ways that create a river
in my own mind. Life is so precious, and so fragile. When someone you love dies, your mind is never quite the same. John would
also say that the one thing that still irked him after all those years
of being a Catholic priest, studying philosophy, and being a teacher
and perennial student of Gaelic mysticism, was that time felt like
fine sand and that no matter what he did, he could not keep time
from slipping through his fingers. These issues of moving freely
with the river of life's uncertainty, of accepting that everything is
transient, and that even life itself is a sand clock whose time is limited are each a fundamental part of temporal integration. And in
these many ways, I feel open to whatever John was and what he
continues to be now in my life—and to these existential issues at
the heart of how our minds and brains track time in our lives.

Openness is an embrace of uncertainty that welcomes the plane
of possibility into the world of awareness. We honor the benefit of
constructed concepts and words and also let our selves move back
to the plane to enable new possibilities to emerge. Being open permits us to relax into the flow of the river of life, wherever it carries
us in its own becoming.

MINDSIGHT SKILLS

Let's dive back into our basic wheel of awareness practice. Sitting with a straight back, let the sounds around you fill your awareness as you let your body find its natural state. Let your awareness ride the waves of the breath, in and out, as it finds its natural rhythm. Let's spend a few moments letting ourselves ride the wave of the breath, in and out. (I need this now too.) Now let awareness rest in the hub, and let the breath go into the background. Unlike in the breath awareness exercise, now we'll invite whatever arises to just fill the hub as we did in the mind awareness exercise in the last chapter. Noticing whatever arises in your field of consciousness, just sit back and take it all in. Whatever sensations, images, feelings, or thoughts, whatever outside perceptions, memories, dreams or worries, just let them arise and fall like ripples on a pond.

This is openness. Rest in the hub, knowing that from this stable place, this inner sanctuary of clarity, you can welcome whatever arises from the rim into your world. This, as we've seen, is the essence of being present. This is the openness leg of mindsight's tripod.

OBJECTIVITY

When we disidentify with the activities of the mind as the totality of who we are, we gain the objectivity we need to see that mental processes come and go within the theater of consciousness. A thought or a feeling does not define who we are—they are merely the present mental activities at that moment of time. We don't need to worry about these being top-down or bottom-up. With objectivity we sense from the hub of our inner mind that whatever we experience in awareness is just something in that moment. It is as if we can sense from the plane that peaks just arise and fall, moving through time, but do not define who we are.

This power to distinguish awareness from the subject of attention enables us to differentiate the hub from the rim. This is the focus of mindfulness meditations, and it is this power of discernment that has the potential to free us from automatic pilot. Developing this leg of the tripod permits us to "sit within the prefrontal cortex" and just watch the array of other neural areas as they fire off in various combinations. To sense these activities as not our identity is the essence of objectivity.

BRAIN BASICS

The strengthened capacity to differentiate different streams of awareness—and even awareness itself from that which it is aware of—is the core neural ability of objectivity. No one knows exactly how this might happen. But we do know from preliminary studies that basic mindfulness training enables the brain to distinguish these various forms of mental life (see Farb et al., 2007; and the discussion of integrating different streams in Siegel, 2007b). For example, the act of practicing internal awareness, of letting oneself rest in the hub of the mind, enables the ability to differentiate incoming sensation from narrative based self-preoccupation. We could guess that this interior knowing is a refined form of mindsight that may be at the heart of what mindfulness training may develop. And mindsight can also be further seen as how we differentiate various mental activities—an ability that relies on midline prefrontal circuitry in its physical correlates and the capacity to monitor, and modify, the internal flow of energy and information. These areas include especially the medial prefrontal region for reflecting on mental experience, in oneself or others. And as we've discussed regarding self-awareness and the von Economo neurons (spindle cells) in the anterior cingulate and anterior insula, these two midline areas are likely involved in our self awareness. It's as if (and this is a cartoon image) we can imagine energy waves flowing through these middle regions as they construct neural maps of an internal image of self-experience—of sensing mental activity, not just having mental activity. This is how mindsight differs from just having a mind.

As Endel Tulving and colleagues have demonstrated (see Tulving, 1993), the orbitofrontal region is also key in autonoetic consciousness as it creates our "mental time travel" in which we link past, present, and imagined future to one another. Again, we can imagine the flow of energy as neural firing patterns in this region that links widely separated zones and their firing patterns to one another as it makes maps of past, present, and future in this self-knowing awareness. We've just identified each of the areas of the middle prefrontal cortex. Orbitofrontal, medial, cingulate, and ventrolateral (which includes the anterior insula) zones each play a role in objectivity and self-awareness. (You can see why it is much more efficient to refer to this mindsight-rich area as the middle prefrontal region. It is this area that is activated and strengthened as we become more mindful.)

Let me offer one point of elaboration here. Some consider mindfulness as a way of becoming immersed in sensory bottom–up data and the shutting down of the narrative chatter of top–down, mediated primarily by the midline prefrontal regions. In this formulation, it would make no sense to then consider being mindful as increasing middle prefrontal functions but rather learning to shut them off. I do not agree with this perspective—from the science, or from the clinical application of mindfulness. Let me elaborate on this by giving you an example. I once had a patient who said that he had been practicing mindfulness meditation for decades and when he entered therapy he refused, initially, to explore his memories of his childhood with me "because that would not be living in the present." I explained to him that one could be in the present with images of the past from memory and make sense of those contemporary neural firing patterns through reflection. Such a way of being mindful of memory, I said, would involve ongoing sensory experience and narrative immersions to make sense of his life. This, after all, was what science had shown to be the case in the world of attachment research. After a bit of resistance, he agreed to try. You can imagine what we discovered: A world of pain from a horrendous past. His journey into meditation had been a "spiritual bypass" in which he sought a hiding place from those memories within the construct of mindfulness as being only about here-and-now sensory input. By embracing a larger view of what being mindful involved—being present with all streams of awareness in one's life—our work could begin to integrate his experiences. He did beautifully in therapy, becoming free to explore his past in the safety of our relationship that allowed him to face those terrifying early demons and emerge on the other side ready to embrace anything from the past, the present, or the future. He was now freed to create a life with a new vitality and open set of possibilities.

MINDSIGHT SKILLS

In our prior mind awareness exercise of resting in the hub and permitting whatever rim activities to arise, we not only supported the tripod leg of openness with this "open monitoring" practice, but by distinguishing the hub from the rim we were also cultivating objectivity. Clearly demarcating the sense of awareness from the subject of attention nurtures objectivity.

Carrying out the body scan can be a useful practice to develop this important tripod leg of objectivity. As we saw in Chapter 2, when we move from body area to body area, we experience different points on the rim from the sixth sense yet experience these within the hub of awareness. In many ways, this enables us to sense our bodies, but also come to experience directly what the objective hub, the central receiver of sensory input, feels like even as we move across the body. We can also engage in a walking meditation, focusing on the sensations of the bottoms of the feet or lower legs. Walking about twenty steps and then slowly turning around to return in the opposite direction, the focus on the feet and lower legs becomes the object of attention. When the mind wanders, lovingly and gently return your focus to the lower legs and feet. Step by step, you can build the "muscle of your mind" to focus on the sensation of walking, noting distractions, returning the focus, again and again. Whether with body scan or walking meditation, you can strengthen the hub of your mind to aim a spoke to a designated sector of the rim. If done properly, this objectivity refines our capacity to sense the power of awareness and to immerse ourselves in the moment-to-moment flow of sensation.

But objectivity, taken to an extreme, has its downsides. It is important to mention here that this discernment, misused, can become a form of dissociation, as some individuals will distance themselves from their own rich inner world. In the body scan, for example, someone can notice himself being aware of a body area but not actually sense the bottom-up input from the body itself. Being objective about life instead of being both experiencer and the one who is aware of the experience can lead to a disconnected way of being. This distancing can be a defense against feeling feelings—another form of spiritual bypass in which people run from living rather than living more fully with discernment. It is important to realize that being mindful can have many nooks and crannies of misuse.

To avoid using this objectivity as a numbing defense, being mindful begins and remains grounded in sensory experience. This objectivity about life is a balancing act—sometimes one that needs intentional suspension to get into the flow of life.

This discussion brings us to the third leg of our tripod, observation.

OBSERVATION

When we have a sense of our self as a witness of our ongoing mental life and even our ability to be aware, we are observing the flow of the mind and the creation of a sense of self. But who, then, is observing? If we can be receptive to mental activities as they emerge (openness) and distinguish them from awareness and our identity (objectivity), what remains of who we are in order for us to know that there is "someone" who is experiencing this whole performance (observation)? Enter the narrator.

BRAIN BASICS

In studies of how human lives unfold, we discover that we are a storytelling creature. We could even call ourselves *Homo sapiens sapiens narrativatas*—the one who knows we know and tells a story about it. Even young children begin to narrate their lives (see Nelson, 1989). Digesting the day's events, weaving them with previous experience and ongoing sensory input, and just harnessing plain creative imagination, our narrating minds lead to the outward expression of our internal neural drama. The physical side—our storytelling brain—has a unique configuration. In our left hemisphere—as we've seen in Chapter 3—we have a drive to tell the linear, logical, and linguistic story of events we experience or witness. Yet in our right hemisphere we have the autobiographical imagery-based representations of memories of the self as lived across time. This tension can be seen to shape the bilateral integration push to create a story of many episodes of our experience. This may be the neural drive of dreams as rapid eye movement sleep states evoke an integration of memory, emotion, and ongoing sensory experience.

You might guess from this view that the left hemisphere is the seat of our neural correlate of a narrator, and this is certainly what Michael Gazzaniga (1998) would suggest is the case. Interestingly, Ruth Baer's and colleagues' (2006) work on mindfulness traits reveals that observation is an independent variable only in those individuals who had formal mindfulness training, but it was interwoven as a part of the other four factors (being nonjudgmental, being nonreactive, acting with awareness, and the ability to label and describe with words the internal world). Add to this Richard Davidson's and colleagues' (2003) repeated finding of a left shift following mindfulness training using the mindfulness-based stress reduction work (see Kabat-Zinn, 1991; Davidson & Kabat-Zinn, 2004). The left shift involves moving the electrical activity of the brain in the direction of a "toward" state rather than "withdrawal." This can be viewed as a neural signature of resilience.

So putting all of these together, we have mindfulness involving the capacity to narrate one's life from the inside out and having an approach left-shift frontal bias that enables one to move toward rather than away from challenging situations. Children with "self-talk" also show more resilience—perhaps relying on the power of a somewhat distanced left hemisphere to comment upon ongoing life feelings and experiences that may be more directly processed in the right. Furthermore, conversations with Mary Main and Eric Hesse regarding the Adult Attachment Interview suggest that the independent measures of a coherent adult narrative map remarkably well onto mindfulness traits. In this situation, the capacity to tell a coherent story that makes sense of one's life may be directly related to one's own capacity to be mindful. So overall we can say that something about being mindful permits us to integrate memory and make sense of our lives: We approach rather than withdraw and we "name it to tame it" so that we reduce subcortical firing with cortical naming (see Cresswell, Way, Eisenberger, & Lieberman, 2007). Here we can see the overlap in independent fields (a process called consilience—see Wilson, 1998) in which observation may be a powerful aspect of a resilient mind.

MINDSIGHT SKILLS

We turn again to our wheel of awareness exercise, this time focusing on an awareness of the whole wheel. First we were being open to the rim, then objective about the rim's activities being distinct from the hub with body scan work, and now we can be observant of the whole of the process.

Let yourself get ready, letting the body settle into its natural state, the breath finding its natural rhythm. Now let the breath be an initial focus, riding the waves of the in-breath and the out-breath.

Next, let the rim become the focus of attention in this "rim review." First bring in the sensations from the first five senses— becoming aware of sounds, of light through your closed eyelids, the touch of your skin against your clothes and where you are sitting, the scents in the room, the taste in the mouth. Let these five senses just fill your awareness as you send a spoke from the hub to this first sector of the rim.

Now let the body become the focus of your attention, letting your sixth sense fill you with the direct feelings of tension in the bones and muscles of your legs . . . your arms . . . your face. Now let your attention move to the sensations inside the torso. Let the center of the chest rise into awareness and fill your attention. You may notice the heart beating and the rhythm of your breath surrounding you in an ever-present rhythm of life. Now let the lungs fill your awareness, sensing the chest expand and the abdomen move in and out. This is the beat and balance of your life. Now let the intestines bring their sensory information up into awareness and fill you with whatever gut feelings arise. These are the visceral sensations of your sixth sense, interoception.

Now let the images of the body go into the background as you let whatever thoughts or images, feelings or memories emerge from the seventh sense of mental activities as you send a spoke to this sector of the rim. Whatever arises in this mental realm, just let it come. You may sense these as worded thoughts, or images in the form of sights or sounds. These mental activities may be quite stable and persistent, or they may be effervescent and transient. Whatever arises from this seventh sense, just invite it into awareness.

Now let your attention move to the next sense—the eighth relational sense. This is the sector of the rim where you may find any sense of your connection to things beyond your bodily self. We have relationships with others we know, with other people we have never seen, and even to people and processes beyond what has ever been or will ever be in front of our eyes. We may even sense our connection to who and what came before us, and who and what will come after these bodies are gone from this earth. You may even sense your connection to our whole planet in the flow of life across time. This is your relational sense. Let yourself just become filled with this eighth sense.

This has been a "rim awareness" tour of the mind, an invitation to have any sense of the rim come into awareness. Now, combining our openness, objectivity, and observation legs of the tripod, we'll move to explore the "space of the mind" by just returning to our seventh sense and observing whatever arises from our mental activities. Here I'll invite you to just notice how a thought, feeling, or memory first appears in your awareness. Does it come suddenly or gradually? How does it stay present? And see if you can just observe how it leaves your awareness. Just notice these mental activities—these points from the rim—and how they appear, stay present, and disappear from awareness.

If you feel up to taking this observation exercise a bit further, we can now move to the intervals between mental activities. See if you can let the mental activities go into the background and instead take note of the spaces between mental activities. What is between thoughts, what is present between memories or images? What do you observe about the nature of the space of the mind within which mental activity emerges? Let these "in between" spaces just fill the front of your mind.

For many, this may be a good place to stop for now and let yourself just come back to the breath. You've explored the nature of mental activities and even the space between. In many ways, this is the way we can take note of the peaks of activation and perhaps the plateaus of probability in the spaces between peaks. You might want to wait awhile before doing the next step—letting this experience just sit with you for a bit. Whenever you are ready, you can continue on to this next phase of the wheel of awareness practice.

Let yourself find your breath and just ride the waves of the breath, in and out, for a few minutes. Imagine yourself resting in the hub, knowing you can bring into awareness anything from the rim from the first five senses of the outside world, the sixth sense of the body, the seventh sense of mental activity, and even the eighth relational sense of the interconnectedness with the larger world.

Now we'll move to an awareness of the hub itself.

As you let these various senses of the rim fade into the background, we'll turn our attention to awareness itself and bring into the foreground the sensation of the hub. Let yourself just rest in the awareness of this spacious center of clarity and calm. As you become aware of awareness, sense what this feels like. Take your time, and just let awareness rest in the spacious hub of the mind.

This can be a good place to now return again to the breath, riding the waves in and out. If you'd like to stop now, that is fine. Letting your eyes come open, just rest in what that experience was like for you. We are quite early in our immersion in these reflective practices, and so for some the awareness of the hub itself is very challenging, sometimes frustrating. For others, an experience of awareness of the hub itself is a mind-opening experience. Whatever it is for you now, exploring this part of the wheel of awareness exercise in the future can deepen as you continue to practice this form of self-knowing.

When you are ready, there is one more global wheel exercise that can help bring a sense of clarity to the connection between the wheel and our sense of observation.

Bringing yourself back to an internal focus on the wheel of awareness, see if you can just get a sense of the wholeness of your experience. You may sense the rim, the hub, and the whole wheel, just being aware of the fullness of you, your connections to yourself, and the sense of connection to things beyond your bodily defined self. This awareness of the whole of your experience gives birth to a you that can narrate your journey across time. Sometimes you may just become immersed in a particular point from the rim: a feeling, a memory, a thought, a bodily felt sense, a perception from the outside world. You can also sense a global feeling of the whole of your experience, enabling you to narrate your life, to observe your ongoing experience with a sense of clarity and perspective. As a scribe of events and as captain of the ship of your life, this narrator plays a central role as both witness and author. Relish the centrality of the narrator, the wholeness of your life, the richness of your experience. This is the center of your narrative gravity—the place where witness and the one who experiences life directly meet, the heart of your inner sea.

SEEING CLEARLY, INTEGRATING OUR LIVES

With a stabilized mindsight lens we are given the ability to see with more fine detail a deeper and clearer view of our internal world. With openness, objectivity, and observation we stabilize the mindsight lens and sharpen our capacity to see inwardly. Building these three foundations of mindsight is like working out at the gym in a balanced way. We don't just work on our legs and ignore our arms and core abdominal and back muscles. We work on all groups to strengthen our body as we move through the river of life. Mindsight's tripod strengthens our ability to monitor and modify the rich inner world of the mind.

When we embrace the idea that developing the mind toward health entails moving our inner world toward integration, then we can see how a strengthened mindsight lens can be essential for identifying when we're in chaos and rigidity. We then also have the ability to clarify which components of our life are not differentiated or linked and promote these elements of integration in our lives.

For our patients, teaching the basic wheel of awareness exercise can be a powerful organizing experience that transforms a previously chaotic or rigid life into one of open possibility. I have been deeply moved by the way the reflective skill of sensing the inner world through the metaphor of the wheel empowers people to develop openness, objectivity, and observation. Learning to rest in the hub, individuals from a variety of backgrounds can learn to see the inner sea with more stability that changes their lives profoundly. We begin this journey with our own inner work, and then we are ready to teach these skills to others. Ultimately we can ask, what are we actually sensing when we peer inside? To address this important question, we'll return to our grounding place in the triangle of mind, brain, and relationships.

Chapter 7

TRICEPTION

The tripod of openness, objectivity, and observation stabilizes our mindsight lens and we come to see reality with new depth and clarity. This perceptual acuity into the inner world illuminates the ways in which energy and information flow in our lives. As mentioned briefly in the introductory chapter, we can conceptualize a triangle of well-being (seen in Figure 7.1) as consisting of the three points of mind, relationships, and brain. What we're about to explore in-depth now is the essence of this triangle and how seeing it clearly can enable us to monitor our interior worlds with more precision and modify them with more agility. This is how mindsight permits us to regulate—to monitor and modify—with more strength and flexibility.

Seeing the nature of energy and information flow may initially seem awkward, unfamiliar, and for some, even bizarre. Close friends of mine, people in the mental health field, have understandably suggested I drop energy and information flow as a topic and instead use more user-friendly terms such as feelings or knowing or sensations. Some don't like the term *energy* because it reminds them that I'm from California and they see this as gooey or soft. Others like the concept of energy but are offended by the term *information*—feeling that it is too scientific or technical. If energy and information are not satisfactory as core concepts, essential enti-

Mind **Brain**

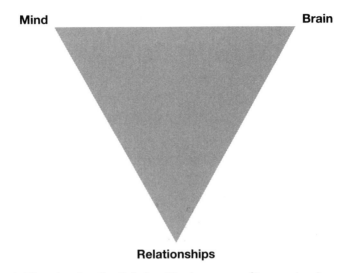

Relationships

Figure 7.1 The triangle of well-being. The harmony of integration is revealed as empathic relationships, coherent mind, and integrated brain. Brain is the mechanism of energy and information flow throughout the extended nervous system distributed throughout the entire body; relationships are the sharing of this flow; mind is the embodied and relational process that regulates the flow of energy and information.

ties, what would the basic elements of mental life be? We could add "awareness" and "consciousness" as well as a "sense of connection" or the "feeling of meaning." Our minds are filled with these and much more: Our mental lives are so rich and textured. Yet I am not trying to be obscure when I suggest we focus on energy and information flow—these we can see as primes, a ground of experience that cannot be further taken apart into its constituent elements. I hear these expressed concerns, and even the one that states that the mind should not be defined at all, and I am open to these perspectives. But defining a core aspect of the mind as an embodied and relational process that regulates the flow of energy and information has powerful implications and useful applications, as I hope you'll also discover.

Learning to track the actual entities of energy and of information as they flow through our mental experience, through our nervous system, and through our connections with one another is extremely useful for improving our lives. This is the essence of *triception*: We track energy and information flow through the triangle of mind, brain, and relationships. Each of these is a real aspect of our subjective and physical worlds.

If eyesight permits vision, mindsight permits triception. Triception is the way we perceive the flow of energy and information in the triangle of well-being. We perceive this flow as it moves through the nervous system (brain as mechanism of flow), as it is monitored and modified (mind as regulation), and as it is communicated among people (relationships as sharing). As this is a triangle of not just energy and information flow, but of well-being, triception is the way we perceive our states of integration and then move the system from chaos and/or rigidity toward the harmony of integrative flow. This triangle is of an integrated brain, empathic relationships, and a coherent, resilient mind.

BRAIN BASICS

Triception is a perceptual ability that can be honed with practice. In many ways, triception is the essential skill for a therapist to explore the inner world with clients. Some people have mindsight skills that are developed well in their families. They are given accurate reflections on their internal world during the formative years of their growth and they develop the middle prefrontal integrative fibers that permit mindsight maps to be laid down early in life. You might be wondering that if mindsight could be the term that embeds these ideas, why use yet another new vocabulary word? You can tell me whether you think as professionals this term is helpful—and I am quite open to us dropping it. But for me and my students, when we discuss in depth the clinical implications of mindsight, it became useful to have the notion of "seeing the energy and information flow within the triangle" as a separate term. In other words, mindsight is a broad notion of how we see and shape the internal world of others and ourselves that could be seen as inclusive of what we're calling triception. Triception is one aspect of mindsight that is the specific perceptual ability to sense energy and information flow in mind, brain, and relationships.

Mindsight has been very useful over these last 25 years of clinical practice. Over this time, the scientific literature has emerged with very useful constructs such as *theory of mind, mentalese, mind-mindedness, reflective function*, and *mentalization* (see Peter Fonagy's research, especially in Allen, Fonagy, & Bateman, 2008). Yet none of these wonderful research terms captured the essence of mindsight as involving the monitoring and modifying of energy and information flow toward an integrated state. And none of them involve how we examine mind, brain, and relationships in one coherent framework—of energy and information flow. And so mindsight found a role in clinical work to help people develop these important ways of regulating their internal worlds more effectively toward health and integration.

Perhaps we don't need triception as yet another new term, but for now let's see how it goes to use the very specific notion of a core dimension of mindsight that is specifically how we perceive the flow of energy and information in the triangle of well-being. Triception brings the triangle to the front of our minds as we think in mindsight terms: We examine neural circuits, relational experiences, and the monitoring and modifying elements of the regulation of energy and information flow. Triception makes the perceptual process of mindsight extremely focused upon these important primes of human experience.

In the brain, repeated training of a skill involves activating neural circuits so that we make maps of whatever we perceive. If I am learning to play tennis, I'll be developing physical maps of the court and bodily maps that embed the racket into my sense of my extended arm (see Blakeslee & Blakeslee, 2007). If I learn to play a musical instrument, I'll likewise increase the auditory maps of sound as well as the finger maps for how I place my fingers on the violin or piano. Studies have even demonstrated that if I imagine myself playing scales, for example, I'll build up the neural architecture I would construct if I were actually using my hands to play those scales along the actual keyboard of the piano (see Doidge, 2007). Interestingly, studies of jazz improvisation reveal that when we improvise, we use the middle prefrontal areas much more than when we play what we've memorized from reading a musical score. The idea here is that improvisation requires that we be more in tune with our own internal world than just playing by rote memory (see Limb & Braun, 2008).

Triception likely involves a similar activation of neural areas that enable us to perceive energy and information flow within ourselves (the brain) and among ourselves (our relationships). We can even perceive how we monitor and then modify this flow (the mind). With this perspective of triception, we gain new powers to use mindsight to shape energy and information flow toward integration and move our lives toward well-being.

But how does the brain do this? What does it really mean to perceive energy flow? What does information flow really mean? And how do we tell the difference between these two, and does it matter? To gain experiential insights into these brain basics questions, to which the objective answers are still forming, we'll need to dive into the subjective side of our plane of reality by further building our mindsight skills.

MINDSIGHT SKILLS

Many of the skills we've been already working on have increased the ability to build the tripod legs of openness, objectivity, and observation. As we develop a stabilized mindsight lens, what is it that we are actually seeing? What is it that you notice from the hub of your mind that is present on the rim? Here's where our discussion can go very, very deep—so hold onto your head and hat. You might say, "Well, I see feelings and thoughts. That's it." And of course, if that is what you see, that is your experience. Fine. But if you use a different aspect of your mindsight vision, and perhaps use a different vocabulary not so trapped by prior top-down definitions, you may find that your perception shifts. Consider what it is like to look up at the sky on a cloudless night before the moon comes up. If you've just been out in the city with its glaring lights, your eyesight will be accustomed to bright light. Literally the specialized receptor cells, the rods and cones of your retina, will be adjusted to large amounts of photons bombarding them as in the daylight so that you can discern the minute details of objects in the world. This is what we can call day vision.

Now imagine yourself out on that moonless night, say, strolling on the beach. (I've described this journey in *The Mindful Brain* [Siegel, 2007a], about a time I first met John O'Donohue in Oregon.) If you let your eyes adjust, your peripheral vision with its rods will become more sensitive to the markedly diminished density of photons bombarding you from the world of darkness enfolding you. With day vision they were shut down and the more central cones enabled color vision and glaring detail to be perceived. But now you're permitting a shift in perception as you relax your intense focus and let the patterns of subtle light falling upon your retina at the back of your eye take hold of the rod receptors now awakening from their daytime slumber. You are now inviting night vision to paint your perception of the world.

As night vision emerges, what before seemed like a black sky becomes filled with stars sparkling in their distant stance in the universe. Yet those stars were there all along. The stars are even present during the day—but the glare of the sun overwhelms your night vision and the more intense data of streaming sunlight obliterates your perception of the stars. In the night, when we let night vision become active in our lives, suddenly a whole new world of perception emerges. As you perceive the stars, you may gather that you are now sensing energy flow from not only gazillions of miles away, but also from disparate times across the galaxies. Stars appear, sometimes only faintly, sometimes becoming stronger ironically when you look slightly away from them. When you relax your vision, not looking intensely for something but just letting the whole of your vision gently receive its light show of black and white and present it to your awareness, a whole new world appears. You may even see a shooting star.

Even the darkened beach can now become luminescent with the ebb and flow of the waves lapping at your feet coming into view. Amazingly, what before you were convinced were formidable crashing waves invisible to your eye but robust to your ear are now seen with your eyes as the gentle undulating folds of water beckoning you to step into the evening surf.

So it is with mindsight and triception. Mindsight sensitizes us to a subtler world motivating behavior. It is wonderful to be at the beach during the day, to frolic in the sun and splash in the waves. It is great to dive into those waves ourselves, floating on the surface of a much deeper sea. Knowing and feeling, being aware and thinking our thoughts, are the large conglomerations of energy and information flow that we can now begin to perceive as we dive beneath the surface and sense these crucial aspects of our night vision of the mind's internal world. These are the subtle flows of energy and information, the internal patterns of motion at the heart of our subjective worlds. This energy and information flow is equally real yet different in its texture from the physical surface of behaviors and elements in the world. Mindsight enables us to sense these subtle waves of energy and information flow that are at the heart of knowing and feeling. Triception enables us to use our more subtle faculties to detect and perceive the deeper essence beneath our mental activities. We can come to be aware that at the very base of our eight senses is the flow of energy and information.

If you do a rim scan right now, as we did in the last chapter, see if you can feel the sensation of the flow of something. Our first immersion into this exercise focused on differentiating the different senses from one another. Now, in this exercise, we'll be focusing on the nature of change. With whatever arises from the rim into awareness, just note its presence in your mind's eye, the hub of the wheel. Notice how an element from the rim stays fixed or moves across time. How does it change? Don't worry about naming whatever arises as energy or information or any other entity. Just let your mind be open to the sense of something changing across time—something moving, something flowing.

Sending a spoke from the hub to the rim sector of the first five senses, notice how sounds and sights, tastes and odors, the feel of your skin against your clothes or your chair, each bring in this flowing sense of something. That something moves, shifts, and changes. Now send a spoke out to the sixth sense and invite anything from the body's interior world into awareness. Just soak that in. What do you notice? How does this sensory field change over time? What emerges, strengthens, softens, dissipates, disappears? And now send a spoke out to the seventh sense as you bring in mental activities of thought and feeling, memory and knowing, all into the hub. How do these "gatherings of somethings" shift and change over time? Is anything fixed, unchanging, unmoving? If you'd like (and this is not as accessible initially for some as the other seven senses are), send a spoke out to the eighth sense to bring into awareness "something" about the relationship to things outside your "self." What do you notice here? How do these elements in awareness change over time? The eighth sense, when felt at the level of "something" flowing, may reveal the perception of our deep interconnected nature. The boundaries of "you" and of "me" become permeable, the steep walls between us come down, and the notion of a wholly separate self begins to dissolve. This may not be a trick of the mind, but a refining of our ability to perceive a deeper level of reality beneath surface and perhaps cortically constructed distinctions.

For many of us, what becomes clear with this rim review exercise in general is that nothing is fixed in the mind. We've learned to distinguish hub from rim, and different senses from one another on the rim itself. Now we are exploring the nature of transience, the way the river of time carries everything forward. Nothing is predictable; everything is forever changing. These "-things" of nothing and everything and something are what? What is it that we are actually experiencing in awareness?

Many people have said to me that they just don't get the notion of energy and information. Even with the definition of energy as the "the ability to do things" in its varied and changing forms, many of us—physicists included—have a hard time pinning down what energy means. And energy for some is just some New Age speak that, for them, means nothing. Yet energy is a real property of the world. All branches of the sciences studying the physical objective world share the concept of energy. And energy is also a fundamental part of our mental world as well. From a subjective awareness viewpoint, energy has a feeling of vitality to it and it moves across time, it flows. The physics connotation of energy is "the capacity to do stuff," whether that means moving a mountain or thinking a thought. Energy enables motion to occur. And even matter ultimately is condensed energy. (Remember energy equals mass times the speed of light squared?)

On one level, we could state that everything is energy. Some swirls of energy have high degrees of probability—like a stone or a pencil—they are likely to be there, as they are, rock or leaded writing instrument. But what of a feeling? What of a sensation of fullness in the belly, loneliness in the heart, excitement in the head? What are these emotions, these textured inner colors of subjective life? Filled with energy, e-motions get us to move, to evoke motion. And notice that beyond the push for motion, we have that which is moved: information. We've seen that information can be defined as something that stands for something other than itself. Like the word *word*. W-O-R-D. What in the world is *word*? Once you dive into the elements of information, the "thing" that is used to convey the meaning beneath the representation is not what the symbolic intention of the thing is.

Okay. So information itself is, well, information that moves us.

We can feel the symbolic nature of the information—and that symbolism creates in us a certain texture, a certain set of feelings, associations, beliefs. Recall our ABCs of meaning in the brain: We associate, believe, conceive, develop, and emote as responses to experience and thus create the meaning of an event. Information flow moves meaning in our minds.

When we receive information from another, we feel the intention to communicate embedded in the symbol as we inherently explore the meaning within the message. And here is an important but little-known aspect of information. Information is a verb. The act of symbolizing catalyzes its own "information processing" so that a symbol produces further symbolizations. Meanings emerge from our meaning-making minds. This is truly the flow of information, propelled along by energy flow, as these fundamental elements of experience arise and shift patterns as they travel across time.

And here is the trick in our subjective and neural realities: Information itself is composed of energy. And any bit of information induces its own cascade of unfolding processes. So why say "energy and information flow" in our working definition of a core aspect of mind? Why not just say "energy" if information is composed of energy? The point of this distinction is that some of our experience is direct: We smell the rose and it is as close to the scent of the flower as possible. It is not the word *scent*. It *is* the scent—or as close as we'll ever really get to it. So that sensory experience involves energy, and the subjective experience in awareness is of something that has data, but not information. It, by itself, is not symbolizing anything. It is itself: the smell of the rose.

Some energy swirls itself into information configurations that stand for something other than themselves. Like the word *rose*. So mind immerses us in both direct energy we might call imagery or sensation and symbolic energy we call information.

Mindsight invites us to soak in the unfolding mind behind our subjective lives and between our eyes. Mindsight permits us to have the perception of energy and information flow as it moves through our nervous system, is regulated by our mind, and is shared in our relationships. Perceiving this flow through our triangle is triception. Using triception to then know how to modify the internal world is the power of mindsight to move our lives toward integration.

TRICEPTION AND INTEGRATION

I hope we are together, at least for this moment, on diving into this more subtle and perhaps deeper level of perception that is fundamental to mindsight. I am typing here, but imagining you there. Yes, time and space separate us now. But at some time and place, these words will pop from the page or out of a speaker and into your subjective experience. They'll move you from the plane of possibility, as you are receptive, into valenced plateaus of probability and then outward to peaks of specific activity. This is how we take in information flow and make it our own. My intention behind this notion of triception is that these peaks and plateaus of this concept will prepare your mind for the chance encounters that can then be seized upon to help move our lives toward integration. We can take the best of science and the sound reflection of subjectivity and help one another acknowledge periods of chaos and rigidity that imprison us. With triception we can then interpret these states as moments of impaired integration and then identify where differentiation and/or linkage has not been cultivated. I know this is sounding familiar—but we are going to move deeply now into levels of energy flow and its transformation toward integrated states. This is the power of triception to enable us to focus our awareness on the dimension of reality that is the flow of energy and information in mind, brain, and relationships.

We can sense, for example, how energy and information flow emerges from the specialized circuitry of the right or left sides of the brain. Can we sense the presence of linguistic, linear, logical, literal, labeling, and list-making language of the left? Can we perceive the nonverbal, holistic, imagery-based, metaphoric, autobiographical, whole-body-mapping world of the right hemisphere? These are the differentiated flows of energy and information distributed horizontally in the neural mechanisms within the brain portion of the triangle.

Once identification has been established, once we've noted rigidity and/or chaos and the domain in which it is arising, we can introduce the next step of intervention. If the specialized functions, say, of left or right modes of processing are not present, if implicit memory is isolated from the integrative explicit forms, or if bodily energy and information are blocked from entering cortical awareness, we can nurture the development of these differentiated functions by SNAGging the brain as we stimulate neuronal activation and growth in these isolated regions. Once differentiation is established, we can then move toward integration by promoting the linkage of these varied functions.

Triception also permits us to perceive how energy and information flow are shared in relationships in ways that support each person being differentiated and then linked. If you and I are in a relationship and I don't value your perspective and our interactions don't involve mutual respect for the internal world of the other, then differentiation is not a part of our relationship. As energy and information flow between us, we'd likely find moments of chaos and rigidity emerging, revealing this impairment to integration. We might periodically explode in rage, become filled with frustration, impatient over minor misunderstandings because of the lack of such respect for each other. Or we may find ourselves not connecting at all, seeing our differences but doing nothing to promote our linkage. Here, too, our relationship would be prone to chaos or rigidity. We might find dullness in our connection, emptiness in our sense of vitality with each other. Soon our friendship might just drift into oblivion. Whether working with our own lives or helping the relationships of our clients, triception permits us as therapists to not only be present in the moment, but to have the perceptual skill to see the whole in front of our eyes.

Triception also permits us to become aware of how we are being aware—of making the mechanisms of mind open to inspection and intervention. We can alter how we monitor and modify the flow of energy and information within us as we move our own lives toward integration. This is the fascinating way in which we can be awake and intentional in how we change even our own internal life. And, as we've seen, we can even tell one another stories of our journeys, and even write books about our narratives to enable this energy and information flow to exist outside our moment-to-moment interactions. We can pass what we've learned about mindsight and the healing power of integration through the very flow of energy and information that triception permits us to perceive. This is how we can find connections with each other across the wide array of streams of energy and information flow that enrich our worlds.

When many of us were trained in medicine in the last millennium, the biopsychosocial model was an important step in combating the reductionist view of illness and having us not forget the "whole" person. Triception takes that goal further by examining those three entities as part of a "whole" system. Energy and information flow is regulated, shared, and shaped within mind, relationships, and brain in a way that we can now perceive and conceive to the benefit of our patients, and our selves.

Chapter 8

TRACKING

With the emerging capacity for triception, we can see the subtle distinctions among previously blurry images of our sea inside. Energy and information flow into our awareness and we become subjectively filled with the sensations emerging from the outside world (the first five senses), the bodily domain (the sixth sense), the world of mental activity (our seventh sense), and even the relationships we have with others and elements of the larger world (our eighth sense). These are sensations we feel across the array of sectors of the rim.

A crucial way that we stay present with our patients is to track what they are experiencing, moment by moment. This tracking involves communicating what they are experiencing in the here and now and being open with them so that we can "stay with" whatever arises in their awareness. Tracking these eight senses in real time is an important starting place to begin the therapeutic communication around being with the moment, together. But why is tracking so important?

We can propose that sharing within awareness across the divide between two people creates a more integrated state of being. In complexity terms, the work of Gerald Edelman and Guilio Tononi (2001) suggests that consciousness emerges when neural firing patterns achieve a certain degree of complexity. We've seen that a deep view of complexity theory suggests that the self-organization of a dynamic system moves toward increased complexity by linking its differentiated elements to one another. In this sense, then, shared awareness raises the degree of complexity even further as it enables two autonomous individuals to become linked within one state of shared consciousness.

In childhood, this tracking experience of shared awareness can be seen as the essence of the attunement and subsequent resonance that enables the child to "feel felt" and to thrive. In our interpersonal neurobiology view, we see that such attunement induces the growth of the integrative fibers of the brain. In other words, interpersonal integration promotes neural integration.

Ed Tronick's work (2007; and see his chapter in Fosha, Siegel, & Solomon, 2010) proposes that a "dyadic state of consciousness" exists within such attuned pairs of parent-child relationships. This dyadic state achieves new levels of intricacy—new levels of complexity—that permit the child to be brought forward into an ever more integrated union in the interpersonal world. We can draw on Tronick and Edelman and Tononi's work in proposing that tracking within therapy is the achievement of more and more integrated dyadic states that bring the client into a more complex and adaptive state of being in that moment. This may be why tracking is so crucial in the therapeutic experience.

But what exactly is being tracked? What are we actually attuning to within such dyadic couplings?

If we pause and consider our internal experience, we may come to layered dimensions of awareness that each may comprise the "element" that we share in the tracking union. Sensory experience in the present moment—sensing our body, perceiving the external world—is a naturally shared element within tracking. See Figure 8.1 for an elaboration of these points along the rim of the wheel of awareness. But there are also aspects somewhat distinct from these streams of sensation that fill us in the moment. The wheel of awareness can be seen to have more than one stream that brings in data

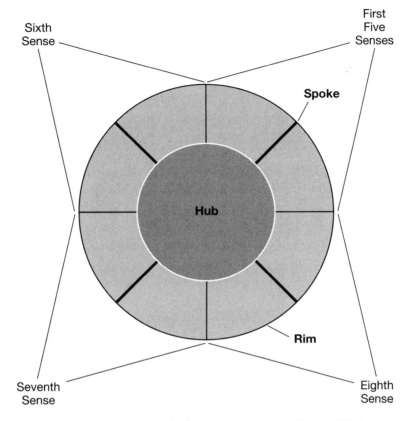

Figure 8.1 The elaborated wheel of awareness. Rim, spokes, and hub and the sectors of the rim: first five (outer world), sixth (body), seventh (mental activity), and eighth (relationships) senses.

from the rim to the hub. For example, we may observe ourselves tasting an apple. Here we have awareness filled with both the sensation of the taste (and touch and smell and sight . . . and even sound) of the apple as well as some other aspect of what we are terming a stream of awareness—that of observation. In Figure 8.2 we can see this notion of filters, or streams of awareness, that enable rim-point data to enter hub-awareness through quite distinctive channels of flow. The feeling of observing is not the same as that of sensing. With observation there is somewhat of a distance, a kind of knowing that feels like a narrator is witnessing an event as it takes place over time. So there is at least a direct sensory stream, and then an

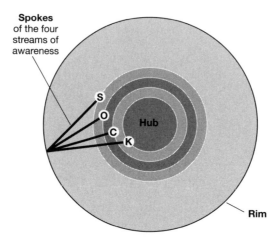

Figure 8.2 The four streams of awareness filtering the flow into the hub of the mind: sensation, observation, concept, knowing. Sensation is the most direct input of inner or outer data into our awareness. Observation is the capacity to sense our selves as witness to unfolding experience. Concepts are constructed ideas and models of how the inner or outer world works and include facts and memories of past events as well as images of imagined future possibilities. Knowing is a nonconceptual inner sense of truth, an intuitive and non-language-based way of perceiving the nature of reality and our place in the larger world and the continuity within the flow of life in which we live.

observing stream. Tracking could involve both staying with sensations and connecting around the stream of observation as well.

But what about these ideas we are sharing—even about tasting an apple? We can have a more *constructed concept*, a frame through which our awareness is filtered. The word *apple* has embedded in it much more than the fruit in your hand. You can have the idea that this object came from an orchard where people harvested this fruit for others, including you. You can have the concept that farmers throughout the world have been working for generations to cultivate new forms of fruits and vegetables to feed our ever-expanding population. You can look inside the apple and notice the seeds, knowing about DNA and reproduction, understanding the concept of genetics and the generational passage of traits. All of this is constructed conceptual knowledge not limited to the important, but different, stream of sensation. And you can even observe yourself thinking your thoughts, and even sense the texture of an idea. So we have now at least three "streams" of awareness that include our sensations, observations, and concepts.

Again, tracking is the moment-by-moment "staying with" the other so that we are present with how events change within awareness. Being present with ideas is also an important way we join with our clients in their unfolding journey to heal.

In my own experience, these three streams of awareness each play distinct roles in how energy and information enters the hub of my mind. If these distinctions help you refine your mindsight lens and support a more highly developed triceptual ability, great. If they can open your own tracking experience so that you embrace a broad range of ways to join with your clients, wonderful. If this does not work for you, then just noting that others may see the world this way may be useful in your work if it does not apply to your own direct experience.

This is a key to being mindful: We each have our own unique inner experience, perceive that experience in different ways, express it with differing terms, and organize it in our "making-sense" conceptual mind in individualized ways. In our conversation in this book, I can only offer you my own experience, some words that depict one way of experiencing, seeing, and making sense of inner life. If we were together, I'd love to hear your experience directly— so you and I could track each other. This afternoon I had a ton of things on my to-do list. My wife came into the room and had a lot on her mind. At first I looked at my "stuff" on the desk and felt distracted; then I put down my paper, shut off the screen of my computer, and turned to direct my attention to her, face to face. I took a deep breath and said to myself (being in the middle of writing this chapter) that I would be present with her on whatever level of experience she was traveling in that moment. I felt an open-

ness emerge inside me, the to-do list faded away, and a deep sense
of being-with her arose. It doesn't always turn out like this in our
interactions, day to day. But we can choose to make ourselves available to join. And this joining is not just about basic sensations. We
can start with our bodily sensations to ground us in the bottom-
up of the present moment, but tracking in our relationships, being
present for and with the other person, brings us to dyadic states of
union across all streams of awareness.

As we continue in our discussion, see if these ideas of various
streams of awareness work for you. Perhaps these discussions will
merely invite you to become more aware of how you do experience, perceive, and organize your own inner seascape—how you
have mindsight for the sea inside.

In my own experience I have also found that another stream of
awareness seems to exist, perhaps better considered a kind of subterranean spring that emerges from beneath the flow of these other
three streams. This fourth stream is that of a *nonconceptual knowing*,
a deep, inner sense of the truth, a coherent impression of the world
as it is. *Knowing* is the term I've used for this fourth stream, and it
has a quality to it that we can point to with words, but it is before
and perhaps beyond words. This is the nonworded way we come to
know the truth. Some of the most profound moments of meeting
I've had with my own patients have emerged as we share this resonance of knowing that is, literally, without words.

Those who share the acronym addiction with which I am
afflicted may see where this is going: These four streams spell out
the word SOCK. In Figure 8.2 you'll find two ways in which
SOCK can be visually depicted. One is as distinct streams that feed
into our overall consciousness of something. The other comple-
mentary view is to envision that the hub of the mind has four
concentric circles surrounding it that represent each of the SOCK
streams that filter whatever comes in from the rim and into the
hub. For example, we can have a sensation of our heartbeat, observe
ourselves sensing our heart, conceive of the importance of the sixth

sense in informing our lives, and know that the wisdom of the body can guide our lives toward truth. This is how the SOCK hub-filters stream a rim-point of the sixth sense into our awareness. And it is this layering of experience that we can track with others as we stay present with our patient's unfolding awareness of experience as it emerges in therapy.

BRAIN BASICS

As no one really knows how neural firing and consciousness cocreate one another, so we are fully in the land of speculation here to postulate how we create the dyadic awareness of tracking. We know, as we've seen, that at the moment we are aware of something, there tends to be prefrontal activation. If we keep something in the front of our minds (like a phone number), we activate the dorsolateral prefrontal cortex—which we are calling the *side prefrontal region*. Please note: The term *side* is just easier for most people to remember, and these English words are very helpful when working with patients and teaching them about their brain. Teaching about the brain—tracking with our clients the inner flow of neural firing patterns—is actually an important part of focusing on our triangle of well-being. Knowing about brain function and structure is empowering for people—and having terms that are not intimidating and relate to everyday life (like side and middle) can be extremely useful. I've tried to avoid what for many nonprofessionals (i.e., our clients) is often the overwhelming experience of being confronted with a bunch of Greek and Latin terms. So *side* is more easily digested and remembered than *dorsolateral*. I'm bothering with these details because as we track, the sharing in awareness can be fluid and free—not filled with fear and dread. Having accurate but user-friendly terms is essential to comfortably "live with the brain in mind" and not overwhelm people so they end up saying and feeling, "It's all Greek to me!"

When we are aware of our bodies, the anterior insula is activated.

(This important region is considered by some researchers to be a part of the ventrolateral prefrontal region—so it can be accurately included as part of what we are calling our *middle prefrontal cortex*). When we are aware of our social connections, a related middle prefrontal region, the anterior cingulate, becomes activated and lights up on a scanner, as it also does with bodily pain. This is an important discovery that Eisenberger and Lieberman (2004) found: Social rejection and physical pain activate the same region of the brain, the anterior cingulate cortex. When we are aware of our own thoughts or our autobiographical memories, our medial and orbitofrontal regions become activated. Here we see that each of these fundamental parts of our middle prefrontal cortex—the anterior cingulate, medial prefrontal, orbitofrontal, and ventrolateral prefrontal (including the anterior insula)—are all important in self-awareness, as we discussed earlier. Other regions, such as the parietal lobe, also play a role in various aspects of being aware of our bodily selves. But when we add to this finding that empathy and attunement involve these similar prefrontal regions, then we see that mindsight is predominantly a "middle prefrontal job." These middle prefrontal regions are profoundly integrative in that they link input from the cortex, the limbic areas, the brainstem, the body proper, and the input from other nervous systems (what we can call "social" input) to one another. Cortical, limbic, brainstem, somatic, and social input become linked into one functional whole. Now that is integration at its neural best.

Tracking with our clients, we can actually empower them to have the concept of the brain as a mechanism by which energy and information flow. I say "empower" because in my own and my students' experience, teaching people about the brain gives them the power to change their lives more effectively. We teach our clients to know their own neural mechanisms, translating energy and information experience within the frame of neural circuitry and relational realities. Ultimately, when we track at this level of conception, we are aligning ourselves deeply with their awareness of the triangle of well-being.

Triception enables us to perceive this flow as energy and information moves within and among these various neural layers in our lives. When we track together with mutual triception, we can share the deep ways of knowing about how integration can be promoted in our nervous systems and our relationships. And this movement toward integration is carried out by the common focus of our minds. This is shared attention—crucial in tracking, and vital in our earliest relationships with our caregivers. As we've seen, attunement focuses on our basic internal states, and attention is the essence of how we direct those states to shape the direction of energy and information flow. Sharing a focus of attention and intention is how we connect with the internal world of another. We can guess that such mindsight skills are harnessing the power of middle prefrontal fibers to create maps of these various components as we track energy and information flow in our patients and in ourselves across these many aspects of our world. For example, as we learn to distinguish at least these five layers (cortical, limbic, brainstem, somatic, social) we are then in a position to link them together as we track their flow across time. Imagine how this highly integrative middle prefrontal neural assembly is further amplified with attunement and tracking. Add to this the dimension of left and right cortical functions, and we've widened the field of integration. We connect with one another across all these fields of differentiated elements of energy and information flow.

The key to tracking is this: Complex systems—such as our minds, our brains, and our relationships—have a natural tendency toward maximizing complexity. This self-organization of complex systems, when unimpeded, tends to have elements of the system differentiate, to become specialized, and then to link together. This is just how a natural complex system operates: There is no programmer, no program, no director, no script. In physics and mathematics, there is generally no use of the term *integration* as a way of describing the linkage of differentiated elements. For those fields, the term is generally synonymous with *addition*. The integration of

3 and 5 is 8—and the features of 3 and 5 are lost. For a mathematician, this integration is the sum of the parts.

But in common everyday language, integration results in the finding that the whole is in fact greater than the sum of the individual parts. In this common use of language, integration is the linkage of differentiated parts in which these parts retain elements of their individual specialization. This in fact is exactly what the mathematics of complex systems predict: that the movement toward maximizing complexity is achieved by way of the linkage of differentiated elements. Putting this together, we can see that complex systems—like human beings at all levels of our experience, mind, brain, relationships—will have a tendency toward integration.

When we're unimpeded, integration is what naturally happens. And here's the key. When systems are integrated, they move in that FACES flow of being flexible, adaptive, coherent, energized, and stable. Out of this flow, we've seen systems tend toward rigidity, chaos, or both. That's the way the self-organization of complex systems gets translated as the self-regulatory patterns of human life. Tracking enables us to lift others out of their stuck and chaotic places and help move the dyadic system toward integration, and ultimately shift the internal elements of the client to liberate the natural drive toward a self-regulation and integrative flow.

Putting this together with tracking, the idea is that something has blocked the natural tendency toward integration—the natural way we move toward healing, toward health. Tracking permits the presence of an attuned therapist to create resonance with a client and in this connection move with attunement and resonance moment by moment through the various layers and levels of experience, now shared. This tracking enables the dyad (the pair) to widen windows of tolerance so that impedances to the natural drive toward integration can be relaxed and ultimately transformed and released. In brain terms, we can imagine that synaptic linkages associated with defensive reactions, implicit retrievals, and restrictive self-states that repeatedly keep the individual in chaotic and/or rigid patterns can now, finally, be changed. The neuroplastic changes induced by this attuned, resonant, relational experience likely not only alter the neural profiles of impedance to integration, but strengthen the integrative fibers of the brain. It is these fibers that link widely separated areas to one another that indeed are the self-regulatory and the social core of the human brain.

With these ideas more deeply in the front of our mind, let's continue to track the various layers of tracking itself. What follows is filled with speculation, but I hope you'll track with me through these imagined steps and see both the fun of this approach and, when in the practice of therapy in real time, the power of this view to help you decipher the many layers of tracking that are both possible and powerfully transformative.

Let's place the hub filter of SOCK into the mix of seeing the wheel of awareness. We can track the sensation, observation, concepts, and knowing into our awareness of these various streams. This view expands the notion of tracking beyond the realms of just sensing together. From a brain perspective, we can only imagine that a sensory stream might be more a bottom-up flow involving input from the lower layers of the cortical colums (layers 6, 5, and 4) and dominating the flow of data at layers 4 and 3 as they mingle and move into our awareness. Recall from the prior chapter's discussion that we humans have more axonal fibers at layer three in the frontal most parts of our prefrontal regions—the middle prefrontal areas—that may enable us to use conscious awareness to alter the nature of the flow of information that balances top-down and bottom-up influences. Building our mindsight skills with mindful awareness may enable us to disentangle the dominance of top-down that overshadows our bottom-up sensory experience. As we take in the observing stream, we could hypothesize that it likely involves more of a top-down middle prefrontal direct input containing a subjective experience of a "sense of self" as narrator. Recall that this narrator function may have a dominance of left-mode processing as it uses language to represent experience across time often in a linear fashion (oh, those Ls of the left are so logical . . .).

For concepts, we may now move to a more fully top-down flow with less influence of the input from bottom-up signals. Here we'd expect a dominance of layers 1, 2 and 3 into the stream of awareness for our constructed concepts. If these concepts are fact driven and word based we'd also expect to see more left-mode activity in the conceptual stream—but certainly we might have more imagery based notions or ideas that are top-down but just without a word basis. And our nonconceptual knowing? Intuition and gut feelings play a role here—and so perhaps we return to some more bottom-up input, but from which regions? As we've seen in the discussion of truth in Chapter 5, coherence plays a role in the experience of being connected to things as they are. Coherence may have a global synchrony embedded in its neural correlates. So perhaps we have some way of feeling this neural synchrony—the gamma waves it might produce and the spindle cell–type activations it might involve as the coordination and balance across a wide range of now phase-shift-synchronized separate but now linked neural regions begins to take form. I know those are a lot of words. Basically they say this: Tracking "knowing" is integrative.

How do we know when we are in such neural integration? I don't know if we are able to achieve that yet from a technical measurement point of view. (We can see gamma waves in some studies such as those with nonreferential compassion meditation [see Lutz et al., 2004], but this may occur at other times as well. We may be able to use future elaborations, for example refinements in the diffusion tensor imaging now used to detect structural connections within the white matter—myelinated—tracks of our long axonal neuronal lengths. This would be a kind of tracking of tracks in the brain, we might imagine. Perhaps we'd find more neuropil—axonal fibers—at layer three and four in those with higher levels of integrative functioning that could be an anatomical sign of their ability to alter information streams with intention. Time and technology will tell.)

On another level, we may detect this knowing on the neural level as we would in our capacity to see a fishtank as a whole and know it as a living system. This aquarium next to me right now has a wholeness to it, its rocks, fish, water, the movement of the various individuals living in their caves, finding one another as mates or foes, standoffs and egg-laying, hatching and feeding. All of this is contained within a flowing whole. When a new fish arrives, the system changes, adjusts, and re-equilibrates into these newly differentiated subgroups and their emerging linkages. This is an integrated marine system. Seeing them in this way through such a holistic view might have a right-mode dominance, a feeling beneath words that emerges in our parallel-processing analogical right hemispheres. Even a study of the cultural impact of development on perception suggests that this might be the case (see Nisbett & Miyamoto, 2005). Time and research will have to tell if these global impressions turn out to be correct, that we have nonconceptual knowing with a right-mode dominance. But two anatomical findings from our evolution are clear: Our two hemispheres, and likely the information processing they support, are much more spatially isolated in us than our primate relatives. And our prefrontal regions are anatomically set up to have some kind of unique axonal processes at the very levels where top-down meets bottom-up.

MINDSIGHT SKILLS

Let's continue with our wheel of awareness exercise and further develop our skills of tracking. By now you know the basic steps: Let your body settle into its natural state, inviting the sounds of the room to fill your awareness as you sense your body sitting or lying down as the earth holds you. Let the breath find its natural rhythm, as you let your awareness just ride the wave of the breath, in and out. Breath awareness stabilizes our attention. With regular practice, this simple exercise, as we've seen, can help steady our mindsight lens and allow us to see deeply into the sea inside.

Now imagine the wheel of awareness, with its hub, rim, and potential spokes linking the activities of the rim to the spacious awareness in the hub. We've done the exercise of tracking each sector of the rim, from the first five senses, to the sixth bodily sense, to the seventh mental activity sense, to our eighth relational sense. We've even let awareness focus on the awareness in the hub itself, feeling that wide-open plane of possibility. Each of these is a way of tracking energy and information flow within the wheel of awareness.

Now let's explore the wheel further by weaving it with a view of the plane of possibility and the peaks of activation. In our first rim awareness focus, we let the points of each sector fill awareness, one by one. We entered a state of open monitoring in which we just allowed whichever activities arose from the rim to fill our awareness as they came. With these rim exercises, we intentionally placed the points of activation in the front of our minds. Now we'll further explore in more depth the "space between" mental activities. Some might call this the "space of the mind" as we peer into what the subjective sense of our mind is when there is no mental activity.

To deepen this space-of-the-mind focus from your prior immersion, let yourself just notice when activities arise—from the first five senses, the sixth sense, the seventh or eighth sense. But now, instead of taking note of how things first arise, how they stay present in awareness, and how they dissipate, just let these factors go to the side. In the front of your awareness, let the intervals between these points from the rim just become the focus of attention. What is the sensation of the space between mental activities? What does it feel like, look like, sense like, to notice what it is like between the various rim points that present themselves to your hub awareness?

This interval focus allows us to feel the space of the mind, the mental openness that is the water within which the fish of mental activities swim. We can even track energy and information flow within this space of the mind and perhaps sense this as the movement from the peaks of activation (the rim points) downward into plateaus of probability on our mental side of reality. Perhaps a corresponding movement matching this flow on our physical side of neural firing is the priming of potential neural firing patterns. The subjective correlate of this may be just a tendency, a feeling of leaning, an impulse or notion in a certain direction that has no clear form, just a sense, perhaps, of intention. This is how we feel the brain readying itself to fire off in a particular direction or sense our mood or impulse, setting us up to respond in a certain manner. This is the valenced plateau of probability—and it may suffuse the intervals with a new sense of fullness, a "valence" or a push in one direction or another. We can then follow the flow outward toward peaks of activation as interval probabilities become realized as peak actualities in our neural firing and our mental experience. Physically we may sense specific circuits becoming active (as in the yes-no exercise) and we may become aware of a certain thought, feeling, or image (as in seeing the Eiffel Tower in our mind's eye). Here we've moved from plateau to peak, from interval to point on the rim of our wheel of awareness.

Some may experience within this interval focus a slightly different texture. Instead of remaining in valenced plateaus, with a sense of imminent movement, the feeling described is more like a vast expansiveness, an open sea, a wide sky. We can imagine that such direct first-person experience may reflect the movement of awareness from the rim to the space between and then to the hub itself: from peaks to plateaus to the wide-open plane of possibility. We'll explore this more directly in the next chapter's exercise as a specific hub awareness practice, but here let me just point out that in any of these practices, we never know exactly what will arise. The key is to bring that COAL state of curiosity, openness, acceptance, and loving-kindness to whatever arises in our experience. This is the essence of a kind and compassionate stance toward our selves.

Resting in the open plane, focusing awareness on awareness itself, can give us the direct immersion in infinite potential. This deep and grounded place, as we'll soon see, may play a special role in the healing process and in helping people grow beyond restrictive habits and identifications of individual personality patterns.

Tracking our clients opens the door to ride with them along these various dimensions from peak to plateau to plane. With time, you may find that feeling these parameters within yourself makes you more open to sensing and tracking them with others.

Next we can move into a new dimension of tracking that helps differentiate even more subtle components of the rim and hub of our wheel, expanding the details of the open plane of reality and the plateaus above it and peaks poking away from it. Now we can also track the streams of SOCK as they filter what enters our hub's awareness. You can be aware of the sensory stream of what is on the rim, right now, sensing the texture of the sounds in the room. You can also let the observing stream fill your consciousness, feeling the fullness of a you that is observing your sensing the sounds. Now consider the nature of sound itself, the energy waves that move particles of air in patterns that bombard your eardrum. The neural signals from your acoustic nerve then transmit those energy patterns as action potentials along this cranial nerve upward into the skull portion of your brain. Waves of neural firing move further up to ultimately be filtered and transmitted to your prefrontal regions and you become aware of the perception of sound.

Sensing sound, observing your awareness of this sensation, conceiving of the nature of sound and of your self and even a mindsight skill exercise, let yourself imagine the purpose, the meaning, the intention of all of this activity. Being aware of the sense of meaning, the ways in which awakening the mind in your own life can also serve to help others, let yourself bathe in this deep sense of knowing. This deep knowing can move from inner knowledge to outer action on behalf of others. This is how intention is the fuel that turns passion into action.

Integrating the streams of awareness from sensation to observation, concept to knowing, brings us to the inner place of clarity where we can turn trouble into triumph, bring inner knowing into interpersonal healing. A lot of words, I know. Try it out for a while, if you're up for it, and see if it works for you. There is plenty of time to discard this framework if it proves not to be useful to illuminate an effective path in your experience.

TRACKING AND INTEGRATION

As we've explored, there is an innate drive for complex systems to move toward integration. Harmony is the natural outcome of this push toward integration. Our job as clinicians is to tap into this native instinct to integrate and free up the constrictions that are blocking it from unfolding. Our role is to join with others' birthright to live with ease and well-being.

Tracking is a step-by-step joining with which we stay present with our clients to help them free up the drive toward integration. This is the way a solitary system expands its complexity by dyadic states of awareness that promote more highly integrated configurations. Integration is enhanced as we move from me to we. It may seem strange that it could be this simple, but when we realize that we are each beings of a larger whole, that the drive to be whole is inherent in our makeup, then psychotherapy can be seen as a deep, transformational form of collaboration. Our clients are our colleagues: We are companions along a journey together toward integration.

The detailed experience of tracking can be private or it can be shared. For example, James Pennebaker (2000) found that when people write in a journal about a difficult event—even if it is never shared with anyone or read again by the writer—there is significant physiological and subjective improvement in the person's life. Likewise, methods such as EMDR (see Shapiro, 2002) do not require that the tracking inherent in the process be articulated with words. Somatic methods (see Minton, Ogden, & Pain, 2006; Levine, 1997) also involve tracking but do not require the verbal expression of what is experienced. The latter two involve the social setting of one person being present while the other tracks. The journaling involves perhaps the narrating self to be present as witness to the tracking of internal details of an unfolding life story. Each of these important methods involves awareness. In fact, I have yet to discover an effective form of therapy or therapeutic intervention that does not have awareness in its essential toolkit for change.

Why is awareness a seemingly necessary part of therapy? Why does tracking require that we place into awareness the moment-to-moment unfolding of our changing internal states? With mindful awareness a state of COAL is created: curiosity, openness, acceptance, and love infuse the sense of experience of what is unfolding. If there is an unempathic, uncaring therapist, research suggests, clients do not do well. And if there is a harsh and critical inner voice distorting the open reception of what is being tracked in private reflections, I would suggest to you that narrativizing may not be so helpful. Each step of the way there would be an internal battle and assailing criticism that could actually make things worse. For many people, it is this harsh inner critic, this internal judge and jury, which keep life stuck in an unintegrated state. It is this non-mindful awareness that makes chaos and rigidity an ongoing trait in the person's life. Harnessing the power of specific interventions to promote compassion for the self would be indicated in these situations (see Neff, 2009; and Gilbert, 2010).

And so tracking can liberate integration only when it brings moment-to-moment awareness within the spaciousness of a mindful state, not just with awareness itself. As we've seen, mindful awareness is distinct from plain awareness in that it involves the integrative fibers of the middle prefrontal cortex, not merely the side prefrontal areas. What this means is that tracking—bringing into the focus of mindful awareness or the hub of the mind—allows new combinations of neural firing to be created. Consciousness in this manner permits choice and change. This may be why open presence, attunement, and resonance within a mindfully aware experience are so central to positive outcomes in psychotherapy.

When we consider the suggestion that as complex systems we have an innate push toward integration, then tracking releases this natural drive toward the linkage of differentiated elements of a system. With tracking, amazingly, we tap into the natural capacity to heal. Dyadic states of mindful awareness move the client out of a rut and liberate the innate drive toward integration.

Chapter 9

TRAITS

 eing a mindful therapist in every one of the three meanings of
that term (conscientious, open-creative, and nonjudgmental consciousness) requires that we embrace the serenity prayer's essential message: May I have the serenity to accept the things I cannot
change, the courage to change the things I can, and the wisdom to
know the difference. As therapists, we need to know our own limitations, to know what we can and cannot do inside of ourselves
and within others. We also need to embrace the reality that not all
aspects of ourselves or of our patients can be changed. As we track
the moment-by-moment experience of our clients, as our patients
move through their experience with our attuned presence, the sky
is, in fact, not the limit for what can unfold. People do have neural
propensities—called temperament—that may be somewhat but not
fully changeable. There are constraints to what is possible, in our
clients' development and in our own. Yet these constraints can be
enabling. Ironically, by embracing our limitations we can achieve
true freedom.

One of those limitations emerges when we examine the concept of traits. Of course we can practice mindfulness exercises and
develop states of mindful awareness within those intentionally
created and temporary states. And with practice, these repeatedly
instantiated states can transform our lives as they become traits—

ways of being that are present without intentional effort. This is how we SNAG the brain: We stimulate neuronal activation and growth to change the very structure of our brain. This is essentially how psychotherapy can indeed change the nature of what we may have believed were fixed aspects of our personality—and even the course of certain mental illnesses. For example, we can create a left shift and alter our baseline to a state of approach that enables us to move toward challenges rather than withdraw from them. This is the essence of resilience. We can have an increase in our eudai-monia as we build a sense of connection, meaning, wisdom, and equanimity in our lives (see Urry et al., 2004). But there may, how-ever, be traits of our personality that derive from our temperament that may not in fact be so amenable to change. While this is an area in need of further study, we can examine aspects of our tempera-ment that we've had since early childhood that may not be quite so open to major transformation. At least considering this possibility, a mindful therapist will be equipped to have both the courage and the serenity to develop the wisdom to know what can and cannot be significantly altered through therapy.

Anyone with more than one child often learns, firsthand, that beyond our attachment relationships and the best of our inten-tions rests the child's temperament. Each of us is born into the world with certain nervous system proclivities—how regular our daily rhythms are, how intensely we react, how much stimulation we need to respond to an event, how moody we may be, how we approach or withdraw from novelty, how we react to changes in our environment. In the classic Chess and Thomas (1990) studies of temperament, nine factors were identified of this kind that could then be sorted out in the majority of children into the groupings of easy, difficult, and slow to warm up. An easy baby was relaxed, happy, flexible, and responsive. A difficult infant was uptight, irri-table, moody, and intense. A shy child took some time to get used to changes and withdrew from novelty rather than approaching the experience like the others. The major finding was that it wasn't the child's temperament that predicted outcome later in life, but rather the match between the child's features and the parents' or school's expectations.

Fortunately, as parents we can alter our expectations, and even ourselves, to become more flexible in seeing the child for who he or she is rather than becoming imprisoned by our reactions that are shaped by what we expected the child to be like. In its essence, this is what being mindful as a parent requires. As I mentioned earlier, we can propose that the relational experience of secure attachment of the child to caregiver and the mindfulness traits of the parent may actually go hand in hand. Mindfulness may be the essential relational component of how we offer a secure attachment relationship for our children. It gives us both the openness to accept the child—whatever his or her temperament—and the approach state to move toward, rather than away, from some of the most challenging demands of being a parent. As we're seeing throughout this book, mindfulness may also be the way we offer presence, attunement, and resonance as the essential starting parts to begin all the TRs of being a mindful psychotherapist.

As therapists, we serve as attachment figures in the development of our patients. We, as parents do with their children, need to identify and release our preconceived ideas and free ourselves to see our clients clearly for who they really are. And one of the ways of seeing clearly is to let go of the idea that all of us are blank slates. Temperament is a true and likely persistent nervous system variable that interacts with our attachment experiences early in life, and with our peer relationships later on, in shaping how our personality develops. Yet it may be surprising to discover that to date there is no overarching model of personality development that provides a comprehensive model that traces early temperament into adulthood. Yes, some investigations reveal persistence of traits such as sustained attention, reactivity, and shyness (see Kagan & Snidman, 2004). For example, studies of shy kids grown up reveal continuing enhanced brain reactivity (with right-sided withdrawal) to novelty. And these studies demonstrate that this internal response of withdrawal from novelty can be overcome with the proper attachment experiences (see Kagan, 1992). The inner reaction to withdraw persists, but the outward behavioral stance can overcome that impulse when children are given enough nurturing support to explore what may have felt intimidating. There is a middle road between excessively protecting a shy child and just throwing him in the deep end of the pool without support. Both extremes of these nonattuned approaches maintain the anxious state and inhibited behavioral patterns. Secure attachment finds the middle road—providing a scaffold of connection and nurturance while pushing the envelope to support further exploration. The child learns, with the attuned parents' support, that he can in fact tolerate what initially appeared to be intolerable. This is how the attachment experiences we have can widen our windows of tolerance and change our behavioral traits. Nevertheless, we may, as Kagan and colleagues have demonstrated, still have the internal traits of neural reactivity.

Several years ago I received a phone call from a clinical professor of psychiatry at Stanford and a genetics of personality researcher who had coauthored one of the most cited scientific articles in the field. They offered to meet me for lunch to discuss interpersonal neurobiology and temperament. How could I refuse? My own work had been in attachment—a set of experiences found to be essentially independent of temperament or genetic influence—so I was intrigued by their request and eager to see if we could incorporate this area of innate traits into the interpersonal neurobiology framework. Ultimately, these Drs. Daniels (David and Denise, father and daughter) also invited me to study a personality system that had been in the popular culture but not a part of the mainstream clinical or scientific worlds in which I lived. At the ensuing weeklong workshop, I was able to conduct preliminary and informal adult attachment research on the over 50 individuals who had gathered from around the globe to study with David Daniels, MD, and his colleagues. Denise Daniels, PhD, was there as well—and I also met up with two other scientists, Laura Baker, PhD (a genetics of personality researcher at USC) and Jack Killen, MD (at the National Institutes of Health). Together, the five of us have now been working over the last 5 years to put together a model of personality that they have given me permission to explore with you here. (See Denise Daniels, Laura Baker, David Daniels, Jack Killen and Daniel J. Siegel, in review: "The Enneagram Personality System: Nine Patterns of Processing.") If accepted, it will be the first article to explore this area in the scientific or clinical professional literature.

The popularization of a nine-pointed figure, called the *enneagram*, as the symbolic representation of a personality system has now been taught to literally millions of people through books, conferences, and workshops aimed at a general audience. An Internet search of this term will quickly reveal a wide array of religious and spiritually oriented interpretations of what has been called ancient knowledge passed down over the generations. Often such search engine results lead my patients, and colleagues, to shut down their interest in the topic, seeing it as too "out there" and not substantiated by science. And this initial response is totally understandable. I had it too. The reality, though, is that there is a fascinating set of subjective experiences described over the last few decades that may have neural correlates that have just not yet been studied. And virtually no one in academia has taken note of this in the professional or scientific literature.

The history of this perspective is revealing. In the 1960s, a Western-trained psychiatrist named Claudio Naranjo met with a mystic in Chile named Oscar Ichazo and together they formed the notion of a nine-part personality system. Naranjo then returned to Berkeley, California, and began teaching this system to various clinicians and others in that area. Ultimately, the notes from those teachings were passed along clandestinely in Jesuit circles and were also translated by Helen Palmer at first—and now numerous others—into the popular literature on the enneagram.

While elements consistent with this system may have been described hundreds of years ago, the full components seem to only have been organized as a whole in the last 50 years. For those of you totally new to this view, let me invite you to explore with me here some of the highlights. For those familiar with the enneagram system, let me suggest that you consider with an open mind that this system may in fact have a neurobiological basis that has never before been described in our conventional literature. The potential first-person discoveries of the "truth" of some of this framework may be at the root of its popularity. That is, there may be a biological truth beneath this fascinating system. As with any exploration, many interpretations of its meanings and origins may be woven into how we as humans make sense and tell the story of our inner experience. Like suggestions from anyone, it is wise to use your own personal evaluation to assess whether there is any merit in these ideas. So I now invite you to consider having a "willing suspension of disbelief" and just see if this framework makes sense in your own world. Just because it fits together in some ways or others does not make it necessarily true. A test will be if there is predictive value in the framework: Does considering how childhood attachment and temperament interact to form personality add anything to your personal and professional journey to move life toward integration and well-being?

Our methodology as a five-member science-based team of clinicians, researchers, and theoreticians was to take our own personal first-person experience, weave this with what we had learned in group settings in which the narratives of others were being explored in depth, and then combine that with an interpersonal neurobiology (IPNB) view of development and recent discoveries in social, cognitive, and affective neuroscience (SCAN). I was able to offer informal assessments of attachment and enneagram type and interview individuals from various groupings in depth to explore these ideas. Our goal was this: Attempt to establish a model that could trace personality development from its temperament and attachment origins in early childhood up through adolescence and then adulthood. If possible, we would then study the predictive value of this framework in a large sample of twin pairs as they grew up. As mentioned, we knew that no model yet exists that provides a comprehensive framework in which to weave attachment and temperament into the development of personality across the life span. No system of adult personality description has such a developmental view. And no system that exists (except the enneagram popular version) has an internally focused organization—that is, a view of how the internal architecture of mental functioning, not just behavior, is organized across developmental periods. And no system attempts to combine the science of SCAN with a model of personality from infancy onward.

We would develop the framework, and then, hopefully with funding obtained, set up studies of over 600 twin pairs we had access to investigating. But in science you first need the theoretical framework and the hypotheses to test in advance, so this was one of our motivations for spending so much careful time compiling this new model. As with any model, it is just a map of the territory. But journeying with a map through new territory can often get you closer to your understanding than totally going at it in the dark.

BRAIN BASICS

So here is the model in a nutshell. As I get into the details with you, let me tell you about one experiment I did. With 120 clinicians one summer, I taught this model without ever mentioning the term *enneagram* and instead just focused on the IPNB/SCAN ideas upon which the model is based. The group revealed that they could then conduct clinical interviews that successfully differentiated nine distinct sets of traits—or what I like to call PDP-3 or just PDP for patterns of developmental pathways, proclivities, and propensities. While our five-person research group ultimately chose not to use the PDP term (and instead use a phrase, "nine patterns of processing"), I like the abbreviation because it has the double meaning of parallel distributed processing (that's how brains are composed in spiderweb-like interconnected networks) and also includes the developmental term (of patterns that are not fixed, but general paths and propensities—our developmental pathways shaped by our proclivities), which I think highlights the unique and crucial aspects of this model. So while it is fully a joint project from the five of us and I've signed on for the title of the paper we've submitted, in my own writing and teaching I'll use the PDP term to refer to this organizational structure. Here it is, for the first time, in black and white.

In my own mind, it is most helpful to outline the major developmental ideas and personality issues. Here they are in linear form for our left hemispheres to soak them in while our right cortices can just sit back and reflect:

1. In the womb most of us had the experience of being in a state of "being at one with the uterus" at some point before birth. In general, all of our needs were met: food, warmth, safety, and oxygen were all supplied without any effort on our part. Not a bad way to start. And our implicit memory likely becomes filled with this sense of *at-oneness*. Let's call this a *ground of being*. (This may have something to do with our open plane of possibility . . . so let's keep that in the back of our minds for now.) This may be the oceanic state Freud described, and may perhaps relate to a sense of oneness that emerges with contemplation. (This does not take away from the notion that this sense of oneness across religions and cultures may in fact reflect a truly accurate perception of our relational interconnectedness with the whole of the world.)

2. We are born into the world. Now we have to work for a living. We need to breathe to get air into our lungs—forever. We have to cry when we're cold or hungry or lonely. Left alone, we'll die. Yikes. Who set up this mammalian heritage?

Okay—this is a big change, one that is quite distinct from our ground of being. This contrast between the ground of being and working for a living sets up a drive to "make things okay again." This is the way we try to create some sense of balance in our lives, some assurance inwardly that everything will work out. It's a longing for that feeling you get when you rest your head on the pillow after a long, full, and fulfilling day and just let your eyes gently shut, sense your breath, and fall into a deep relaxing sleep.

3. As we experience the tension between being at one and working for a living, negative affective states arise. These "aversive states" have distinct circuitry, and most of us tend to have one circuit or another be more prevalent in our lives from early on and persisting throughout our development. These include negative states involving three neural pathways that become more or less dominant in our lives. Jaak Panksepp (1998) has described these in his seminal work on affective neuroscience and explores them further in his new IPNB series book (Panksepp & Biven, 2010). Here are the relevant three we feel are central to understanding personality development: fear, distress, and anger. At a very minimum, the PDP model suggests that some of us are more prone to experience fear in response to events in life; others experience distress, especially at social disconnection; and still others readily feel anger. It is striking how quickly most people can recognize which one of these three is most readily experienced in their reactions to various events—disappointments, frustrations, irritations—in their day-to-day life. Think of people you know and their innate first response to emotional slights or misunderstandings. Where do you yourself first go in your emotional response to such experiences? Do you generally first feel fear (anticipatory anxiety or vigilance for danger), distress (especially sadness over loss of connection), or anger (especially in response to limitations to feeling in control)? When we take

each of these three broad clusters and find that some of us are generally externally focused, some internally focused, and still others are both internally and externally focused as a proclivity of our attention, then you can see where we move from the broad three groupings to the fuller nine categories.

4. Here is an abstracted paraphrase of how we've described the essential features of these nine types in our collaborative paper (used with permission from Daniels et al., in review):

> Each of the nine personality types has a strong propensity for attention to be drawn to specific aspects of the events in everyday life, particularly in the realm of interpersonal interaction. Examples across the nine types include focusing attention especially on: (1) right versus wrong, errors, and mistakes, (2) other people's needs and desires, (3) tasks, goals, and achievement, (4) that which is missing and longed for, (5) potential intrusion and demands of others, especially regarding time, space, and knowledge, (6) potential hazards and worst case scenarios and how to deal with them, (7) positive or pleasurable options and opportunities, with a general emphasis on planning; (8) injustices and the need for control or assertiveness, and (9) maintaining harmony with one's physical and social environment.

Generally, we may have a tendency to live with one of these as a predominant modality of being—a way in which we tend to first focus our attention in new situations, patterns in which we prioritize our emotional evaluations, and ways in which we engage with others socially. Some people have more than one type, and depending on this combination, it can be facilitative or quite challenging. Overall, these tendencies are an internal focus and others may be unaware that this is where your attention tends to go. What this means is that determining your own PDP type is a personal job, not something someone other than you can determine accurately.

5. The PDP system has the following features. We've hypothesized that distinctive patterns in which attention is organized and

selectively focused emerge in early life. As mentioned above, this system is really an "inside job" in that these PDP categories are revealing how the inner world—the mind—is structured, not just how another person can view our outward behavior. This model is all about where attention tends to go. In this way, I can be one way internally but have learned to mask this proclivity from others, and so you wouldn't necessarily pick up what my PDP was just from your observations from afar. (I've interviewed family members and some were shocked to learn of another's type—but this system is truly only something the person himself or herself can ascertain. It is not observable by external behavior alone.) The PDP is a system of how we orient to aspects of our internal and external world—how we shape our ebbs and flows of orientation and arousal, our primary emotion. Over time, this general propensity to orient to certain features of our experience shapes how we develop.

As we've defined a core aspect of the mind as being a process that regulates the flow of energy and information, then attention—the governing of information flow—is what the mind is. In the PDP model, discernible patterns of where attention tends to go and what emotional states follow that attention are the essence of this developmental system. This is truly a developmental model of traits of the mind. Naturally, as we develop over time, a PDP grouping can reinforce itself and become more or less rigid in its internal focusing. In our larger picture as mindful therapists, we may have propensities that stay with us our whole lives, as may our clients. The notion of psychotherapy is to make us feel comfortable in our own skin and not to lose our skin. PDP is like the skin that defines the bodily structure of the mind. We can make our skin flexible, but it wraps a body that has a certain characteristic shape. Therapy's focus would be on increasing the flexibility of how our mind focuses its attention. Herein you can sense how all of our work with the wheel of awareness and developing observation, openness, and objectivity might be useful in relaxing the grip of a PDP type on a person's life.

6. It's likely that our innate temperament and our experiences in attachment and peer relationships together mold our personality. In the PDP model, inspired by doing direct Adult Attachment Interviews with a number of people knowing their PDP type, it appears that the way we are constricted in our type is what attachment coherence seems to determine. In other words, you can be securely attached and have any of the nine types. But a person with ongoing insecurity of attachment (as revealed in adults by incoherent AAI findings) may have marked dysfunction that amplifies the restrictive aspects of their type. With therapy, the type does not disappear; rather, it seems to move to a more adaptive, flexible, and coherent flow.

How can we understand this notion that attachment insecurity is likely associated with PDP inflexibility? Here is one explanation. We may have greater or lesser degrees of integration based on how supportive our relational experiences were, and how we've come to make sense of them. Our research group's impression—consistent with the preliminary investigations and clinical work we have done with adults—is that attachment category and PDP grouping are independent in category, but interactive in the *freedom within each type*. Secure attachment was associated with someone feeling at ease with his or her own particular proclivities, the PDP type. They would own who they were and even have a sense of humor about it.

Yet if people had insecure attachment histories and continued to exhibit incoherence of their adult narratives (a sign of continuing impaired integration and adult insecurity of attachment), their PDP pattern seemed to restrict them; they appeared to be imprisoned by their own temperament, irritated by their own personality. In many ways, insecure attachment and being not-mindful went hand in hand: When you are insecurely attached, you may not be able to have kindness and compassion toward yourself. Rather than being curious, open, accepting, and loving to your persistent proclivities, you buck up against them and create an internal war that no one can win. Recall that insecure attachment leads to impaired integration developmentally in our general IPNB model. The result of lack of integration is chaos and/or rigidity. If we as adults remain insecure, this can be viewed as a continuing lack of integration and the persistent life of living out of harmony and ease. With the development of security—with both interpersonal attunement in relationships and internal attunement with mindfulness practice, which each promote neural integration—people don't lose their personality; they become more at ease within it. In fact, they seem to come to take pleasure in their own makeup rather than feeling compelled to try to jettison it. This is the goal of therapy and it is the outcome of integration. We come to treasure our traits. And as we do, we loosen how restrictive they are in our lives. We "stretch" and become freer in our relationships, more comfortable in our own skin, more at ease in our lives.

7. There are several elaborated components to these patterns of developmental pathways (PDP) that can be identified and that shape subsequent processing: (a) core motivations, (b) emotional reactivity, (c) primary orientation bias, and (d) resulting adaptive strategy. We don't have space here to review these elements in their full detail, but let me just mention that with these elements of the model we can illuminate the ways in which our developmental paths start early in life and then continue to shape our inner experience throughout our lives.

Core Motivations

Above and beyond physical nurturance, infants need to feel (1) secure/assured, (2) loved/connected, and (3) valued/comforted (Brazelton & Greenspan, 2000; Daniels & Price, 2009). The need to feel secure becomes elaborated as children grow and develop and then comes to include the broader realms of safety, certainty, preparedness, and opportunity (dominant in the Fear group); the need to feel loved and connected comes to include notions of recognition, approval, and pair/group bonding and affection (dominant in the Distress group); and the need to feel valued and protected comes to include notions of respect, power and control, congruence, comfort, and harmony (found in the Anger group). Satisfaction of these social and basic biological needs from the inside leads to the outward expression of motivation that organizes behavior into the distinctive patterns for each large grouping. In other words, our internal focus of value and meaning governs where our attention goes, which in turn influences our behavior. The inner workings are the characterizing driving force while the outward manifestations follow and vary a great deal.

Emotional Reactivity

The general initial emotional reactions of anger, sadness/distress, and fear help organize initial orientation to stimuli and then focus attention toward basic needs and desires. The model's proposal is that anger, distress, and fear are the uncomfortable or aversive emotions that function shortly after birth and exist in each of us long before the emergence of our more complex cognitive functions (Panksepp, 1998). These aversive emotional responses characterized by fear/anxiety, sadness/separation distress, and anger/rage arise in the course of our lives, especially when those we depend upon fail to fully satisfy our needs and desires. In this way, we move from being at one with the uterus to working for a living with these emotional reactions being common in our everyday experience— no matter how good a caregiver is. This is just the reality of being out of the womb and out in the air-filled busy planet.

The PDP model suggests that in each of us, during the first months and years of life, one of these three systems becomes more dominant than the other two in organizing our early inner life. As all three are available to us, some people may have a relatively even distribution of tendencies; but the observation from interviewing dozens of people myself, and thousands of people as a group, is that people tend to lean toward one grouping or another. Why this seems to be the case is unclear. It may be that neuronal development favors specialization—even of a basic emotional response. Just as we tend to be either right or left handed, socially or mechanically inclined (see Baron-Cohen, 2004), the brain will favor the "most aggressive bidder" like a real estate market that responds to activity. So we may activate one emotional reaction and simultaneously inhibit the others. We're excited to explore whether in fact this can be researched to determine if this proclivity for a certain pathway (see why I like the PDP term?) is related to classic notions of temperament and genetics, or a combination of these factors plus family setting and which emotional reactions are evoked or tolerated. Our guess at this point (there is no validated and controlled research on this yet) is that the ultimate determination of which pathway becomes salient or dominant in a person's life is likely influenced by both innate temperament and the particular life experiences we have. This is a view consistent with an IPNB perspective on how we become who we are.

Primary Orientation Bias and Adaptive Strategies

Each pathway biases us in two aspects: content and direction. The content relates to the ways in which attention is drawn toward particular information or features of our experiences, minimizing attention to other less salient aspects of our experience. The directional dimension involves our strategies of self-regulation, especially of the aversive emotional reactions. This strategy can be directed internally (e.g., self-soothing in early childhood or the development of internal rules, self-sufficiency, and idealization in adults); externally (e.g., needing other people to soothe us in early childhood or asserting power and actively pursuing safety or interpersonal relationships as adults); or both simultaneously (this is the inward/outward dimension). These are the sources of the three variations of biased direction described above—inward, outward, and combined—within each of the three content orientations (based on salient needs driving the dominance of anger, distress, or fear). The result of this PDP model is the nine patterns of developmental pathways. These are our adaptive strategies that enable us to live within our families, find our way through school, and then create our patterns of living in the world of relationships and work.

MINDSIGHT SKILLS

As mindful therapists we have the ability to begin with reflection on our own PDP tendencies so that we are familiar with these patterns of pathways ourselves before we work with our clients to help them understand their own. As with each of the mindsight skill exercises in this book, we can first explore our own internal world and then apply this internal education in direct ways as we offer these skills to our patients.

The notion of personality and of PDP is that we have innate proclivities of neural firing, mental activities, and interpersonal interactions that emerge from our inborn temperament and our attachment histories. On our plane of reality, we can see these as vectors that valence our plateaus, setting us up to experience repeated patterns of particular peaks that activate and prime us in specific ways. The PDP model proposes that at a minimum, we have propensities toward anger, separation distress/sadness, or fear. These three broad categories are then further subdivided into plateaus that focus our intention inward, outward, or combined.

In Figure 9.1, you'll find a set of questions that explore the subjective nature of these various groupings. Rather than strictly identifying one type or another, these inquiries are meant to open a discussion about the nature of where your attention might go, and what patterns may emerge across the nine different clusters of information. You can try this out for yourself now, and after reflecting on these various questions, you may find diving more deeply

Please tell me three adjectives that would describe yourself. (Relevant for and asked of each of the groupings)

Group S – c
What does success mean for you?
What does approval and acceptance mean for you?
Are you task oriented?
Do you ever cut corners in doing a task?
Is how you appear to others important to you?
Is it important to you to be competent, strong, or the best at something?
How important is being recognized by others to you?
Can you adapt to your environment easily?

Group F - c
Does worrying play a big part in your life?
Do you have doubt about things in your life?
Does fear come up easily for you?
How important is security for you?
How do you protect your security?
How does trust play a part in your life?
Do you find yourself questioning authority?
Do you scan the environment for danger?
Do you find yourself confronting things that otherwise would seem
    intimidating?

Group A - c
How is comfort important you?
Where does your attention go in relationship to others?
How easy is it for you to do things for yourself?
What is harmony to you?
How do you deal with conflict?
How does conflict feel to you?
Do you stand your ground easily?
How easy it for you to take action to do things for yourself?
Do you find yourself seeing from all points of view easily?

Figure 9.1 PDP interview. These are general questions that can be used to distinguish nine types of patterns of developmental pathways. They are listed here just for a sense of the range of interview questions that may evoke differing proclivities that an individual may have in where her attention goes. You can begin by asking yourself these questions, then perhaps some friends and colleagues. Until you are familiar with these in yourself, it may not be prudent to use this

Group S - i

How do you compare yourself to others?

Do you ever feel the grass is greener on the other side?

How does envy play a role in your life?

Do you ever feel that there is something missing in your life?

How do you feel when other people are in pain?

How easy is it for you to feel hurt?

How is it for you when you feel misunderstood?

Do your partners and friends feel that they are not enough?

Does the feeling of inadequacy play a big role in your life?

Group F - i

How important are knowledge and skills to you?

How important is it for you to spend time alone in your own space?

Do you think that it is important to be self-sufficient?

In what ways do you find other people to be intrusive?

Are you concerned that others might be wasting your time?

Do you find collecting things to be important?

Do you get think more about an experience after it is over than when it is
    happening?

Do you find yourself figuring out things on your own?

Do you feel that when you are with people for a long time you need to with-
    draw from them to restore your energy?

Group A - i

Do you find yourself noticing what is not right in the world?

What kind of reactions do you have when you see the imperfections in the
    world and the things that are wrong in others?

Is it easy for you to identify what you should do rather than what you would
    like to do?

Is there more than one right way to do things?

Does correcting others often lead to conflict?

Do you ever feel resentful toward others?

Do you have a harsh inner critic that it is hard to live up to?

Do you ever find yourself cutting corners in completing a task?

Do you find yourself feeling responsible for fixing things and sometimes notice
    that you say, "Why did I do that?"   *continued*

---

to conduct a formal clinical assessment. For your education—and not necessarily needed in this order—these are clustered along the major groupings of primary emotional bias: Group S (Sadness/Separation Distress), Group F (Fear/Anxiety), and Group A (Anger/Rage). After the letter grouping is the inward (i)/outward (e) focus or combined (c).

Figure 9.1 continued

Group S - o

How much time and energy do you spend on relationships?

Do you need to have someone in your life to care for?

What do you do to get connected to people?

What happens when you don't get the connection that you want with others?

How are you needed by other people?

How do you know what people need?

How do you feel when others do not appreciate you?

How quickly can you access your emotions?

Do you ever feel other people's emotions before your own?

Group F - o

Is it important for you to have something to look forward to?

How easy is it for you to know and get what you want?

How do you feel with limitations?

How important are choices and options to you?

What is it like for you when you have no options or are stuck?

How do you deal with pain and suffering?

Do you feel comfortable getting what you need?

How does negative feedback feel to you?

Do you find yourself rationalizing what you do?

Group A - o

Do you find strength an important characteristic of a person?

Do you feel you have to right the injustices of the world?

To what degree do people find you intimidating or accommodating?

Do people find you excessive in your behaviors?

Do you see yourself as exuberant or passive?

Do you handle conflict with anger?

Are honesty and truth important to you?

If you feel someone is not honest with you, how do you respond?

Do you ever feel that your reaction gets out of control?

into a reflective mindsight practice with inner reflection on your innate tendencies may be a helpful way to proceed to a deeper understanding of your own internal patterns of being.

To explore this inner world of personality, here I'll introduce you to an exercise that focuses on the triangle of mind, brain, and relationships. Recall that mindsight in its refined, most basic view is the capacity to sense energy and information flow in the triangle so that we can monitor and modify how we regulate, shape, and share this flow with one another and within ourselves.

For this mindsight skill training exercise focusing on the triangle, I'll invite you to get set up in your hub: Sensing your breath, imagine the wheel of awareness and let your body settle into its natural state, sounds around you filling your awareness. Now focus your attention on the in-breath and the out-breath. The hub is the place we've been cultivating for all of these practices, and it is the place we begin for our deep work of knowing the inner world.

A triangle exercise entails being in the moment with present sensation, but also taking in all aspects of our streams of awareness—from sensation to observation, concept, and knowing. And so we are embracing the fullness of the hub, surrounded as it is by the four concentric SOCK circles that filter what enters our moment-to-moment awareness of what arises.

For this triangle focus, I invite you now to begin first with relationships. Naturally we'll be inviting elements of memory into awareness as you rest, alone, in this reflective exercise. But in the future, when actively interacting with others, it is possible to have a dual focus and enact this exercise in real-time engagement with other people. (This can be especially useful when exploring old, engrained patterns of communication with family members.)

Consider your attachment history, much of which we've explored in detail in the first chapters of this book. We can work to make our adult attachment narrative become secure as we integrate our internal life and create empathic connections in our interpersonal worlds. As we do this, we relax the rigid and chaotic reactions of a nonintegrated life that would have intensified our PDP proclivities. If you've already done a lot of that work, then determining your specific PDP type may be more difficult. As we've seen, sometimes it is helpful to think back to your way of being when you were younger, just leaving home, and before you may have carried out your own reflective growth and personal change. As we do grow, we become more integrated, our PDP type may loosen, and we become more at ease with ourselves. That is wonderful, but may make finding your PDP category a bit more challenging. Becoming integrated does not mean losing these tendencies; rather, it means coming to appreciate them, in part, as aspects of our temperament, our neurological propensities, which we may have as a baseline for all of our lives. That neural side of the triangle, as we'll see, is often felt to drive both the mind and the relational points in particular patterns.

What do you notice about your history of relating to others? Can you sense that anxiety and fear have dominated your response to intimacy? Do you often withdraw from closeness, becoming overwhelmed by the needs of others? Is counteracting these fears drawing you to making continual plans, thinking of the future and not feeling in the present? Or, is distress and sadness more your homebase emotional state? For some, separation is painful and a longing to feel whole permeates much of interpersonal relationships. For others, the drive is to be sure others see them as good, worthy, important, impressive. For those where distress is dominant, meeting others' needs may be a primary way of feeling important, of guaranteeing social commitment by being the source of comfort and connection in others' lives. Perhaps instead you tend toward relationships where anger—or avoiding it—is a central theme. Here you may find that you get easily irritated when others, or you, fail to meet expectations for how things should be. Others in the anger grouping avoid conflict at all cost, finding themselves as mediators to be sure everyone just gets along. Or you might find you direct your anger outward, asserting your opinion easily to let others in relationship to you know that you are in charge and do not need them. These are the many ways a PDP type can influence the relational side of how we share energy and information flow with one another.

Now consider the brain point on the triangle. As you feel right now or as you reflect on memory, can you sense how energy and information tends to flow within particular uncomfortable emotional valences? Does anger, separation distress or sadness, or a feeling of fear dominate your internal seascape? If one of these aversive states establishes a pattern of response, you may become familiar or at home with one affective state or another. These innate temperamental tendencies can become so much a part of who we feel we are that we just feel resigned to the regularity of these responses. This is the neural side of the mechanism of energy and information flow in our lives.

To examine the mind point of the triangle, we can look toward the way energy and information flow is regulated. Here is the tricky part: The mind is both embodied and it is relational. In this way, our PDP type can be sensed both in how particular mental activities may be molded by the neural proclivities and how relationship patterns unfold over time. Do you sense ways in which this valenced response has influenced how you share energy and information flow to sculpt repeating patterns in your relationships with others? The mind uses relationships and the brain to create itself. The key is that mental activity rides along neural firing patterns without much intervention when we're on automatic pilot. The secret to transformation is to awaken the mind so that we can regulate these patterns intentionally, shift how the brain fires and alter the ways we approach communication within our relationships.

Sensing these elements of the triangle, see if you can just rest in the larger awareness of how energy and information flow is shaped by these neural mechanisms which may, in this case, be driving your experience of regulating and sharing this flow. This is taking in the whole triangle within the hub as you just sense, observe, conceive, and open to a sense of knowing how these patterns have been emerging in your life. I invite you to take a deeper and more intentional breath and let your eyes come open if they're closed and let's pause for a moment.

We flow along patterns of energy and information as it moves through time. Our mindsight skills enable us to become deeply aware of this flow—as it is shared, structured, and regulated—and ultimately to use this awakened awareness to integrate our lives more fully. Yet engrained patterns of this flow emerge from innate synaptic circuitry and repeated learning and response. And even our relationships with others form an enduring system that can continue to reinforce particular patterns of being. To explore these patterns of PDP influences on our lives, we'll now move to a second exercise.

To build on this awareness of the triangle exercise, we'll explore the PDP history you may have by applying further our baseline wheel of awareness practice. This will be a more directed elaboration of the triangle exercise we just performed. Now we'll dive specifically into features of each of the PDP types. Finding or staying in a comfortable place to sit, let your attention take in the sounds in the room, feeling your body sitting on the chair or floor, and letting your eyes go closed. Let your attention just ride the waves of the breath for a few moments, your body settling into its natural state, your breath finding its natural rhythm.

Now imagine the wheel of awareness with its central hub and outer rim. The hub is where we have that inner space of awareness and stability, of calm and clarity, from which we can just experience whatever arises. Sometimes we just have a nonfocused attention, taking in things as they emerge, stay present, and fall away from our attention. Now, I invite you to send a spoke out to the seventh sense—that part of the rim where we have our thoughts, feelings, perceptions, and memories. Let your autobiographical memory become the target of attention for this exercise.

We've been exploring the notion of a model of personality—the PDP view—that enables us to see if there are general patterns of attention and emotion that have organized our internal world. We can explore these patterns in our daily interactions with others, noting if we tend to react initially with emotions of anger—or sadness and distress—or fear. We can also look deeply into memory and assess these same patterns.

Looking toward the rim, see if you can imagine sending a spoke to the seventh sense and inviting memories of yourself in the past to enter your awareness. Ask yourself the question, where does my emotional reaction tend to go first in interacting with others? Do I feel anger readily, becoming irritated when others have not kept up to my standards of behavior? Do I avoid anger in myself or in others, trying to moderate arguments so that anger is minimized and people just get along with one another? If anger is a primary emotion for you, ask yourself if you tend to project it out toward others—or do you tend to be hard on yourself, especially when you haven't lived up to your own expectations? Just let whatever responses to these questions rest in your awareness and soon we'll move on to another set of exploratory inquiries.

How are you with distress at separation from those you care about? Do you get sad easily as a first reaction? For some, avoiding this emotional state can be achieved by focusing on how they perform and please others; for other people, being needed by others is of vital importance—to be of service, to help out at times of distress or become a crucial part of supporting others' work. Another PDP pattern is to feel that things are always better for others— that the grass is always greener on the other side of the road. Often there may be a feeling that no one understands who you really are. Are any of these patterns your particular proclivity? Again, let your responses to these general questions just fill your hub, resting in awareness of whatever has come up.

With fear, there may be an anticipatory anxiety that tends to dominate an individual's life. Fear and dread can come in many forms. For some, the focus of attention goes outward on the many ills that could befall a life—this is the worst-case-scenario thinking that has the benefit of making sure you are always prepared for what might come, with a vigilant focus on the outside world. The focus here is also inward, on the internal sense of dread that something bad might happen and one always needs to be ready for anything, doubting even one's own thoughts. The downside, of course, is to become a "Debbie Downer" and always spoil a positive experience with negative concerns. Others in this broad fear grouping are focused on protecting their time, space, or knowledge, often needing to go inward to recharge their batteries. A primarily outward focus of the fear group is to avoid the feelings of fear, and most other feelings as well, by always planning. Anticipation of external activities, organizing one's mind to focus attention on details, sometimes to the exclusion of inner awareness of feelings, is a pattern in this grouping. This outward focus has the sense that the fear of feelings has organized a person to continually focus outwardly on projects and plans that enable him or her to live an externally oriented life. Let these responses just fill your awareness, floating in a sense of whatever has arisen.

As you explore each of these major three spheres of experience in the anger, sadness/distress, and fear groupings, what did you notice? Which direction of focus seemed to fit with your autobiographical memories—a tendency toward looking inward, outward, or combined? Did one emotional reactive pattern seem to resonate with your experience more than the others? Whatever your PDP proclivity or proclivities, the idea is that you can move toward a more flexible life at ease with your own personality through exercises that enable you to disengage from automatic pilot and awaken your mind. This is the essence of integration.

In the next phase of this mindsight practice, let yourself move back into the hub and let go of the spokes to the memory aspects of the rim. Imagine the following view as you rest in the open hub of the wheel of awareness. Recall that we've been exploring a visual image of an open plane of possibility. As we move outward away from the plane, we go from wide-open potential to valenced plateaus of probability that increase the likelihood we'll respond in a particular way. These plateaus are literally a graphic representation of neural propensities and mental proclivities. As we've inherited neural pathways of emotional reaction over millions of years of evolution, certain aversive circuits are available to us. Indeed, sometimes they entrap us. These independent paths, as we've seen, are the anger, distress, and fear circuits.

For example, you may have used the anger circuit predominantly in your childhood, and the "neurons that fire together wire together" principle of neuroplasticity led to the strengthening of that particular circuit over others. As your anger circuit became the more likely neural circuit to be activated under stress—like walking down a snow-covered hill and following the previously laid down path of prior travelers—you've found over these many years of your life that this was an "easier" and more readily taken path. This increased likelihood creates a valenced pattern of response and is depicted as a particular set of plateaus of probability. Here, anger is your plateau: This is the familiar place you go, the underlying propensity, the repeated pattern emerging from your temperament and learned experiences. Getting angry at a particular moment of time is depicted as a peak of activation—a mental activity or neural firing profile. So in a nutshell, our personality from the PDP view is merely the ways repeated neural firing and mental experience have shaped our plateaus and peaks into repeating and enduring patterns over a long period of time.

Some elements of these patterns have been acquired genetically, some by chance, and some by reinforcement through the neural firing of experience. This is how we developed personality traits. Another dimension of this view is this: As we move from the open plane of possibility outward, we are shaped by personality. Personality, then, is the hidden proclivities, propensities, and pathways that shape our motion from possibility to probability and then on to activation. This model enables us to see, directly, how a process of relaxing the stranglehold of rigid personality patterns would involve mindfulness practices that move us from peaks and plateaus toward the plane of possibility. Moving back to the open plane, we "relax" our personality, become more flexible, and more readily enter a receptive state of wide-open potential in which we rest in the expanse of possibility rather than being imprisoned by the patterns of the past. While we may never rid ourselves fully of these proclivities, with a harnessed hub—with mindsight engaged—we can awaken the mind to sense these pathways we're on, to relax the propensities and widen our base of possibilities, so that the actual activations of thought, emotion, and behavior are more flexible, adaptive, and coherent. Instead of our proclivities being reactively defensive, we become proactively receptive to ourselves and to others.

From your open hub, see if you can imagine this: We all share the ground of being, the spaciousness of the hub, the openness of the plane of possibility. This is how we can say, from a scientifically grounded point of view, that personality is necessary but it can be restrictive; the ground of being, the hub of the mind, is where we can find one another—and even find our own selves.

Let yourself find your breath and take a few moments to ride the waves of your in-breath and your out-breath. Knowing that sensing the breath brings you to the open spaciousness of the hub of your mind, this deep space of clarity and calm is always there for you. As we go forward in our journey together, let the hub of your mind become an ever-strengthening sanctuary to which you can return from your various journeys through the peaks and plateaus of personality that we all inhabit in our daily lives. This hub of your mind is the refuge to which you can turn to rejuvenate, and it is the spacious awareness from which you can rest to sense the ongoing experiences of your life day by day, moment by moment.

From the hub, we've practiced how to let yourself move from a focus on activated points of the rim to the intervals between thoughts, feelings, and impulses. As this skill becomes practiced over time, you may find that you'll be able to develop a more refined way of feeling the activated peaks (rim points) and the valenced plateaus (the feel of the intervals between points). We've also practiced how you can move your awareness from this rim focus (on points and on intervals) inward, to the hub itself. This visual image, the metaphor of our wheel of awareness, can also be seen as reflecting how you can let the focus of awareness move from peak to plateau, and now from plateau to plane. We can move from an activated point of the peak (rim point) to a valenced plateau (interval) to the open plane of possibility (the hub). Let yourself sense again, even for just a moment, what this hub awareness feels like. What do you notice? As we've seen, for some this is a difficult step in our mindsight journey, so don't worry if nothing particular arises that is different from the rim as in past exercises. But you may find that by reflecting on our various visual metaphors, these maps of the territory of the mind, some new light will be illuminating the path. These are not maps to restrict, but guides to open your own direct experience to receive and decipher the internal world as it is. More practice building mindsight's tripod, as we've described earlier, will help in supporting you in this hub awareness/plane of possibility exercise.

With practice, some begin to feel a wide-open spaciousness of the mind, a feeling, we can imagine, of the open possibility of resting in the plane. And so here is the notion: Awareness of awareness, so central to mindfulness practice, brings us directly into the plane of open possibility. This is what our metaphors of the hub in the wheel of awareness and our plane of reality may truly represent. And this hub of our mind is where we can turn to get beneath the propensities of our PDP proclivities. Harnessing the hub is how we can relax the imprisonment of personality and integrate our brains, our minds, and our relationships with others, and with ourselves.

INTEGRATION AND GROWING BEYOND TEMPERAMENT

While the PDP model may help us embrace our starting place, reflective practice stabilizes our mindsight lens and develops the hub of the mind to bring us back to the ground of being, to the open plane of possibility, so that we relax into a more receptive place in our lives. We can view the PDP types as being the way we've both learned and have been born with a general topogra-

phy of our valenced plateaus of probability and propensities to particular peaks of activation. When we are not integrated, the peaks
become steep and the tendency to rigidify those patterns is strong.
Integration relaxes those peaks but may never erase the general
pattern of the plateaus. With integrative practice, as we use mindsight to track the energy and information flow in our lives, we can
move toward the plane—returning to the ground of being with
daily practice.

In these ways, we may be able to develop what have been called
mindfulness traits. In ourselves, reflection may cultivate these ways
of being; in our clients, helping them develop mindsight skills may
assist them in weaving such personality features into their day-to-
day lives without effort. In other words (and this is not yet proven
but is conceptually clear): With mindfulness practice, an intentionally and repeatedly created state can become an effortless trait of
our being.

These are the traits Baer and colleagues (2006) have identified
in individuals with or without formal mindfulness practice. This is
a natural history, if you will, of what a general population (of college students) revealed when being offered a conglomeration of
several questionnaires about traits of being mindful. Here is the
list: Acting with awareness, being nonjudgmental, having emotional
equilibrium ("nonreactivity"), labeling and describing with words
the internal world, and self-observation (this last feature was only
an independent variable in those with formal mindfulness practice). We don't yet know from research itself if these mindfulness
traits perhaps can be cultivated with formal practice.

From a different set of reasoning and data, we do know that
mindfulness meditation does promote our nine middle prefrontal
functions: bodily regulation, attunement, emotional balance, fear
modulation, flexibility of response, insight, empathy, morality, and
intuition. And so we can say that helping our clients, and ourselves,
to practice mindfulness can be considered a form of brain fitness in
that it stimulates the growth and presumably maintains the func-

tioning of our integrative prefrontal circuits (see Lazar et al., 2005; Luders et al., 2009). The daily creation of a state of mindful awareness with specific skill practice can create these integrative traits in our everyday lives. The magic of states becoming traits is elucidated in the neuroplastic principle that repeated firing increases synaptic linkages and may lay down myelin as we become an expert in the skill of knowing the inner world. We can create this repeated firing, coupled with a close focus of attention and sense of emotional engagement, as we voluntarily engage in mindfulness practice on a regular basis. You can see why we might consider this a most basic form of life fitness, one that cultivates integrative functioning and improves the health of our bodies and brains, relationships and minds.

As we conclude this section on traits, let's recap some dimensions that may seem contradictory. Yes, we've said just now that with the practice of creating mindful states we may be able to alter synaptic connections in the brain so that we have more integrative traits—in ourselves, and in our patients. What was once an effortful activity to intentionally create a state (regular mindful practice) becomes an effortless, automatic aspect of our "personality," and we call this a trait. This trait we've cultivated on purpose so that we have all these nine middle prefrontal functions as our baseline. This can be seen as how we now would have more flexible valenced plateaus, making balanced self-regulation, kindness toward ourselves and others, and all the other features of middle prefrontal functions a part of our makeup.

We've also explored the PDP model, which proposes that synaptic connections laid down early in our lives result from a likely combination of genetically influenced temperament, chance, and relational experiences with parents and peers all embedded in our synaptically shaped circuitry. Suboptimal experiences may have impaired integration and may have made the plateaus and peaks of our experience more rigid, less flexible (and hence prone to chaotic outbursts), and our personality more of a problem in our lives—and the lives of those we interact with. In contrast, we may have had the same PDP pathway but instead had optimal interpersonal experiences earlier in life and then our personality is part of our natural way of being, a plus in our lives, and not a hindrance. As mindful therapists, knowing that these personality traits may be lifelong features of our plateaus and peaks—our innate tendencies—lets us accept that the goal of therapy is not to lose our temperament and personality. Instead, the goal can be to promote integration so that we can help others, and ourselves, make our personality features assets rather than liabilities.

The PDP model and this general discussion of personality lets us see that some traits we can loosen up and even truly learn to love; other traits emerging from neural integration, such as those of mindsight in general, and of mindfulness in particular, we can actually learn to cultivate. For example, as we develop mindfulness as a trait we can move the brain to a left shift as we learn to approach and not withdraw from life's challenges. This can be seen as a neurosignature of resilience. And no matter what our temperament, we can create more equanimity, meaning, and connection in our lives as happiness flourishes for the benefit of not only ourselves, but those for whom we are devoting our lives to help move toward integration.

Chapter 10

TRAUMA

Being mindful as therapists, we remain open to whatever arises. But at the same time, we're exploring a framework that embraces the central concepts of mindsight, integration, development, neuroplasticity, and the relational nature of the mind and the brain. We've now even journeyed into the notion of a PDP model that traces early innate features of temperament into the development of patterns of personality. And so we've filled our minds with ideas and concepts that can serve as top-down limitations to being fully open to what is as it emerges. This is the challenge: to use mindfulness in its creative context to avoid premature hardening of the categories that can constrain how we perceive, make sense, and act. On the one hand, we have an open mind; on the other hand, we have a way of knowing about how health may emerge. Before we explore the major role trauma can play in human development to impair health, let's briefly review our major conceptualizations so we see them clearly together and then apply this view to an understanding of how trauma may fit into this framework. "Chance favors the prepared mind" is our basic reason for having these maps of the territory, so as we move into the murky and chaotic waters of unresolved trauma we don't lose our bearings along the way.

You may have noticed that as we move forward in each of these layers of exploration of being a mindful therapist that we are scaffolding our knowledge so that we review and synthesize where we've come so far before we take the next chapter's steps into expanding the ideas and experiences of mindfulness, of mindsight, and of integration. This is a kind of tracking to be sure that we are together as all of these first-person immersions, second-person descriptions, and third-person concepts unfold. In many ways, this is the feedback process research suggests we need to do to inquire into where we as a therapeutic relationship are in the moment. Perhaps this is a way of bringing in the streams of sensation, observation, and concept so that our shared knowing can occur and integrate the experience. The same kind of integration is likely implicitly true for friendships and relationships between parent and child, teacher and student, work colleagues, and romantic partners. Here, though, we have the opportunity to put this process into words that reflect these layers of our journey. While such meta-communication—communication about the communication—takes us a step away from the flow of new information, it is crucial in illuminating where we've been so we can be sure that where we actually are enables us to take the next step, together.

In our triangle of well-being we've seen how we can define certain patterns of energy and information flow. The mind has a regulatory function in which energy and information flow is both monitored and modified. The brain entails the nervous system distributed throughout the entire body and is the physical mechanism through which energy and information flow is structured. And relationships are the way we share energy and information flow with one another.

We've also offered the conceptualization that mental health emerges from integration, the linkage of differentiated elements of a system. When integration is present, the system moves in the FACES flow of being flexible, adaptive, coherent, energized, and stable. When integration is impaired with the blockage of linkage and/or differentiation, the system moves toward chaos, rigidity, or both.

In our discussion of the patterns of developmental pathways (proclivities and propensities), the PDP model, we've explored the notion that certain traits are a part of the individual's temperament and genetic contribution to the development of personality. While these traits may endure a lifetime, shaping the patterns of our plateaus of probability and peaks of activation, therapy can promote integration and create a more flexible pathway within which these patterns emerge. While the essence of our personality may not be changed, the way we come to live within these constraints can become enabling rather than imprisoning. The path toward freedom involves expanding our experience within the plane of possibility, to relax the constraints of those propensities symbolized by steep and narrow plateaus and rigid and inflexible peaks, and open ourselves to new ways of being. By acknowledging our patterns as just a part of who we are, ironically they loosen their grip on our lives. We get freedom from knowing and owning our limitations.

But how do we distinguish a personality pathway from a historical adaptation to a suboptimal set of experiences? How can we discern when a particular proclivity is an aspect of unresolved trauma—major or minor—in need of change through treatment versus a fundamental feature of a genetically shaped, temperament-organized personality pattern?

These are not just academic questions—they are at the heart of what we face in our daily work as therapists. I often like to think of the old story of Willie Sutton, the bank robber, and his response when they asked him why he robbed the bank. Willie allegedly said, "That's where the money was." Similarly, as therapists, why shouldn't we just go where the money is in terms of assessing what is going on with specificity and then offering interventions that focus directly on the issue creating suffering in a person's life? That's the notion of having a truth-based coherent framework, an accurate yet flexible map of the territory, so that we can address these important questions and make our work most effective and efficient.

Trauma, I'll suggest to you, offers an example of an extremely important developmental experience that illuminates how we can distinguish what needs to be done in therapy. As we try to differentiate a PDP trait from an unresolved trauma, we are faced with the most fundamental of challenges. How do we know what can be changed and what cannot? And how do we develop the wisdom to know the difference?

In this chapter I'll use an example of my own traumatic experience to offer you a view from the inside out. You may find useful discussions in our many IPNB books and the other texts mentioned in the introduction that deal directly with trauma and its treatment. Here we'll focus on the mindful therapist's role in distinguishing traits from trauma.

BRAIN BASICS

I am having breakfast with my family before our two teenagers head off to school. I'm treating a sinus infection so I have some antibiotics to take, and the kids are finishing their cereal and juice before our son drives his sister to school. I'm distracted by our engaging conversation about the weekend's upcoming events and lose track of what I'm doing and a capsule of antibiotic drops to the floor. No big deal. I lean over to reach down for the medicine and, before I know it, one of our dogs has leaped from her cushion and swept up the pill into her mouth.

Okay, no big deal, right?

Well, I explode out of my chair, chase her around the house, pry open her jaws and try desperately to get the antibiotic out of her mouth. My heart is pounding, I'm sweating up a storm, my hands are shaking, and I'm clearly in an altered state.

My kids ask what in the world is wrong with me. I tell them that she can't swallow that stuff, that it will kill her, and that I have to get it out of her mouth. My daughter finds the pill under the leg of the table, hands it to me, rolls her eyes, and tells me to get a grip.

They go off to school, and I go to take a shower before heading to work. What I really should do is head to therapy—which I ultimately did—and figure out what was going on.

Now you might supportively think, "Be kind to yourself, Dan. You thought the pill could kill your dog so you tried to protect her." Well, thanks. While you certainly may be right—the possibility that one antibiotic that I take two times a day for a week could actually kill a canine is in fact quite unlikely. But even so, my fear of her taking that pill had made it so that I actually didn't see that she in fact had not swallowed the capsule. Fear puts us in a fog, taking over our perception, capturing our attention, and focusing our mind on the most endangering aspect of an experience. In short, while fear can save our lives, it can also imprison our perceptions and make us see what is not there.

The amygdala has been studied extensively by many, including Joseph LeDoux (2002), and has been shown to monitor the incoming stream of perceptual input. If we've been sensitized by a past painful event, such as a trauma or a loss, then the amygdala adds that context to its laundry list of things to watch out for in our day-to-day lives. Screening incoming data, if it detects something similar to a past list condition, a past trauma, then it amplifies attention to the salient aspects of the current event. If the subsequent analysis assesses an ongoing match between event and past-encoded memory, then its creation of the physiological state of fear will also increase. This is how fear is helpful to rapidly mobilize our resources to avoid danger. This sympathetically driven state of alarm—of fear—can also accelerate into a state of panic with its sense of dread and impending disaster. I was certainly in panic mode when I saw my dog come for the pill after I dropped it on the floor.

But was she coming for the pill, or just a grain of cereal that had fallen moments before? When I saw her coming, my amygdala responded with an emergency switch on full throttle and in my panic I did not even assess if she had eaten the pill or just come for a human-food snack.

Why did this occur? Do I just have the trait of someone who thinks of the worst-case scenario? Well, yes, I do have that PDP proclivity. And is that the end of the story—this is just some personality quirk that my family and I have to live with: I'm just a nut when it comes to pets eating pills?

Or is there something more? Is this not merely a trait, but a remnant of trauma? If it is unresolved trauma, what would that be? In this case, an unresolved overwhelming past event was creeping into my present life. When I was 14 years old, I had the sad and painful experience of putting out snail poison for the garden I was in charge of and then forgetting to warn my parents not to let my puppy out in the backyard after I went to bed. When I awoke, my dog, Prince Junior, was dead. The pain of the loss and the profound guilt over forgetting to warn my parents and protect my best friend were horrendous emotions that tormented me for years. I think I always had the trait of fear and worrying about things, but this traumatic event built on those prior propensities and made me a bigger worrier. After that, when I was in school I did everything I could to be prepared. When I was in medical school, I studied like crazy and felt deeply responsible for every aspect of my patients' care. Personality traits and professional commitments went hand in hand—which in some ways was a good thing. But what role did the trauma play in all of that?

An integrated system enables equanimity to be established. In the brain what this means is that waves of neural firing reflecting deeply moving memories or feelings can occur throughout the nervous system, but our regulatory regions, such as the middle prefrontal areas, enable coordination and balance of these diverse firing patterns. Work by Richard Davidson and his colleagues at Wisconsin (personal communication, 2009) reveals that a part of the middle prefrontal circuit, called the uncinate fasciculus, releases inhibitory transmitters that diminish the firing of the lower limbic amygdala during reactive states. Other studies by David Creswell and colleagues (2007) at UCLA have demonstrated that middle prefrontal areas including the ventrolateral prefrontal cortex are activated when we name an emotion accurately. This internal labeling is associated with diminished amygdala firing following the observation of an emotionally expressive face (primarily, by the way, in those who exhibit high mindfulness traits revealed in a questionnaire—they are the ones who can most robustly name it to tame it). All in all, the integrative middle prefrontal region plays an essential role in monitoring and modifying the firing patterns of the lower limbic and brainstem areas. It is this regulation that we need in order to live with coordination and balance of our nervous system. And it is such neural integration that permits a FACES flow of living to be achieved.

Here is the basic proposal: Trauma impairs integration. Unresolved trauma results in persistent chaos and rigidity. My panic attack after dropping the antibiotic capsule was an example of a chaotic reaction. My vigilance about people or animals being poisoned may be laudable given my profession in medicine, but the rigidity of that stance even when a pill is dropped during breakfast reveals an inflexibility to adapt to the context of my interactions. This chaos and rigidity reveal a brain with impaired integration—and a mind with unresolved trauma.

We can postulate that the neural representations associated with dogs and poisoning within my brain then gave rise to a cascade of out-of-control reactions. This could result in the panic/chaos, and it could result in excessive vigilance/rigidity. It's hard to put this into words, but imagine this: Neural associations in my unresolved state gave rise to subsequent firing patterns that lacked the FACES flow. They were not flexible, adaptive, coherent, energized (in the sense of feeling full of vitality), and stable (in terms of leading to a solid set of interactions that supported their own unfolding in an adaptive way). Naturally, there was energy in the panic, and the repetitive nature of the vigilance could be understandably interpreted as stable in that it was recurrent in my life. But the use of *energized* and *stable* here is more about enriching with vigor and grounded in long-term strength and steadiness.

Unresolved trauma makes a mind incoherent. The acronym of coherence was not met: My internal world did not feel connected, open, harmonious, engaged, receptive, emergent (like things emerging fresh and new), noetic (with a deep sense of knowing), empathic, or compassionate. From my kids' vantage point, what I did was incoherent: It did not make sense. I was on automatic pilot, not mindful, and, literally, becoming "out of my mind."

MINDSIGHT SKILLS

One of the basic reflective exercises for detecting and resolving unresolved trauma is to explore the ways in which memory is impaired in its integration. Posttraumatic stress disorder and impairments to resolution of overwhelming events can be seen as an outcome of the separation of the two major domains of memory: implicit and explicit. As Figure 10.1 reveals, implicit memory develops first and has the six aspects of perceptual, emotional, behavioral, sensory, mental modeling, and priming.

After the pill incident, I took some time later that day to sit quietly in my office and explore what might be going on regarding this issue. Having burst into chaos, I knew that something was up in my mind; something remained unresolved in my brain. Moving to the hub of my wheel of awareness, I could follow my breath and let it find its own natural rhythm. Once feeling the clarity of the hub, I could invite the rim elements of memory into my awareness. I know this may sound strange, but having practiced the wheel of awareness exercise repeatedly in its many dimensions, you may also see how effective this approach can be. Patients often take to this visual metaphor of the mind with remarkable speed and use it with powerful effect. When we can apply our knowledge of the layers of memory to the interpretation of rim events, then we can come to see our inner experience from a new and liberating perspective.

Implicit memory lacks the sensation of something coming from the past. Yet with this knowledge, it is possible to just observe what-

Implicit Memory
Present before and after birth—and throughout lifespan;

Does not require focal, conscious attention for encoding;

Does not require the hippocampus for encoding or retrieval;

When retrieved in its "implicit-only" or pure non-integrated form, it enters awareness but does not have the internal sensation that something is being recalled from the past;

Involves at least six aspects: Perceptual, emotional, behavioral, and likely sensory; Plus mental models (schema) and priming (readying for a particular reaction);

Is automatic and thus not flexible.

Explicit Memory
Develops in the first years of life;

Requires focal, conscious attention for encoding;

Requires the hippocampus for encoding and for retrieval of non-consolidated, long-term (but not permanent) memory;

When retrieved, enters awareness and does have the sensation that something is being recalled from the past;

Involves at least two aspects: Factual memory (left-sided dominance) also called semantic memory and Autobiographical memory (right-sided dominance) also called episodic memory, for oneself in an episode of time;

Is flexible and can be retrieved with intention, re-organized and categorized, and new meanings extracted as the basic building blocks of memory are sorted and people "make sense" through the process of autobiographical narrative.

Figure 10.1 Levels of memory.

ever arises and track the sensations that emerge with each new image. I like to think of the term SIFT, for how we can track the sensations, images, feelings, and thoughts that come up in our various streams of awareness. In this case, a sensation in my abdomen of dread and doom emerged as I considered the panic that morning. That's what panic entails, I thought; but knowing about implicit memory, I tried to stay open to the possibility that this was some sensory representation derived from long ago. And in fact, these elements did not have a feeling that I was remembering that morning—or any time. So perhaps they were a current assessment, or perhaps they were unresolved implicit sensations. Even considering these questions from the hub enables our experience to move from being swept up by the rim and instead to develop the discernment to just notice whatever arises, even if it feels like it is here-and-now sensation rather than some seventh-sense-sector memory configurations. We can know that this is from the past and not about the present.

Then what arose in my reflections from the hub were images of the table, the pill, and my hungry dog looking for food. These felt like memories of that morning, explicit representations that were tagged with "this is something from the past." Then a picture of my dog Prince Junior came to mind—and while it felt like an explicit memory (I had dealt reflectively with this trauma before), it had an inner quality of something much more alive than just a memory. It's hard to describe the distinction, so let me diverge to another story to try to clarify this.

When I was 20 years old, I was working in Mexico for the World Health Organization studying folk healers. A colleague and I were headed up to the mountains to interview a renowned curandera, and as we approached the mountains at a full gallop, the saddle of my horse became loose and it slipped to his belly. My feet stayed in the stirrups and I was dragged for a long way. They were amazed I survived, left with a bunch of broken bones and teeth. Decades later, I was watching the movie *Seabiscuit* and suddenly felt this sharp pain in my face and arm and felt my muscles tighten as I bent over to the side. Though I had ridden horses since that accident and hadn't recently felt that twinge of pain I used to feel when I'd see horses for the first few years after I'd returned to the States, now watching the movie I felt overwhelmed by feelings out of my control. And even though I quickly realized that the accident in *Seabiscuit* was just like the one I'd had, these feelings felt in the here and now. It did not feel like I was remembering anything from the past. That is the emergence of "implicit-only" memory.

Back to the poisoning experience. In this reflection exercise, now the feeling of seeing the image of Prince Junior had a shimmering quality. I was intentionally searching for memory and knew about the snail-poisoning trauma, so I had a narrative primed to look for connections to the antibiotic-on-the-floor panic. That narrative had a distant internal quality, like a story that's been repeated so much it no longer feels fresh and alive. But at the same time, this image of Prince Junior also felt frighteningly real, like no time had passed since he died, like I was there, now, with him.

We have many layers of neural processing that parallel the mental side of subjective experience. One view of what this mindsight skill exercise was doing is that it was evoking two streams of awareness simultaneously. One was the narrative stream of conceptual knowledge (the C of SOCK). In this case, concepts were in story form. The other stream had the quality of sensation, of feeling something raw, as if the image were a perception of what was happening now. This was the sensation of the implicit reactivation of memory.

As the Farb et al. (2007) study reveals, mindfulness training enables us to distinguish the various streams of awareness. In my discussion of that article in the *Journal of Social, Cognitive, and Affective Neuroscience* (Siegel, 2007b), I suggest that mindfulness is a powerful tool that promotes integration. It seemed that in this study what was revealed was the effective manner in which different streams could be differentiated from one another following mindfulness training. In the case of my experience of the image of Prince Junior, I was feeling both the narrative knowing and the implicit sensory stream of awareness. With a conceptual knowledge of these two streams and the nature of explicit versus implicit memory, we prepare our minds to distinguish the many dimensions of our inner world. It is through this process that we can begin to make sense of the mind, to observe our sensory and conceptual streams and move to integrate implicit memory into its next, more integrated, explicit form. And then with this step, we can weave into our life story the fuller sense of the meaning of events in our lives. This is the first step toward the resolution of trauma.

Naturally we could go through many similar stories of unresolved trauma and the movement toward healing and resolution.

In this chapter, what I'm offering to you is the invitation to consider areas in your own life where trauma may remain unresolved.
Moments of chaos or rigidity may suddenly or insidiously constrain
your otherwise harmonious life as signs that a traumatic experience
in your past may have had lasting impediments to integration.

Sometimes the ongoing adaptation to trauma persists not as just
moments of incoherence, but as lasting habits of being. If these are
in fact experientially related, we may find that doing the work of
integration deeply alters their ways of entrapping us. Our more
innate features, ones that may have genetic origins and embed
themselves in our PDP propensities, may in contrast persist a lifetime no matter what our work in therapy. These proclivities are
distinct from the adaptations to trauma that remain unresolved and
can be a focus of therapy and invite us to promote integration of
these posttraumatic states. In the case of our PDP proclivities, the
notion is to free ourselves from their rigid hold on our lives and
realize that these are just the fabric of our skin that can become a
companion and not a prison warden as we move through life.

UNRESOLVED TRAUMA, HEALING, AND INTEGRATION

From the open plane of possibility we move outward to plateaus
of probability that prime our minds to interpret events through the
lens shaped by prior experience. This is how we create a state of
mind that filters perception and structures how we respond: This is
a plateau of probability. I had a trauma-induced state with a mental model that dogs ingesting substances beyond their usual diet
was a lethal action. These top-down influences shape what aspects
we attend to in our environment, bias our perceptions, and create
the rapid and specific associations to what we see. Our perceptual
interpretations, emotional responses, behavioral reflexes, and even
sensory reactions can each be created as part of the implicit filters
that lack an awareness that anything is being shaped by something

from the past. When we've experienced a trauma that remains unresolved, these top-down implicit influences are not integrated with the factual and autobiographical aspects of explicit memory. We experience the peaks arising from such an unresolved plateau as just our here and now experience, not something coming from a past event. The antibiotic falls to the floor and then my brain goes on high alert and my mind experiences terror. I become convinced the dog has swallowed the pill and is bound to die. I've lost reason and am on the automatic pilot of unresolved trauma. Here lack of resolution immersed me in the chaos of an unintegrated brain.

Our mindsight skill discussion was a brief immersion in the first steps of identifying how implicit memory in its unintegrated form can feel quite distinct from the blend of implicit/explicit processing that emerges with autobiographical knowledge and the resolution of trauma. In my situation, resolution was clearly not achieved even though I had spent time at various points in my life reflecting on that loss. But this episode at breakfast inspired me to return to my own therapy and go more deeply into that time in my life. Ultimately what those sessions were able to do was to find the deeper meaning behind the loss. For me, not only had I lost my attuned, unconditionally loving companion, but also I could not forgive myself for being responsible for his death. Even after all those years I still felt profoundly guilty—and ashamed—that I had forgotten to warn my parents of the need to not let him into the yard. That stance of nonforgiveness created a harsh inner critic inside of me, a vigilance to avoid any similar kind of oversights, tense and disturbing sensations in my body, and continual monitoring of the worst-case scenario in my vivid imagination.

Now if my PDP proclivity had been to lean toward anger instead of fear, perhaps my post-poisoning life would have become more intensely filled with being furious toward others who hurt animals or forget to protect people. Or if I had a PDP leaning toward sadness/distress, perhaps I would have become preoccupied with relationships, excessively concerned with being rejected, socially abandoned, unloved. But my PDP tendency was for fear, and so vigilance was heightened in anticipatory dread of yet again forgetting what should have been remembered.

In my own therapy, finding a way to accept that a 14-year-old boy has a lot on his plate with friends and family, homework and chores, and a prefrontal cortex in the midst of reconstruction, I was able to reach out to him and, finally, forgive him/me for what had happened and what had not been done. I forgave myself for having forgotten to warn. In holding onto the resentment toward myself and my perceived failures, I was locking onto a war with myself. Without a truce created in my own treatment, I could not transcend the trouble (oh no, not another set of TR words). I had done the best I could.

This time around, the presence, attunement, and resonance with my own therapist could be created in my stance toward myself. I needed to come to terms with the ways in which that loss could be truly integrated into my ongoing narrative of who I'd been, who I am, and who I could become. I had to identify the feelings of shame that locked me into a painful inner sense of both dread and disgust, a feeling that I was bad, that not only had I done wrong, but that there was something wrong with me. Reaching out to that young boy locked in an implicit prison was the crucial step of liberation that needed to happen in order to set myself free.

But freedom does not remove our personality; it brings us into harmony with who we are. It frees us to be more ourselves, not less. And so I don't expect that my leaning toward the fear side of a PDP path will change. That tendency can just loosen up and not imprison me. What has happened is that I find myself more at ease when things drop on the floor—literally and metaphorically. I think even my adolescents have noticed that I'm less reactive to their own comings and goings, more at ease with their place in life, as I've come to accept where I was when I was their age, and where I am now.

Chapter 11

TRANSITION

Being a mindful therapist requires that we be open to not only how things are, but how they change moment by moment. One of the profound insights of mindful reflection is that nothing ever stays the same. Whether we gain access to this perspective through meditation, letting go of premature categorizations, or just conscientiously paying close attention to our inner and outer worlds, being mindful entails awakening the mind to the ever-changing nature of inner and outer reality.

Our own minds change constantly. One of the first great surprises for people who take the time to do a basic inner reflection exercise is to notice that what they thought would be the internal sense of stability and predictability was indeed not the situation that confronted them. And when they thought they'd nailed down what their mind was like—voilà, it changed yet again!

This dynamic nature of life seen clearly from the inside out evokes the fourth dimension, the feature of time, as we sense how things evolve over a span of years, months, days, hours, minutes, or seconds. In many ways, noting transitions is the essence of temporal integration—how we confront the important existential issues of life ranging from our longing for certainty and impermanence to wrestling with our mortality.

Each moment—what Dan Stern (2004) has suggested bridges up

to 5 to 8 seconds—has within it what some call "the whole universe in a grain of sand." Phrases in music or movements in dance each capture this moment in time. Even in the brain, the notion of an electrical object representing our image of something in awareness in that moment reveals an assemblage of neural firing patterns that correlates with our deepest subjective sense of how we experience the world. These assembled moments may be worlds unto themselves, constructed wholes in the river of time, but the transitions between enfolded moments are also an important dimension of reality to which we can attend as mindful therapists. Bringing the transitions between moments into focus enables us to hone our perceptual abilities and learn how to see the mind with more acuity and depth—to cultivate mindsight in ourselves and then in others.

Transitions are important to have in the front of our mind so that we are prepared to monitor shifts in states with clarity. When shifts occur, a window is open to discover important opportunities for modifying. In other words, some innate process makes a change happen; and when this shift is noted, an intentional sculpting of the direction of that change becomes possible. This is how we harness mindsight's power of monitoring and then modifying the energy and information flow that is the essence of strengthening the mind. When we offer this to ourselves, we enhance our ability to be mindfully present. When we provide such mindsight skill training for our patients, they have the opportunity to transform their lives.

If we reflect back on the chapter on trauma, we can see that attending mindfully to my unresolved state of leftover traumatic issues revealed sudden shifts in state. I am taking an antibiotic for an infection, the medicine falls on the floor, my dog moves, and I enter a sudden immersion into panic. This is an example of an automatic shift from a coherent state of mind at breakfast to one of chaos as I chase my dog around the house. Monitoring this change afterward, I could sense the movement from integration to disintegration. This perception of the flow of energy and information revealed, as we've seen, an unresolved trauma from my adolescence. It is this noticing of transitions between states that highlights their configuration. Naturally a moment moves through time, continually reassembling elements of experience and constructing a sense of a continuous whole. But a state of mind—a larger assembly of related moments—may have longer duration than its separate components. It is these transitions in state that permit us to see how we can take rigid peaks and narrow plateaus and create more flexible movement in our lives. First, though, we must note the transitions. Just as contrasting colors with one another enables us to more fully appreciate the hue of different shades, focusing on shifts in states enhances our ability to perceive the detailed textures of the states themselves.

Focusing on transitions across states is an essential component in the treatment of unresolved trauama. With mindsight we learn not only how to perceive energy and information flow more clearly but we also learn to shape it with more specificity. This modifying aspect of mindsight is revealed in how state shifts can be modulated. Various forms of therapy have postulated ways of doing this modification, called by various names such as shuttling (Cozolino, 2002, 2010), pendulating (Levine, 1997), and "staying with" (Minton et al., 2006; Shapiro, 2002). From an IPNB perspective, the underlying notion here is that people can learn to grow from passive observers and victims of their own unresolved trauma to active molders of their internal state. They can learn to modulate their internal world from the edge of chaos or rigidity to the harmonious state of integration. Naturally, this often involves the close and collaborative attention of the mindful therapist who offers guidance and companionship along the path toward healing. Shifting back and forth from the edges to the center of the window of tolerance for a feeling state or memory, the patient experiences the empowerment of mindsight. This is how we shuttle, pendulate, stay with, or use safe-place imagery to expand our windows of tolerance. We widen the boundaries of a window by providing the intentional experience of being at its edges yet remaining in an integrated state with the expanded dyadic complexity that emerges with the mindful presence of therapist with client. When the patient senses that it is safe to sit together with whatever feelings or images arise, that dyadic sanctuary widens the window internally for her. And from the neuroplasticity perspective, such experiences of tracking transitions at the boundaries of the window harness the active power of attention to catalyze changes in the brain's self-regulatory capacities around the implicitly embedded elements of traumatic memory. These alterations that accompany the focus of attention toward transitions widen the window of tolerance and ultimately alter the imprisonment of a person's life by the traumatic experience and adaptations to it. As my old memory mentor, Robert Bjork, would say, "memory retrieval is a memory modifier." Here the active modulation of transitions can produce synaptic changes that literally integrate the nonintegrated elements of unresolved trauma into a more coherent state. They can also be the focus of loosening the restrictive hold of insecure attachment in maintaining narrow plateaus and rigid peaks in a personality pattern that is unyielding and inflexible.

BRAIN BASICS

A state of mind is the phrase we use to encompass the notion of a cluster of functions ranging from mood to memory that shape our subjective internal life. This state can be expressed to others in various ways, coloring the texture of our interactions and communicating the internal world externally within the nonverbal signals we send. Eye contact, tone of voice, facial expressions, gestures and posture, the intensity and the timing of these responses, each reveals our inner state of mind.

As we move away from the plane of possibility out to our plateaus of valenced probability, we've entered into textured states of mind and brain states of activation. This is just the way life is lived: We don't remain only in the open fluidity of the plane of possibility, but we engage in the world fully with our range of plateaus of personality proclivities, our states of mind in a particular plateau, and our ever-changing instantiated peaks of particular mental activity that make such interactions with others fully possible. At the most basic level, the subjective side of this movement from plane to plateau creates our experience of mood. On the physical side we experience neural readiness, called priming, as we neurologically become more likely to activate specific synaptic patterns that underlie our peaks of activation. Our plateaus set up a tendency for particular peaks to arise as personality makes certain valenced states of mind readily available. A plateau, in turn, makes a particular set of peaks more likely: Our state leads to specific thoughts or feelings or memories that are state dependent.

As a review, we'll have our Figure 11.1 as the plane of possibility here (from Chapter 1) and examine this from the point of view of transitions. Each movement away from the plane puts in place an increased probability of neural firing or mental experience. The further away from the plane (on the y-axis) we move, the more certain specific firings/experiences are likely to occur. The narrower the base of a plateau, then the more restricted our range of possibilities is for a particular state of mind or neural firing to occur. Here we've narrowed along the z-axis, and the diversity of experience—neural or mental—becomes more limited. By the time we've entered a peak, the probability becomes certain, or 100%, that at that moment we'll have that thought or emotion, or that neural firing profile. The notion here is that transitions can include softening our proclivities for repeated patterns of peaks that may imprison our lives, and to lower and broaden our plateaus, our states of mind and neural priming, so that we have a wider range of possibilities in our lives.

Therapeutic efforts to focus on transitions from peak to plateau to decrease engrained peak reactivations, and clinical movements to lower and broaden our plateaus, are exactly what the process of deep transformation involves. Mindful practice bathes us in the

Subjective Experience

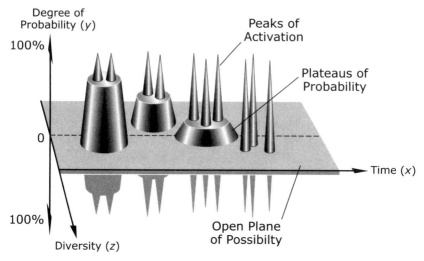

Neural Firing

Figure 11.1 The plane of possibility and transitions across states. This is the visual metaphor for embracing several dimensions of human experience we saw in Chapter 1 (see the original legend for this figure there). Here we'll focus on the plane and transitions. Recall that a peak represents a specific activation of mind or brain instantiated in that instant—activations that are committed to manifest as that particular activity in that moment of time. Softening peaks means helping transition away from repeating patterns of specific activations that are imprisoning our lives. A plateau represents a state of mind or profile of neural firing that may have various shapes and degrees of height and broadness: Lower means less certainty of which firings might be possible and wider signifies more variety, a wider set of propensities. In this way, we try to help ourselves and our clients to lower and broaden their plateaus, to make aversive and repetitive emotions, thoughts, or behaviors less likely to occur, and to open up the range of possible states available to us in various situations. Mindful practice involves the intentional movement of our minds and our brains into the open plane of possibility. We can have new peaks arise directly from this state—experiencing thoughts, memories, emotions, and perceptions from a more flexible and adaptive vantage point. Transitions are aided in this way as mindful awareness and a receptive neural profile are created in that state in that moment—and repeated practice of creating this state of mind and neural firing can then cultivate an enduring trait of these helpful features across time in our lives.

open plane of possibility, making such conal transformations (softening peaks, lowering and broadening plateaus) the target of our personal work.

Recall that the visual model of our plane of possiblity is based on the essential notion of probabilities. This is a topography of mind and brain based on a deep view of reality illuminated by both the science of quantum mechanics and the knowledge from first-person subjective experience. Each mental state and each set of activated neuronal circuits shapes and configures the likelihood of the unfolding of what comes next, the emergence of movement in a particular fashion in either the mental or neural side of probability above and below the plane. Within the plane, we rest in that open space where any potential is possible, and all are equally likely to occur. But as we move into our personality—into the particular pattern of plateaus in our model—we set up the shift in likelihood that movement through time will unfold in a particular fashion. From our proclivities of personality, we then have a movement in a particular direction—a valence—toward a set of states, our plateaus in the plane model. Then from particular state plateaus, we have an even more refined set of peaks that might arise.

If I am sad, I may be more likely to activate memory configurations related to past events in my life when I felt down and blue. The specific memories are my peaks; my sad state is my plateau. And if I am in the sad PDP grouping, that would be my broad cluster of plateaus. At a given moment in my sad mood (a particular plateau), there may be no particular memory activated, no peak instantiated. But at a moment's notice, I could recall sad periods in my life in an automatic way or with intention. I am primed to move toward particular peaks from that plateau. The overall result is that my subjective experience of the present and recollections of the past are filled with a down, sad, dejected feeling and I begin to feel hopeless and in despair if this state persists or deepens. As I move from peak to peak, I can reflect on how terrible my life seems to be. I feel imprisoned, hopeless, and in despair. Brainwise, priming toward sadness evokes state-dependent synaptic firing and the cascade of neural representations of memory, imagery, reasoning, and social affiliations become imbued with the music of sadness. My mood is my plateau, my down preoccupations my peaks.

Yet if I do not have a sad PDP grouping, a temporary feeling of sadness may be less likely to consume my overall patterns of plateaus that evolve. I may have a few peaks of feeling blue, but my PDP of anger or fear has not reinforced plateaus of being distressed in this sad way. I move more quickly out of those peaks, lower out of that sad state plateau, and onto other ways of being. Perhaps I am not inclined toward getting depressed, whereas my sad PDP cousin has that proclivity. Instead, if my PDP leans toward anger, I may get rapidly stressed and explosive, vulnerable to a set of difficulties other than sadness and depression. How our aversive circuitry of sadness/separation distress, anger/rage, and fear/anxiety make us prone to the specific forms of enduring difficulties that we call mental disorders when they create dysfunction in our lives can be a subject of future research. And how, knowing this, we as therapists can harness the power of neuroplasticity to utilize our presence within an attuned and resonating relationship to help guide the patient's focus of attention in ways that change the brain toward integration is a framework ready for us to explore.

Transitions in and out of enduring states of mind and brain activation are moments of opportunity in therapy. Clients' experiences can move from peak to peak—the intervals we explored in our wheel of awareness practice—and they can be taught to sense the plateaus in which such peaks arise. As we discussed earlier, windows of tolerance reveal that a given state may have more or less broad spans of degrees of activation in which the individual can remain in an integrated and functional state. Outside the window, chaos and rigidity or both result. I can learn to experience sadness, to be in a particular plateau, and not fall apart. This would be seen as the way we broaden our plateau and thus widen our window. (I know, your window for visual metaphors may be narrowing here, but please bear with me as these visual models are quite useful, as I hope you'll soon discover as you apply this in practical ways in the immediacy of your work and life.) But at other times or in other people, the window may be narrow for sadness and a small hint of such a narrow and elevated plateau, of this rigidly engrained sad state, puts me into a tailspin. Trauma is an important form of experience that narrows our windows, especially for current contexts, internal and external, that resonate with the specifics of the past event. Integration is compromised, and our states rapidly transition from coherence to the incoherent states of rigidity, chaos, or both. Noting these transitions within and between states is a key aspect of our monitoring as mindful therapists.

Within the brain, neural integration involves the coordination and balance of widely distributed areas to one another. When integrated, these systems achieve a harmonious flow; when the differentiation and/or linkage necessary for integration are impaired, harmony is replaced by dysfunction in the form of emotions out of control, impulsive behaviors or intrusive memories, and by a shutting down of mood, restrictions in a sense of vitality, feelings of being stuck. These chaotic or rigid states that reveal impaired integration can be sensed like a pulse and enable us as therapists to know when and where integration is blocked.

Guiding the nervous system back to integration is a direct method by which we SNAG the brain toward health. How we do this depends upon our capacity to sense energy and information flow within our extended nervous system (the brain), as it is shared among ourselves and others (relationships), and how it is regulated (the mind). This is how being a mindful therapist requires we hone our triceptual abilities to perceive this flow within the triangle of well-being. Much of this triception rides the waves of energy and information flow across transitions from harmony to chaos and rigidity and then using mindsight to guide such flow back to the integrated state.

As we've seen, there are domains of integration that can become the focus of attention within an IPNB approach to psychother-apy. Individuals can have suboptimal attachment experiences, overwhelming trauma, or innate features of temperament, some inherited and some just developed by chance, which may be inhib-iting these various domains from achieving coherent states of inte-gration. Noting transitions in states, and even across domains, a mindful therapist can discern which domains of integration may be impaired. We sense, for example, that an individual does not often rely on right-mode nonverbal signals for communicating his or her own internal experience to others. Helping this person tran-sition from a left-mode-dominant life to one that includes both hemispheres would be a way of approaching bilateral integration and improve interpersonal integration at the same time. Similarly, people may be "cut off from the neck down," not taking in the data from the body proper, and leading a vertically nonintegrated life. In this case, using a mindful focus of attention—bringing a compas-sionate consciousness that is conscientious and creative—together, we can move to a more vertically integrated state as these impor-tant bodily signals become a part of the cortically created awareness of everyday life.

Yet another example of riding the waves of transitions comes in when examining temporal integration. Our prefrontal cortex enables us to represent time. We come to know that the past is not the present, and we come to sense that a future is just around the corner. These prefrontal temporal maps give us the empower-ment to plan, the pleasure to ponder the nature of reality, and the at times burdensome worry over the purpose of our existence and the meaning of life. The seemingly contradictory drives for certainty, permanence, and immortality and the realities of life's uncertainty, transience, and mortality are the challenge of temporal integration.

Integration, as we've seen, is the linkage of differentiated parts. In temporal integration, the idea is not to jettison our drives and replace them with realities. Instead, we can embrace the natural desires for certainty, for example, and also yield and accept the reality of uncertainty. Shifting between reality and desire and back to reality, we can help the mind transition across these sometimes warring poles of experience. Learning to modify shifts in our internal state, to modulate these important transitions in patterns of the flow of energy and information, in this way is itself an important part of the path toward integration.

MINDSIGHT SKILLS

Bringing yourself into hub of the mind, let the breath find its natural rhythm, and the body settle into its natural state (this is hopefully getting to be a natural practice for you now). We know now from experience that it is possible to rest in the open awareness of the hub, letting ourselves attend to whatever subject of attention we intentionally choose. While we do this as a formal mindsight skill exercise, simply envisioning the hub and sensing the breath can reinvigorate this sense of the wheel of awareness, separating hub from rim, and inviting whatever is unfolding to enter the field of awareness. We can focus on the breath, riding the waves of the in-breath and out-breath. We can do a review of the rim, taking in the first five senses of the outer world, the sixth sense of the body, the seventh sense of our mental activities themselves, and the eighth sense of our relationships.

We can also take in the totality of our rim's state, sensing the larger whole, our state of mind. When we sense the intervals between activations on the rim—from whichever sense sectors these activities arise—we can glimpse directly the way our brain is primed to fire in a certain manner. This is the plateau from which peaks arise as various points are activated in awareness.

To deeply explore a state of mind, let's synthesize a number of our wheel of awareness exercises. As you ride the waves of the breath and enter the hub, notice how the spaciousness of this open awareness can fill you with what some people have described as a sense of the wide-open sky, the deep ocean, the limitless spectrum of possibilities. These are all the mind's way of representing the experience of open potential. This is the awareness of an open mind, the plane of possibility.

Now invite into your awareness how time moves experience across this open plane. However you experience this sensation, take note of what we've been calling a plateau of probability, that valenced state that makes some types of thoughts or feelings more likely than others. Sense how you experience this state of biased firing, this internally textured frame of mind. You may notice that specific feelings, thoughts, or memories emerge in the mind's eye, arising and becoming prominent in awareness. Let these mental activities, these peaks of waves of brain activations, just arise, stay present, and then fall away, out of the focus of attention. Noticing the intervals in between these peaks, these points on the rim, see if you can feel the texture of these spaces. Do they have a color, a tone, a warmth? As peaks move forward in succession, do you notice the sense of a familiar interval, the common plateau from which nearby peaks may arise? Or does it feel as if peaks arise from the plane itself, moving upward from the spaciousness of open possibility?

As other waves of mental activity enter awareness—as they become the peaks of activation present in this instant—see if you can follow them now into presence, and then into disappearance. Notice how nothing is permanent; everything shifts and changes. The plateau from which they each arise—our primed neural condition, our state of mind—or the open plane of possibility provide the links that form the transitions between peaks.

As these patterns of peaks arise and fall away, you may get a sense of a common plateau from which they arise. This is the valenced state of mind, the enhanced state of probability, which shapes the often vague if not outright invisible texture of mental life. If this formation can be felt, let it become the subject of your attention. See if you can find the shared ground from which thoughts and feelings arise. For some, this feels like a random set of associations—

a memory of a birthday party, a recollection of the political party of their choice, the importance of democracy as an idea, and then of images of the soldiers fighting for freedom. There is no seemingly cohesive state of mind—or is there a shifting in states? With each peak of activation, a different state of mind may be the origin of that particular mental activity and the result of its presence in our lives. You may sense that you can move from one plateau's state up to a peak of specific mental activity, but then find yourself moving back to a different plateau. This is how a mental activity can sometimes serve as the link between two states of mind. This bridge reveals how a peak itself can function as a transition from one state to the next.

States are global tendencies that rise and dissipate in parallel to the transitions of specific mental activity. Yet a state is related to a probability, a priming, a readiness to act; an activity is a specific neural firing pattern/mental activity that has manifested itself as it arises from the wide open set of possibilities and the more limited but still varied probabilities. When we move from the plane of possibility to peaks of activation, we may have fluid states that rapidly change moment by moment as they emerge in the transition from zero to 100 percent probability. But sometimes our states are more enduring. You may feel now, or have felt recently, the pressure of an anxious state, the deflation of a down state, or the elation of an elevated euphoria. Right now, what bodily sensations, images, feelings, and thoughts seem to swirl together in an inner dance moving to the rhythm of the music of your mind? These are the patterns of peaks of activation, our points on the rim. SIFTing the mind and then opening our perception to the spaces in between sorts through these various elements of our internal world and reveals the underlying state that may be present at this moment.

Once a sense of this organizing movement becomes clear in your awareness, notice how you can let shifts in this state become the focus of attention. Now instead of the state itself being your primary subject, let those move to the back of your mind and let the changes in state become of primary interest. What do you notice now? Can you sense the transition between sets of intervals, ways in which states feel stuck or fluid? Consider the situation of being in an enduring state of depression. Here, the various thoughts and perceptions and memories may be skewed toward down, deprecating, low-energy forms, and the state of being depressed is persistent across the intervals bridging these peaks of activation. Here you can see that we can declare an overall state's lack of flexibility, its lack of transitions, to be a primary problem in a person's life.

After learning to monitor these state shifts—or lack of them—it is time to explore how we can modify them. If a state feels low in energy during a reflective practice, see if you can raise the arousal level by opening your eyes more widely and letting in more light. Even looking upward can shift a bodily state, raising energy levels. Try exploring how positioning your eyes to one side or the other can also alter states of activation. Other bodily modalities for shifting state include taking deeper breaths, stretching your arms up above your head and then out to the side and slowly leaning down to the floor. A whole world of shifts in body posture within yoga or qigong provides ancient practices for shifting state.

The key to modification begins with monitoring when shifts in state are blocked—or when shifts are chaotic and disruptive. With rigidity, we can use our bodily movements to change levels of arousal, and we can harness the power of attention to move through painful states. For example, if you focus your attention on pain or discomfort, you may notice that it intensifies initially. If you stay with that focus, and especially if you name that state (e.g., aching, worrying, doubting) you may find that the global state you are in begins to shift. This is the "name it to tame it" experience of being present and labeling with words the internal world.

As we ourselves stay present with whatever is in awareness and also learn to modify these states toward flexibility, we are finding a way to make transitions in our state of mind a part of the way we integrate our experience. We can picture such transitions as the way we have come to intentionally shift our plateaus to become broader and less restrictive in which peaks they permit to arise. We can also see this as how we've brought ourselves adaptively out of a stuck plateau, moving perhaps to the plane and then creating another plateau with new and more flexible peaks that arise in this new configuration.

THE INTEGRATION OF STATES

We have various states of mind that become routed through ancient circuits created by genes and modern pathways carved by experience. Our basic motivational drives arose in our evolutionary history and organize our behaviors to find comfort and connection, to explore and play, to garner our resources and master challenges, to be sexual and to reproduce. Each of these basic motivational systems influences our present state of mind. Meeting our needs requires that we follow the vector of such states with the aim of creating a life where our necessities are met.

We have many states of mind that form the foundation of who we are. If a particular state is not integrated into the rainbow of available states of being, if I've excluded play or sexuality or aggression or mastery from my repertoire of states of mind, then I may not be open to those same states in someone else. As I soak up like a sponge the signals revealing the state in my client, they will drive his or her internal state down through my insula and alter my subcortical firing patterns into states of neural firing beneath my own awareness. As those bodily, brainstem, and limbic patterns of priming and firing shift, these changes will be registered via the insula into my prefrontal regions. Ultimately I may gather hints as to this internal state through interoception and come to know how I feel. These internal feelings—if I am open to them and not defended against them in some reactive way—can then give me an accurate internal sense of what is going on in someone else. If I've excluded some state from my own personal range of ways of being, then these internal sensations I soak up from my patient will not be readily acknowledged or accepted in me. Even beneath my own awareness, the client may get a sense that she is not in a safe place, that I cannot see her, that something is amiss in our connection. Being mindful requires that I myself as therapist and companion along the journey toward transformation be open to my own impediments to integration. In this case, I have blocked state integration and the chaos or rigidity of that situation will not only be my private incoherence, but it will create a rupture in the possibility of therapeutic progress. What I cannot tolerate in myself I cannot tolerate in someone else.

As a mindful therapist, I must bring the curiosity, openness, acceptance, and loving-kindness to my own states of mind in order to be mindfully attentive to the states in my patient. Notice how this view suggests that we need to attend to both rim points and their intervals that reveal our overall state of resonance. These activations and primings dominate our internal world—and it is being open to these shifts in our own internal state that may be the likely gateway through which we come to know the other. It is here where we see that knowing ourselves with self-compassion is an essential starting point in being present. If a patient is stuck in a valenced plateau that I cannot tolerate in myself, then helping that person transition more flexibly in and out of that state will be hampered by my own nonintegrated status. My window is narrow and I cannot take my patient "in" and instead push back or ignore. My patient feels rebuffed or discounted, I feel lost and unaware of his pain, and I remain stuck in an interpersonally nonintegrated state.

With integration, I enable differentiation of my various aspects to be cultivated, including states of mind. If I am not open to parts of myself, to these varied states, I will not be open to receiving them from my client. The subsequent linkage of these states involves an embracing of their distinct natures, even if in conflict with our expectations. For example, if I am feeling angry at an unfair treatment of a client, I can allow myself that state of mind while simultaneously being aware of a need to remain open to my client's inability to defend himself from such treatment. I do not have to deny my own emotional reaction for fear of flooding my patient. I can own the need to remain calm, perhaps not even mentioning my anger (at least not yet), and encourage my patient to explore his own experience without inducing him to take care of my fury. That is something for me to do on my own time. Yet of course the therapeutic encounter is so intense and immediate that we as therapists are vulnerable to placing our unresolved issues and leftover garbage into the field of our relationship. This is a professional hazard that needs to be high on the agenda of what to watch out for and avoid: This is how we respect therapeutic boundaries.

But many of us as therapists have found that the most powerful moments have come when we spontaneously feel joined with our clients. Knowing the power of transitions among states can facilitate that joining while fully respecting the therapeutic relationship and its important boundaries. As one of our domains of integration, the linkage among and within states enables us to work directly on bringing a new sense of coherence into our lives. A given state needs to have its own internal cohesiveness—and flexibility. If you review your own needs, you can explore the ways in which you permit such states to flourish in your life. Between states we also look for coherence, only this time in the transition between states. How are your various disparate states able to achieve collaboration? How do you find time in your day, your week, your month, to cultivate your many ways of being?

Let me take a small step to the side to explore a fun, useful, and, I think, fascinating example of applied integration that involves transitions. This discussion directly involves the many states we have inside of us and can serve as a useful guide to how to promote integration of states.

I have been fortunate in my work as an educator to meet and work with a variety of people in various disciplines. One of those groups is the multimedia entertainment company called the Blue

Man Group. Matt Goldman, Phil Stanton, and Chris Wink (the original three founders of the Group) asked me to become a consultant for their newly forming primary school. The task was to find a way to promote creativity in the course of a solid education in social, emotional, and academic learning. There is much to say about that task—but not here. In the course of working together we have explored a wide array of ideas, from issues of the brain and creativity to humor and spontaneity. What they shared with me illuminates further the nature of state integration, and so I'd like to share that with you here.

When I asked about the foundations of their creating the Blue Man show, they described to me that in retrospect they had come to realize they'd created archetypes of characters that had tension between them. These mind-sets that the "bald and blue" actors on the stage take on have six different names—and, as we'll see, they seem to fit the notion of different states of mind. Transitions between these states, I'll suggest to you, reveal a profound and compelling example of integration of polar opposites that may have its neural correlates in the brain. When a given show would have participation of each of these mind-sets, somehow, Wink said, the audience seemed more involved and the show more compelling and complete.

Here are the six, placed in pairs: The Hero and the Innocent; the Group Member and the Trickster; the Scientist and the Shaman. The way Chris Wink recently depicted these in a presentation at the Vancouver Peace Summit was not only entertaining, but it captivated the imagination of the audience and made me think about this archetypal differentiation and then their linkage on stage as a wonderful—and fun—depiction of integration and its importance for collaboration.

The Hero is the state of mind of the character who has goals he is trying to achieve with efficacy and direction. In contrast, the Innocent is the state with a "beginner's mind" that takes in the world without preconceived notions. For me, the transition between Hero and Innocent reveals the tension between top-down and bottom-up neural processing. Life requires both the Hero and the Innocent: We need to learn from our experiences and also take in the world with an emerging openness to see things as they truly are. Either state by itself does not permit a full and balanced life.

The Group Member is the mind-set that enables the character to fit in with the flow of group consensus. Much can get done as a group—but sometimes that "group-think" can lead to destructive behaviors (think racism and genocide) and certainly limit creativity in the push toward conformity. The Trickster is the state that violates expectations, noting rules and bending them, pushing the envelope beyond group norms. Our creative life, even as a group, requires that we think out of the box at times, pushing our boundaries and inspiring us to try out new ways of being. Blending the best of group membership and trickster living, we can transition between these two important but distinct ways of being.

The Scientist uses logic to analyze in a linear fashion the data he carefully collects. Syllogistic reasoning, the search for cause-effect relationships in the world, is an important way of making sense of things as they are. But there is another way of seeing reality using the intuitive mind. This is the role of the Shaman mind-set. Immersed in gut feelings and intuition, the Shaman is driven by a nonlogical, nonverbal sense for how life can be, interacting with others based on a feeling of spiritual connection. Both ways of knowing are important—and perhaps represented primarily in the left (Scientist) and the right (Shaman) sides of the brain. Syllogistic reasoning is a left-sided affair while gut feelings and heartfelt senses are processed in the middle prefrontal regions, predominantly on the right side.

In fact, the other polar mind-sets may also have a bilateral predominance. Social display rules make the Group Member's drive for conformity a possibly left-side-dominant state, while the Trickster may be driven by the imagery and novel thinking of right-mode processing. The Hero's planning and attempts to achieve goals may

be a left-mode-dominant state of mind. This is a goal-directed aiming of spokes of the wheel of awareness to achieve a particular
end in mind. In contrast, the Innocent may be more of an open
monitoring, entering what perhaps could be seen as a right-mode-
dominant, bottom-up reception of whatever arises from the rim.

If these formulations are correct, it may be that the Blue Man
Group's spontaneous creation of these mind-sets or states of mind
may reveal their unintended exploration of integration. Witnessing
their compelling and entertaining performances, the audience is
immersed in transitions between states as they soak in the wonder
of integration at its harmonious and captivating best.

For our work as mindful therapists, we can take in the notion
of these three pairs of mental states and reflect on how we permit,
encourage, and even cultivate such mind-sets in our lives. How do
we permit ourselves to be both the Hero and the Innocent? Do
we encourage different ways of knowing as Scientist and Shaman?
And can we cultivate the important dimensions of being a Group
Member and also have the courage and spontaneity to be a Trickster
at times? The inspiration of these varied states for me is to realize that
each is important and to facilitate the transitions across these various
ways of being to enable ourselves to live a more integrated life.

Chapter 12

TRAINING

Training is an essential component in both the life of the mindful therapist and in the work of mindful therapy. We've been exploring the concepts, brain basics, and mindsight skill exercises in the process of being a mindful therapist. The same skill training that you've been learning for developing your own mindsight skills can be applied with your clients in helping them become more integrated in their brains, coherent in their minds, resilient in their lives, and empathic in their relationships with others. Here we'll have the chance to review the underlying mechanisms by which training the mind alters the brain through our mindsight skill training exercises and go a bit more deeply into how to weave them into your life and your work. We'll also have the opportunity to examine directly how we can use the mind to alter the structure of the brain toward a more integrated set of circuits through the course of mental practice. This is how with training we use the mind to rewire the brain. Knowing this firsthand through your own experiences in where we've come, you'll be in a position to offer such skill training for others.

To unwrap the inner workings of training, we'll be exploring some exciting new findings about the inner wrappings of the brain. Training involves the purposeful harnessing of the power of experience to change the function and the structure of the human brain. As we've seen, the experience we're utilizing is the power of awareness to focus attention in certain ways to shape the flow of energy and information. As this flow occurs, our mental regulation process drives the firing in the brain by initiating activity in specific patterns of neural connections that can then induce structural changes in the brain's connectivity. This process of neuroplasticity involves at least three components: We can create and strengthen synaptic connections; we can stimulate new neurons to grow; and we can increase the sheathing along the axonal lengths to enhance conduction speed of neuronal electrical impulses. These aspects of neuroplasticity—synaptogenesis (including synapse modulation), neurogenesis, and myelinogenesis—each contribute to how a state of neuronal firing in the moment can become a long-lasting trait of changed neuronal architecture.

We've heard that neurons that fire together wire together. This is the fundamental notion of Freud's law of association and of the Hebbian synapse. Novelty can also stimulate this process along with the differentiation of neuronal stem cells into fully specialized neurons within integrated circuits in the brain. And a process of practice that we'll soon discuss in greater detail can induce the supportive cells—called glia—to produce the myelin sheath that wraps around the neurons' axons. When we establish synaptic connections, through the growth of synapses linking existing neurons or newly developed neurons from neurogenesis, we are laying the foundation for an integrated circuit. When the neurons in that circuit become repeatedly activated, the oligodendrocytes and astrocytes (the supportive glial cells) sense that firing and wrap myelin around the interconnected neuronal circuit.

Here is the essential issue: Myelin can increase conduction speed by 100 times. And while all neurons need to rest after firing, myelin can reduce that resting time—called a refractory period—by 30 times. The end result, you can imagine, is that if you and I are neurons in a circuit and we've been training well, our communication with each other will be 3,000 times faster than an unmyelinated pair of connected neurons. Three thousand times more efficiency in the brain means that our functional connectivity will outshine other neuronal communication. The brain overall can be considered a competitive real estate market: Action goes to the most active bidder. In this case, our enhanced communication will dominate over our competitors and our circuits will become a prominent player in the overall impact of neuronal firing in the brain as a whole.

You may be wondering then, how do we lay down more mindsight myelin? How can we practice activating the brain's specific circuits so that whatever being mindful means mentally, we push the physical side of reality to fire off our specific neuronal clusters so that we encase those circuits in myelin wrapping? This is exactly what we'll explore in this chapter.

BRAIN BASICS

At the turn of the millennium, a new technology called diffusion tensor imaging has enabled us to create computer-assembled images of myelinated circuits within the living human brain. These cutting-edge views reveal what animal studies had previously suggested: The number of hours of practice is proportional to the amount of myelin wrapping the relevant circuits. Expertise, practice, and myelin go hand in hand in hand. To become a mindsight maven, to learn to see and shape the flow of energy and information within our subjective lives, we need to train the mind to myelinate the brain in specific areas.

The study of myelin reveals that increases in this fatty sheathing go along with increases in synaptic connections in enriched environments. As myelin is white, these changes are reflected in enhanced "white matter" in the brain in specific regions that have been active. We can learn rapidly by establishing new synaptic linkages among neurons that are firing simultaneously. This is the basis of memory formation. But the synapse story of memory does not

Areas of the "Middle prefrontal cortex"

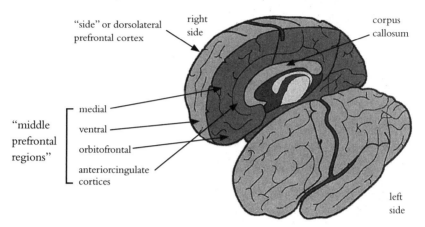

Figure 12.1 The two halves of the brain. This figure also reveals the locations of the areas of the "middle prefrontal cortex," which include the medial and ventral regions of the prefrontal cortex, the orbitofrontal cortex, and the anterior cingulate cortex on both sides of the brain. The corpus callosum connects the two halves of the brain to each other. From Siegel (2007a).

tell the complete picture about skill acquisition. In a recent illuminating book on talent and skills, Daniel Coyle (2009) presents a set of fascinating insights from scientists exploring this aspect of neuroplasticity. In *The Talent Code,* Coyle repeatedly asserts the following notion about myelin and skills: "Skill is myelin insulation that wraps neural circuits and that grows according to certain signals" (p. 33). Coyle interviews a number of individuals, including my old memory mentor Robert Bjork, and quotes him about skill training as saying, "Things that appear to be obstacles turn out to be desirable in the long haul" (p. 18). As we'll see, Bjork's notion of the benefit of facing obstacles—and not avoiding them—turns out to be a key to stimulating skill development and likely promotes the wrapping and maintenance of myelin sheaths to create well-honed integrated circuits. This is a principle we can embrace in approaching our own mental training.

A classic notion is that expertise emerges from 10,000 hours of disciplined study. While many of us have been learning to see the mind, more or less, over many years of interacting with others and reflecting internally within ourselves and our clients, we can hone those skills even further with specific training. We likely don't need 10,000 new hours of practice to create more refined skills; but we do need to train in a certain way.

Daniel Coyle uses a term that can be of great use in our exploration of training as mindful therapists: deep practice. Here is how he describes the essence of this form of mental or physical training. "Deep practice feels a bit like exploring a dark and unfamiliar room. You start slowly, you bump into furniture, stop, think, and start again. Slowly, and a little painfully, you explore the space over and over, attending to errors, extending your reach into the room a bit farther each time, building a mental map until you can move through it quickly and intuitively" (Coyle, 2009, p. 79). The essence of deep practice is to immerse yourself in an experience—in our case, the awareness of the flow of energy and information. As we dive into the sea inside, the dark room in Coyle's analogy, we need to build a map of the territory. We've been exploring this territory by stabilizing our mindsight lens with openness, objectivity, and observation. These legs of the tripod are themselves mental skills and likely involve the wrapping of myelin around our various circuits, especially in the prefrontal regions. With this new tripod in place, we can learn to move through the space of the mind with more intuition and efficacy. As deep practice proceeds, we learn the language of the mind as we can sense energy and information flow with more fine detail and depth—with more acuity.

At first, this may seem difficult for us, and certainly for our patients as well. But in skill development, Coyle notes, "by trying hard to do things you can barely do, in deep practice—then your skill circuits will respond by getting faster and more accurate" (2009, p. 45). While this may be difficult for us and for our clients, the effort may be essential to develop a true skill of mindsight. "Struggle is not optional—it's neurologically required: in order to get your skill circuit to fire optimally, you must by definition fire

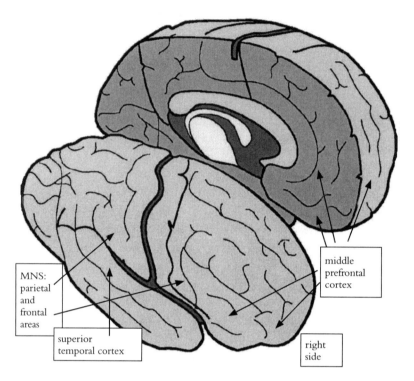

Figure 12.2 The "resonance circuitry" includes the mirror neuron system (MNS), the superior temporal cortex (STC), the insula cortex (IC, not visible on this drawing, but beneath the cortex linking these areas to the inner limbic region and the body below), and the middle prefrontal cortex. From Siegel (2007a).

the circuit suboptimally; you must make mistakes and pay attention to those mistakes; you must teach your circuit. You must also keep firing that circuit—i.e., practicing, in order to keep myelin functioning properly. After all, myelin is living tissue" (p. 44).

Struggle is not optional. The essential idea of deep practice is that you approach mistakes rather than avoid them. In Coyle's view, the "hotbeds" of talent—for music performance, athletic skill, chess playing, mathematics—each share this one common approach. These training sites offered a different attitude toward "failure." "Deep practice is built on a paradox: struggling in certain targeted ways—allowing yourself to make mistakes, to seem stupid—makes you smarter. Or to put in a slightly different way, experiences where you're forced to slow down, make errors, and correct them—as you would if you were walking up an ice-covered hill, slipping and stumbling as you go—end up making you swift and graceful without your realizing it" (2009, p. 18).

To adapt these insights for our training in the skill of mindsight, we can see that a mindful therapist can move his or her own level to new layers in a systematic way. "The trick is to choose a goal just beyond your present abilities; to target the struggle. Thrashing blindly doesn't help. Reaching does." This notion is parallel to Lev Vygotsky's (1934/1986) zone of proximal development. This zone is the difference between what we can do on our own and what we can accomplish with the assistance of a guide, a teacher, or a mentor. In the Renaissance, Coyle points out, great genius was achieved by apprenticeship in which younger individuals were offered collaborative relationships where they learned by doing, not just by conceptual understanding or by reading alone. Diving into the mind is an immersion we've been exploring throughout these chapters. In many ways, we as therapists can serve as guiding mentors that attend to the zone of proximal development in our clients as we assist them to push their mindsight skills further than they can do on their own. The notion is to develop the skill of seeing this internal world, and then being able to shape it toward integrative functioning.

Which are the circuits we are recruiting to develop mindsight? Which regions of the brain are active when we sense the flow of energy and information? How do we harness neural circuits to shape that flow toward integration? The resonance circuitry appears to be the core component of how we make mindsight maps and then modulate our mental life toward well-being. To explore this in more specific depth, let's now turn to a review of our mindsight skill-building exercises and see how the internal mental side of these experiences may correlate with the physical side of neural firing. As we do this, let's keep in the front of our mindsight map-making minds the triangle of well-being with its integrated brain, empathic relationships, and resilient and coherent mind.

MINDSIGHT SKILLS

In understanding our own mindsight skills, we can see an overview of our efforts as this: We learn to sense and shape energy and information flow within our internal experience, our relationships with others, and our neural circuitry. This is how we sharpen our triception to see energy and information flow within the triangle of well-being.

A first step in this process is to stabilize the mindsight lens with its tripod of openness, observation, and objectivity. In our exercises, we worked on this skill by confronting the "mistake" of how our intended focus on the breath repeatedly "failed" as we were distracted by other targets. Redirecting our attention was the task—and accomplishing this with kindness and understanding was essential to achieve a state of openness. As we paid attention to our intention to focus on the breath, it is possible that we were utilizing a similar set of circuits that enabled us to attend to the intention of others, the mirror neuron system that is part of our resonance circuitry. Simultaneously, we need to maintain awareness of awareness, tracking when our attention wanders, and then lovingly returning our focus to the breath. While this skill training may seem painfully simple, it is profoundly life altering. This, as we've stated earlier, is what William James proclaimed would be the "education par excellence." If nothing else were to be taught, within ourselves or for our clients, we'd still be offering an important major step in creating a daily form of brain fitness to support our brain training program of encouraging neural integration.

With a somewhat stabilized lens, we could move on to the next step of mindsight skill training. Taking these steps in small chunks and bringing into awareness the challenge points or "growth edges" for us—but what Coyle might term a "mistake" in athletic training terms—we can now begin to differentiate the hub from the rim of the wheel of awareness. We're moving from the simple but important awareness of awareness (meta-awareness) and attention to intention to be able to distinguish the architecture of our dark room of the mind. Yes, we'll be bumping into the furniture of that room quite a bit, but as we've stated, such struggle is necessary. "Targeted, mistake-focused practice is effective because the best way to build a good circuit is to fire it, attend to mistakes, then fire it again, over and over. Struggle is not an option: it's a biological requirement" (Coyle, 2009, p. 33). Here let's be clear: "Mistake-focused" for us means bringing us to the edge of our comfort zone and playing at this point of near chaos or near rigidity. This is how we push the window of tolerance for sensing the wide-open potential of the mind and developing the skills of mindsight through deep practice.

Deep practice involves our coming to the edge and paying close attention. In neuroplasticity terms, paying close attention may be associated with the secretion of chemicals—such as brain-derived neurotrophic factor, BDNF, from localized firing neurons or acetylcholine from the nucleus basalis that enhance the growth and solidification of neuronal connections to one another (see Doidge, 2007). The emerging glia story may reveal how these supportive cells detect repeated neuronal firing and wrap myelin around those cells that are active. When we practice deeply—moving at our growth edge and paying close attention—we may then be very specifically myelinating the resonance circuits which are active during the practice. Notice how close attention at our growth edge, "attending to our mistakes," is the essential feature of pushing our skill levels higher in a powerful and effective manner. This is how we become mindsight experts with training.

Let's walk our way through how training may recruit, activate, myelinate, and then reinforce interconnectivity within our resonance circuits. This is how training can integrate the brain. First, we begin with our own individual work to be sure we've experienced and established our own mindsight circuits. Then we are in a position to offer such deep training to our patients. Notice how ultimately the goals for ourselves and for our clients are parallel: to focus our attention to activate specific circuits that change their connections so as to integrate the brain.

Close attention sets the stage for neuroplasticity. This may involve synaptogenesis, neurogenesis, and myelinogenesis. Mindsight skill training starts with the careful paying of attention to energy and information flow patterns. As we've seen in our exercises, this perceptual practice does two things: Awareness enables us to intentionally focus the flow of information, which specifies which neuronal circuits will become active, and close attention promotes neuroplasticity.

As we focus on distinguishing the eight senses along the rim of the wheel of awareness, we are chunking mental activity so that the small elements of the rim can be distinguished from one another and from the mental sensation of awareness itself. We highlight the distinction among rim sectors, and between rim and hub. In Farb and colleagues' (2007) study, just 8 weeks of mindfulness training enabled individuals to differentiate separable streams of awareness. The hub itself, as we've proposed, has differentiated input streams of at least four types: sensation, observation, constructed concepts, and nonconceptual knowing. This SOCK differentiation can help our mindsight skills as we embrace the wide spectrum of ways of experiencing the world. Unlike some views of mindful awareness, our stance presented here is that being mindful is not just about sensing alone. While the sensory stream is vital in bringing us out of the top-down prisons of prior learning, being mindful is about embracing all these ways of experiencing awareness of the world.

We can be in the present with our past, approaching it with curiosity, openness, acceptance, and love (COAL). We can experience past memories even with the sensory stream. In the treatment of trauma, in fact, it may be necessary to integrate all streams of awareness in exploring the layers of memory of an overwhelming event as we sense the recollections, observe them from a bit of a mental distance, and then understand them conceptually and embed them with a deeper, nonconceptual knowing as we create meaning from madness.

Deep practice in our mindsight skill training involves moving into these distinct steps of the dance of the mind, but then also seeing the larger picture. This is how we can choreograph the minute steps, movement by movement, and also create the overall pattern of the dance. Much like the chunking involved in memory retention or language acquisition, we first learn to see the letters *l, e, t,* and *r* and then later can read the word *letter* as one chunk. So it is that we can work with the components of the resonance circuit.

BRAIN FITNESS: HOW STATES BECOME INTEGRATED AS TRAITS THROUGH MINDSIGHT TRAINING

We've seen in earlier work that the nine functions of the middle prefrontal area are the chunks, if you will, of what we experience in the course of mindsight skill training. Those functions include regulating the body, attuned communication, emotional balance, response flexibility, fear modulation, insight, empathy, morality, and intuition. You may be able to sense that our skill-training practices have involved many of these building blocks of middle prefrontal function already.

The body scan enables us to focus close attention on the internal state of the viscera and of the muscles and movement of the limbs and face. The careful focus of attention, part by part, on this sixth sense likely builds a tract of communication from the flow of information and of energy from the body proper up through Lamina I of the spinal cord and then into the subcortical brainstem and hypothalamic regions. The focus of attention on sixth sense data may increase Lamina I input from these lower, subcortical areas upward, to the anterior cingulate and the insula. First going to the posterior and then anterior insula, the body data between the anterior portions of the cingulate and the insula, along with the parietal input of the body in space, may contribute to our bodily defined sense of self. The careful focus of attention may also ride along the rapid conduction of spindle cells that link these two anterior zones and contribute to our self-awareness. This may play an important part of our observing leg of the mindsight tripod, stabilizing attention as we tune in to the observing stream of awareness.

Attuned communication as a chunk of our mindsight skills serves to align the experiencing self with the observing self. Here we see that the openness to whatever arises as we experience moment-by-moment sensory lived events comes into the focus of the hub of the mind. We focus attention on the sensory stream, letting our inner attunement blossom as we let go of expectations and judgments and bring bottom-up into the close focus of awareness in that moment. Such internal attunement may produce a reflective coherence in which we stimulate the firing and ultimately growth of integrative fibers of the brain. An interpersonal neurobiology perspective suggests that attunement—interpersonally between parent and child or inwardly between observing and experiencing self—stimulates the activation and growth of integrative regions of the brain. With such repeated firing in deep practice, we can imagine that these integrative circuits become wrapped in myelin and increase their impact on the overall integrative functioning of the brain.

This is the essential point of our whole approach: Inner and interpersonal attunement stimulate the neuronal activity that links differentiated areas to one another, which in turn would promote the neurogenesis, synaptogenesis, and myelinogenesis that would literally create a more integrated set of neural circuitry. This is how integrated neuronal firing in the moment becomes strengthened integrated circuits in the long run: how intentionally created states become long-term traits.

Emotional balance as a portion of mindsight skill training focuses our minds on the river of integration and the parallel notion of windows of tolerance. Within the river's flow across time, within the window's open span in that slice of time in the moment, mental functioning is harmonious and coherent, interactions with others are empathic, and the brain is integrated. On the two banks of the river, or at either end of the window, we move toward chaos or rigidity. Emotional balance focuses on the ways our internal affective states achieve levels of arousal in which life has meaning and vitality. With too much arousal, life becomes chaotic; with too little energy, life becomes depleted and depressed, stuck in rigidity. Even neuroplasticity can be shut down in such depleted states. Emotional balance as a focus of skill training builds on the monitoring of chaos and/or rigidity, and moves us to the second aspect of mindsight: modifying. We come to learn to modulate our internal states, to raise arousal levels when too low and to shift them down when too high. Monitoring and modulating our internal states is the essence of mindsight's capacity to promote self-regulation.

Response flexibility is the way we pause before acting. This is the temporal space between input and output, between perception and action. In training, we can allow a full acceptance of internal states—emotional feelings, intense thoughts, behavioral impulses. But with the important capacity to monitor these internal mental activities, we can then introduce a space between mental activity and physical action. We can decouple automaticity, awaken the mind, and create the essential pause of emotional and social intelligence. This space can be pictured as the strengthened hub of the mind that enables all rim activities to be present, but we can choose to inhibit action. The act of sensing the breath, returning the focus again and again to this target after the mind has wandered, is a basic training in this important flexibility dimension of executive function. Breath awareness practice along with other basic training exercises serve to cultivate our objective leg of the tripod. With this training, we become able to distinguish rim from hub, making mental activities one aspect of our present experience and not our total identity. It is this practice of differentiating rim activity from hub awareness that is at the heart of becoming flexible in our responses.

Modulating fear has now been demonstrated to involve the activation of middle prefrontal areas to downregulate the activity of the fear-generating limbic amygdala. This is good news for our skill training, as we can learn to harness the hub to "squirt more GABA-goo" onto our inflamed limbic region. GABA, gamma-aminobutyric acid, is one of the inhibitory peptides that is likely secreted with cortical activation. This is the "cortical override" that enables awareness to modulate subcortical fear states. And this is how we name it to tame it at times, as research with those with mindfulness traits reveals. (This is the study by David Creswell and colleagues, 2007, that demonstrated that stating the name of an emotion can decrease amygdala firing following medial and ventrolateral activations during the naming process—especially in those with mindfulness traits.)

Empathy for others is stimulated when we perform the loving-kindness exercises directly—and likely when we develop attunement internally as well. Offering a compassionate and caring stance toward others within our internal mental life may stimulate the circuits of compassion to become activated. In studies of universal, non-goal-directed compassion, the highest states of neural integration as seen with gamma waves (see Lutz et al., 2004) were discovered. Future research will need to explore further the notion that neural integration and compassion indeed go hand in hand. On the mental side of reality, embracing the internal mental state of another with kindness and concern is certainly a form of the linkage of differentiated centers of mental gravity—the integration of individuals, interpersonal style.

Insight from a middle prefrontal perspective refers to a self-knowing awareness, called by Endel Tulving "autonoetic consciousness." Tulving also coined the term "mental time travel," in which the individual connects the past with the present and the anticipated future. It is in this sense that we use the term *insight*, focusing our awareness not only on sensation in the present, but freely and intentionally on elements of the past (as in our various early reflective exercises on presence, attunement, and resonance) as well as imagining a desired future (as in the loving-kindness exercises). It is perhaps in the chunking of past, present, and future that we come to ride the stream of the constructed conceptual awareness. We can imagine a self that is, in fact, a concept of our own construction. We can examine observed patterns, derived facts, and complex ideas, and construct theories and unveil principles, from all of which skilled action can emerge. Concepts in this light, seen for what they are, can give us freedom and offer insights into ourselves, and into the world in which we live. While this indeed is a top-down-dominated stream, it is an important dimension with which we integrate our many ways of knowing the world within and outside of us.

When we speak of a moral imagination, we are evoking not only the you-maps of empathy and the me-maps of insight, but the we-maps of our eighth, relational sense. Morality involves our awareness of being a part of a larger whole, that we contribute to the well-being of others not for our private benefit, but because "they" are "us." As with the various differentiated organ systems of the body, an organism functions under healthy conditions as an integrated whole. Heart cells don't extract resources away from the quite distinct kidney cells; skin cells don't try to dominate muscle cells. Each collaborates with the others as if they were part of the same body . . . which of course they are. Just so, morality is based on mindsight maps that create a sense of a "we" that embeds the individual directly into membership with a larger whole. But integration does not involve losing one's identity—it is not the same as becoming homogeneous. In this way, morality deeply reflects this integrative foundation—we are unique and linked, and we are more than the sum of our individual parts. Contributing to the whole gives a sense of deep meaning because it is revealing the truth of our interconnected nature.

With this awakening of new levels of awareness, what enters our sensibility is a sense of intuition. Seen from the middle prefrontal lens, when we open our hub to the input of the sixth sense, we bring the "wisdom of the body" up into our cortical consciousness. But the sense of this wisdom is not a logical thought or even a constructed conceptual category. The wave of information, perhaps flowing from the parallel-distributed processors of the intestines (a gut feeling) and the heart (a heartfelt sense) as well as from the integrative circuits throughout the brain may give us a deep sense of nonconceptual knowing. This is the K of our SOCK and completes our full complement of the streams of awareness.

With deep practice we turn the challenges of the journey within the sea inside into myelin-coated circuits of integration. Across these nine aspects of middle prefrontal function, we can harness the power of careful attention to let the mind promote the neuroplasticity that can integrate the brain and transform our lives. This is mindsight's power to move our lives toward health.

Chapter 13

TRANSFORMATION

With training we are reinforcing how intentionally created states become skillful traits in our lives. As mindful therapists, we bring this regular—hopefully daily—practice into our care for ourselves. Similar to a physical fitness program, a mindful awareness practice done every day can keep our brains healthy by creating and maintaining the integration of our neural circuits. On the mind side of our plane of reality, deep mindsight skill practice can be seen as a form of mental training that strengthens our capacity to monitor and modify energy and information flow within the brain and in our interpersonal relationships.

And so transformation of our personal lives is an invitation to awaken our awareness and create coherent minds, integrate our brains, and bring kindness to our relationships. And these relationships begin with the one closest to us, the relationship we have with ourselves. Being mindful is woven seamlessly with self-compassion: treating ourselves as we would treat our own best friend. Both self-directed and other-directed compassion enable us to offer kindness under stress, forgiveness with mistakes, tenderness with vulnerability, and perspective when confused. Altruism, as the monk Mattieu Ricard (2005) urges us to consider, is a larger construct than compassion. Yes, we want to help others (and ourselves) alleviate suffering. Becoming integrated can also involve an altruistic sense of taking joy in others' joy, pride in their pride, of wanting to give positive energy to the world. These are all sensibilities that move us to embrace the full complement of experience, from joy to suffering, as we join with others as truly a part of ourselves. This is the power of the concept and reality of integration to embody kindness, compassion, altruism, and gratitude for the miracle of this life.

Mindsight enables us to cultivate these positive traits. We can offer help and take joy; we can see the internal world of ourselves and of others and find deep pleasure in those inner visions. It is truly a gift to be alive, and cultivating integration expands our sense of self to become a part of the larger flow of humanity, to share our place in the order of life.

Mindsight focuses on how we can see the inner world more clearly and transform that world toward integration. By separating hub from rim, the internal state of awareness becomes a sanctuary where we can move in and out of states of resonance with the pains and pleasures of each day. Transformation is about freeing this inner sanctuary to become the home in which we live. From this place in our heart, we garner the resilience to approach life's challenges with a deep sense of commitment and engagement. This is how we move through our lives, navigating the currents and winding our way between banks of rigidity and chaos in the ever-emerging flow of a harmonious and integrated life.

BRAIN BASICS

It may have become natural for you by now to move from an overview into considering our two sides of the one plane of reality. You may imagine that here in this Brain Basics section on transformation we'll see how the integration of neural circuits leads to the harmonious functioning of a coordinated and balanced nervous system. We've seen throughout our discussions in this book that the overarching concept of neural integration offers a profoundly useful framework for viewing well-being. If you detect in your own life, or in those of your clients, periods of rigidity or chaos or both, you can be sure some aspect of integration is being impaired. The blockage of differentiation and the impairment of linkage each can contribute as impediments to integration.

Areas in the brain that are harnessed in intentionally created states to cultivate moments of integrative functioning are varied and include our friend, the middle prefrontal region, that connects cortex, limbic area, brainstem, body proper, and even the social signals of other brains. As we've seen, cortical, limbic, brainstem, somatic, and social are woven into one functional whole through the integrative fibers of the middle prefrontal cortex. And as we've explored in depth in the prior chapter on cultivating the nine middle prefrontal functions, even a mental practice that highlights awareness of these can help promote their development. As Jon Kabat-Zinn said to me the first time we spoke in a public setting together in 2005 at the Psychotherapy Networker meeting, these nine functions are not only the outcome of mindfulness practice, they are the way of being mindful.

Other integrative regions of the brain that are harnessed in integration include the corpus callosum linking the two sides of the brain, the hippocampus weaving implicit elements into explicit memory, and the cerebellum, connecting body balance with cognitive and emotional processing. We've also seen other aspects of the nervous system playing significant integrative roles, such as the spindle cells linking anterior cingulate and insula to one another, and the parietal lobe and its important role in body and self-awareness. Science will likely reveal ever-new findings that illuminate the nature of the linkage of differentiated parts into a functional whole.

Transformation, we can propose, is how we move from nonintegrated ways of being toward integration. As we've suggested that emotion itself is a shift in integration, transformation is an emotional renaissance. The key is, how do we "inspire to rewire" the brain—of ourselves, our clients, our world? If transformation leads to a life well lived, to that state of eudaimonia, of well-being that has meaning, connection, wisdom, and equanimity, how do we nurture this integrative change in our personal and collective lives?

To address this question, we turn to the amazing capacity of the mind to change the brain. Without this revolutionary perspective from the field of neuroplasticity, we'd be left shrugging our shoulders and wandering aimlessly for answers. Knowing that we can use the intentional focus of attention in specific ways to cultivate integration empowers us as individuals, therapists, and world citizens to awaken our lives toward health.

MINDSIGHT SKILLS

Mindsight is the capacity to see and shape the flow of energy and information within and among us. We've defined a core aspect of the mind as the embodied and relational process that regulates the flow of energy and information. Although defining the mind is not widely done in mental health, education, science, or philosophy, by offering a working view of a central aspect of the mind as regulatory we are able to identify its essential monitoring and modifying components. Without a definition, or with just a description of mental activities, we would be in the dark as to how to strengthen these regulatory mental functions. As therapists, we are prepared to help our clients to refine and strengthen their emerging capacities to monitor and then modify the flow of energy and information in their brains and in their relationships. This is the transformative power that having a definition of the mind—especially as mental health professionals—offers us to help others, and ourselves, move our lives toward health.

We've seen that transformation requires that we stabilize mindsight's lens so that we can perceive energy and information flow with more stability. Once stabilized, we can see with more clarity, depth, and breadth. Openness, objectivity, and observation are mindsight skills that can be cultivated and form the three legs of the stabilizing tripod. Without being able to see clearly, it is difficult to shape effectively. These skills can be intentionally developed so that individuals are helped in how they can monitor energy and information flow.

Modifying this flow is also a skill that can be nurtured in each of us. As a part of mindsight training, we've seen that developing this skill well may involve a form of deep practice that grows myelin to wrap the linking neural circuits. The myelin encasing of synaptically connected integrated circuits enables skills to be developed. Modifying abilities require that we ride waves of energy and information flow and then have the ability to alter that flow: We can reduce or elevate states of energy arousal and we can shape the direction and content of energy and information movement through the brain and through our relationships. This reveals how the mind is both embodied and relational.

When we use our growing capacities to see and then shape energy and information flow with a strengthened tripod of mindsight's lens, we can then address the question, "How are we to mold our minds toward health?" Here is where the framework of integration becomes essential. Mindsight includes but is not just about being mindful or seeing the inner world. The mindsight framework enables us to take the step of not only defining the mind, but also making a working definition of mental health as integration. We detect moments of chaos and/or rigidity, and then we explore those aspects of our subjective lives for ways in which linkage and/or differentiation are not occurring. To achieve deep transformation, we come face to face with life's challenges. To approach and not withdraw from these critical aspects of our lives, we can embrace these challenges as opportunities to grow.

At least eight domains of integration can be the intentional focus of attention in the experience of transformation. As we'll see, a ninth domain of transpiration is also a part of the larger picture, one we'll discuss in the final chapter of the book. These eight domains offer a framework for approaching the process of personal transformation and are the main focus that organizes an interper-

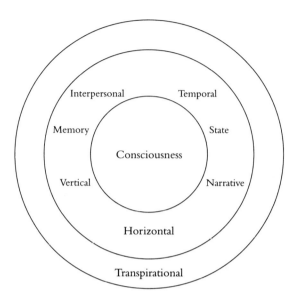

Figure 13.1 Domains of integration.

sonal neurobiology approach to psychotherapy. As you may have gathered from the flow of the chapters of this book, we have actually already covered each of these eight domains by examining the many facets of the TRs of being a mindful therapist.

Each of our mindsight skill-training entries builds on one or more of the eight domains of integration. In your own personal growth and in your professional work, you can naturally be creative in exploring new forms of deep practice that are guided by these fundamental principles. The idea is simple: take these ideas, if they suit you, and make them work for you in your own individualized (differentiated) manner. Ultimately, as mindful therapists we are integrators. Our main job is the releasing of integration from the entanglement of impediments to differentiation and linkage. Focusing awareness on the challenges, not just rehearsing what is already in place, supports the deep practice essential for skill development and myelin growth. We have the opportunity to create this in our own lives as we prepare to join with others in cultivating integration in theirs.

What follows is an overview of the domains of integration that have been touched upon throughout our prior discussions. Applications of these domains in clinical cases are available in other texts (see Siegel, 2010); here we'll review how these domains can be a part of how we transform our own lives as mindful therapists.

CONSOLIDATION AND THE DOMAINS OF INTEGRATION

The *integration of consciousness* essentially involves cultivating the hub of the mind so that we can distinguish the mental activity of the rim from the essence of awareness symbolized by the hub. Rim elements of the first five senses bring the outside world into our awareness. The sixth sense sector brings in the interior data of the body to enable interoception. Our seventh sense permits us to experience the more classically defined mental activities that range from thoughts, feelings, and memories to beliefs, attitudes, and intentions. An eighth sense permits us to gain awareness of our interconnected nature, the way we relate to others and the world at large. Perhaps you can imagine other senses, as well—and I'd love to hear about those experiences and ideas, too. Our wheel of awareness exercises directly cultivate this important starting point of the domains of integration.

Mindsight skills that support the integration of consciousness can also be nurtured through the other mindfulness practices, such as walking meditation, yoga, or tai chi. We've seen that while mindfulness is practiced throughout the world, East and West, ancient and modern, it is a human skill that religions use—not itself a religious practice. While some educational programs appropriately shy away from bringing uninvited religion into a secular setting, it is in fact the case that research has now demonstrated that mindful awareness practices, such as mindfulness meditation, are actually ways of strengthening the healthy functioning of the body, the brain, the mind, and interpersonal relationships. As we've seen,

practicing physicians who were taught mindfulness skills were better at dealing with stress and had less burnout; medical students had
more empathy for their patients. Not bad. (See Krasner et al., 2009;
also Shapiro, Schwartz, & Bonner, 1998.)

But mindsight abilities are more than these important mindfulness skills. Being aware intentionally of the present moment without being swept up by judgments is one aspect of our first domain,
the integration of consciousness. In contrast, as we've seen, mindsight involves developing triception so that we can see and shape
energy and information flow in our relationships, our brain as the
extended nervous system distributed throughout the whole body,
and our regulating mind. We take our triception and then use these
reflective skills of mindsight to both monitor the internal world
clearly and then strategically modify it toward integration. Once
we've stabilized our mindsight lens, we can begin to harness the
hub of the mind to explore and cultivate the other domains of
integration.

Horizontal integration links the bilaterally distributed elements of
neural functioning to one another. This form of integration can
take place on both sides of the brain, and also includes forms of
integration within the same side but spatially distributed in the
nervous system. For example, we can link high levels of visual processing with similar levels of audio processing in sensorimotor integration techniques. This would be considered horizontal in that
these differentiated elements are at similar levels of processing, even
though they may be each on the same side of the brain. Even left
and right differentiation is more about modes of processing, distinctive flows of information, which can be linked to one another.

For the bilateral form of integration, we can view the many
ways in which right and left hemisphere modes differ from one
another. The right mode is earlier to develop, holistic, nonverbal,
visuospatial, and also has a dominance in autobiographical processing, contains an integrated map of the whole body, and is primarily responsible for the stress response. The left in contrast is later to

develop, linear, linguistic, logical, literal, and loves lists. For our left sides, it's easier to remember with all those Ls.

Having separated hemispheres gives us the experience of having two cohesive systems of energy and information flow. The nature of sensing reality through the left is quite distinct from that of the right. And naturally, many people want to avoid dichotomania—exaggerating these differences. And this concern is quite warranted. Naturally, the whole brain works to combine its functioning. Yet for hundreds of millions of years, our vertebrate cousins have had distinctive asymmetry in the physical and functional aspects of their nervous systems. Right and left have been different in their features for literally millions of generations before us. Even if functional imaging reveals blood flow patterns that are increased on both sides of the brain, neurological insults (trauma, strokes, tumors) support the comparative zoology findings that our human brains are also quite asymmetrical. At the very least, we are using the term *mode* to respect the many contributions both sides make to many functions—but acknowledging that distinctive patterns of information flow do in fact exist in our experience. Ultimately, the key is integration and not playing favorites to one side or the other. But our modern culture seems to favor the left mode of processing, and since the right mode generally cannot (literally) speak up for itself in court as it does not have the linguistic language so easily expressed, the linearity or the logic of compelling forensic presentation, it is up to us as whole people to "speak up" for what can appear to be an underdog.

Integrating left and right is like a good marriage. No one should expect the two partners to become exactly like one another. Instead, two individuals find that their whole is greater than the sum of their separate parts. And so linking left and right is about honoring differences while nurturing collaboration. We've seen here and in many other texts the many ways that such bilateral integration is cultivated and nourished: Autobiographical narratives become coherent and relationships flourish. Even a sense of wholeness and vitality blossoms.

Each of the domains of integration supports the others. *Vertical integration* is no stranger to left and right differences. The body's input moves up Lamina I in the spinal cord to deposit itself in the brainstem and limbic areas and then to move primarily to the right side to make interoception a right anterior cingulate- and right anterior insula-mediated process. Even our right parietal area has an integrated map of the whole body—not the left. And so neural findings suggest that the somatic signals move from body to brainstem to limbic area to right cortex first, and then to left. This intimate linkage of the right side of the cortex to the body makes vertical integration overlap with the cultivation of right hemisphere awareness. We take in the nonverbal signals of the body and bring them up, literally, into cortically mediated awareness. That is the essence of vertical integration.

A variety of developmental adaptations can make this and the other domains of integration impaired in their unfolding. Identifying the experiential factors that induced a vertical dissociation can be important for beginning the process of reconnecting body and skull-based brain. But deciphering reasons for developmental adaptations are just a beginning of the journey of discovery and change. The next step is to SNAG the brain toward integration: to stimulate neuronal activation and growth in a way that harnesses Lamina I input and enables the cortex to not only tolerate this data, but to cherish it. Widening the windows of tolerance for receiving these bodily states into awareness is the essence of vertical integration. As therapists, this open presence to whatever arises is the beginning place for us before we can invite our clients to journey into their own bodily experience. As we've seen, when we can enter dyadic states of attunement, we widen the window of tolerance and enable our clients to move into emergent states of trust and safety with their own internal states that before were terrifying or shut-down.

Past events become encoded into our lives through the laying down of synaptic connections first in the various forms of implicit memory. These forms include our emotions, perceptions, behavioral reactions, and perhaps bodily sensations (I say "perhaps" because this is just not a topic of formal study yet). We develop mental models as summations of these experiences, and then filter our ongoing interactions though this model-making lens of the past. Priming is also an implicit process as our brain readies itself to respond in a certain way based on these top-down filters of experience.

Memory integration involves building a flexible form of memory from these more automatic and fixed elements of implicit encoding. The hippocampus, deep in the medial temporal lobe of our limbic area, serves as an implicit puzzle piece assembler as it integrates those pieces into the larger frames of factual and autobiographical memory. Now when we recall explicit memory we have an internal sensation that something in awareness is derived from a past experience. And with explicit processing, we can flexibly retrieve elements through an intentionally shaped search process that enables us to "know" the facts of the world and of our self-in-time life.

Riding the waves of information flow, we can sit back and sometimes get a clear sense of when this flow is in the free form of implicit layering. . . . It shapes our sense of the here and now without being flagged as something coming from the past. Part of the key to memory integration is to take in what is, but at the same time have the conceptual knowing (the C of SOCK) that what may feel real in the moment is actually an implicit retrieval. Bringing in the O of observation also helps to pull us out of automatic pilot (this is the YODA of "you observe to decouple automaticity"). It is this multilayered integration of the various streams of awareness that liberates us from the stranglehold of unresolved issues. We learn to name it to tame it and find that placing stressful states or uncomfortable emotions into the receptive field of awareness actually calms our subcortical storms. Studies even suggest that the right ventrolateral prefrontal cortex plays an active role in most forms of regulation, including affective calming with emotion labeling (see Creswell et al, 2007). Sensation brings in whatever is, to accept things as they are, including a present nonintegrated state of unresolved issues. Knowing enables us to feel the reality that integration is around the corner, it is our birthright to permit the natural flow of our lives toward harmony. We sense our memories within this open space of awareness, often naming them and enabling them to be calmed and contained.

Narrative integration takes the observer function to another level. We have a "narrator" function, perhaps with a left-mode dominance, that oversees our lives from a third-person perspective. Even when saying "I" did this or that, there is a quality that I could just as easily be saying "Dan" did this today. At an extreme, narrating our lives can be a form of dissociation that locks us into the observing stream. We live a distant, cold, and disconnected existence. But narrative integration is about weaving the observer with the observed, of intimately linking bodily experience and the nonverbal realm of right-mode processing with the logical, linear, linguistic, and observing left mode processes. Coherent narratives are not the same as the logically dismissive cohesive narratives of intellectualization. Coherence is literally a way of making sense of our life, of feeling fully the sensations of our lived experience, moment by moment, and weaving these with memory and with our visions for a new future.

Part of making sense of life involves reflecting on the past. We've seen that the best predictor of how children become attached to their parents is in the ways that the parent has made sense of his or her own life. My own perspective on this, supported by preliminary investigations and communications, is that the mindfulness of the parents is reflected in their own presence with the child as well as the capacity to be present with themselves in telling their life story. Internal attunement in the narrative coherence of the Adult Attachment Interview parallels, I believe, the interpersonal attunement of the parent–child relationship that cultivates security.

Being present with yourself also occurs as you approach your various states of being. *State integration* is the way we link the differentiated states that define our self across time. A "self-state" emerges as various needs, desires, and interactive patterns coalesce into repeated patterns of being. We can have a self-state of playing tennis, making love, studying the cosmos, cooking food, gardening. Each of these states is a cohesive whole that makes functioning efficient. Yet often people feel they are supposed to be "whole," by which they often mean "homogeneous." This image of singularity is in stark contrast to the natural reality of our multiplicity.

State integration involves *intrastate* ways in which we make each self-state function well as a cohesive whole. If I have ambivalence, for example, in honoring my need for solitude, I may become irritated with others because I have not given myself the integrative initiative to embrace a natural need to also be alone. *Interstate* integration focuses on the ways we can find cooperation across our various states so that our spectrum of needs is met well and with minimal animosity and maximal collaboration. Another dimension of state integration is the support of the "we-state" in which our own sovereignty is honored while becoming a part of a social connection—with one other person or with a group.

Interpersonal integration is exactly this notion that we can be fully grounded in a sense of self yet become a part of a "we" that enhances our sense of vitality in life. The "neurobiology of we" is the sense that we can promote the integration of two or more individual systems into a larger functional whole. This sense of a "we" is at the heart of "feeling felt" that may be the simplest way of describing love. It is perhaps this deep sense of interpersonal integration that is also the heart of healing. A professional form of love is often not spoken of directly, perhaps for fear of confusing boundaries or bringing inappropriate connotations of romance or sexuality into the clinical setting. But as mindful therapists, we need to, well, be mindful of the notion that this human experience of caring for others (and ourselves) with curiosity, openness, and acceptance can be seen to be the core of what we may experience as "love." This is the aspect of mindfulness in which we avoid premature hardening of our categories for what love means. COAL is what we bring to our awareness with mindfulness of the conscientious and contemplative consciousness forms as well. And COAL is indeed what we bring to our caring concern for our clients. And so it is important to distinguish this healing love from romantic love in that in the professional setting we bring our full selves, hub wide open, to our engagement with the patient. What could be more deeply connecting than this in our unambiguous, nonthreatening, boundary-respecting professional role? This intimate dance between healer and client is the essence of the therapeutic relationship. And yet this dance is intimate in the most nonphysical but existentially most meaningful ways we can be as human beings together on the planet.

I am so profoundly grateful for the connections I have had with people who have come to me over these 30 years of being in clinical practice. What other sense can we use to articulate this deep gratitude for our connection than some form of love? When all is said and done, we are all journeying together on this winding road of life. Being a mindful therapist gives us the grounded presence to embrace the uniqueness and vulnerability of our clinical connections, and to give a deep bow of thanks for the privilege of helping one another heal.

These existential issues of meaning and connection also find a focus in our eighth domain, that of *temporal integration*. The prefrontal cortex enables us to make maps of time. This ability gives us the benefit and the burden of being aware that nothing is certain, nothing is permanent, and we all die. Sorry to be so heavy. But avoiding these temporal realities is a form of impairment—of not facing reality. Yet so often we tend to want certainty, long for permanence, imagine immortality. Temporal integration is not about just shirking away from these human desires; instead, we can come to embrace our understandable longings and weave these together with a true openness to actual reality. Certainty-uncertainty, permanence-transience, immortality-mortality: These are the polarities in the central focus of temporal integration.

A very practical implication of temporal integration emerges when we examine our 200 million-year-old "checker system" that attempts to scan, alert, and motivate us about danger. As mindful therapists, monitoring and modifying this checker system within ourselves can be especially crucial as we make clinical assessments and interventions driven by our own concerns for our clients' safety. Exploring the checker system in our patients' experiences can be a powerful way of investigating the ways in which temporal integration may be impaired in their lives. After a trauma, our checker system may go on high alert and continually seek certainty around issues related to that event. Knowing our past, sensing the ways in which this drive for certainty is shaping how we perceive the ongoing factors for our client, and being open to our own persistent temporal concerns is vital in returning to presence when we've been swept up by checker-driven preoccupations.

For temporal integration, as is true with each of the other seven domains, mindsight is crucial. From the perspective of the plane of possibility, mindsight enables us to see patterns of repeating plateaus of probability and peaks of activation that are locking us into rigid or chaotic ways of life. With the focus of our attention on these tendencies, we can move our lives in new directions that enable us to link differentiated elements in each of these domains in powerful new ways. Softening incessant peaks and lowering restrictive plateaus, we can bring more fluidity into our lives by visiting the open plane and re-setting the course of our journey across time. Without mindsight, we may merely live on automatic pilot and be constrained by these engrained patterns of neural proclivities and mental habits. With clear seeing, we are given the choice and the channel to redirect our mental life and neural firing patterns toward more flexible and adaptive states of integration.

And here is the fascinating flow of the process of transformation.

The more we develop our capacity to see and shape the internal flow of energy and information within the triangle of mind, brain, and relationships, the more we can free our lives toward integration. And the process of integration itself, as we're seeing, sharpens our mindsight lens. This is the way in which integration and mindsight mutually reinforce one another. Time and time again, it has become apparent in patients, colleagues, and my own personal life that releasing the transformative power of integration and mindsight together leads to a positive cycle toward a more harmonious way of living. As a client and his wife said to me recently, this approach brings a "deep smile to the hearts and faces" of all of those benefiting from the transformative power of mindsight and integration.

Chapter 14

TRANQUILITY

It's hard to know how to put this chapter into words. You and I have been through a journey in our conversation about being a mindful therapist. We've been exploring the essential PARTs of being: presence, attunement, and resonance, and all the TRs that followed: trust, truth, tripod, triception, tracking, traits, trauma, transition, training, and transformation. Now we've come to the eleventh TR, to tranquility. I feel it, but I'm not sure how words could ever describe it accurately.

Deep within there is a sense of wholeness that permeates everything. While events in day-to-day living come up evoking reactions of worry and concern, disappointment and sadness, or even of excitement and surprise, elation and fulfillment, beneath and beyond these responses there is a sense of fullness. The best word I can find to encapsulate this sensation is tranquility.

Tranquility has the formal definition of being composed and free from commotion. It has the synonyms of calm, calmness, motionless, stillness, quietness, quietude, serenity, sereneness, repose, rest, restful, peacefulness, harmony, harmoniousness. It also has the synonyms of composure, self-possession, coolness, equanimity, poise, sangfroid (calmness under pressure), steadiness, self-control, and level-headedness (Rodale, 1978). Tranquility is the word that captures the sense of being deeply in the hub of awareness, centered in the open plane of possibility. From this tranquil place we feel the wide-open potential of awareness and can sense, observe, conceive, and know all the elements of the rim, from the external world to the deepest sense of connection to others across time.

Presence has at its core tranquility.

BRAIN BASICS

From the neural side of the plane of reality, we can imagine that tranquility is a state of open presence within the plane itself. As we move beyond the plane into the valenced plateaus of our various states of neural priming, we move away from this tranquil openness of possibility and toward various restraining places of probability. Moving further outward into peaks of activation, we can experience our various thoughts, feelings, and actions as they carry us into their evolving paths along time.

But the flexibility to move back to the plane of open possibility is the essence of tranquility. It is this free motion in and out of the plane that gives us the equanimity to face life's challenges, whatever they are and whenever they occur. This is the power of tranquility to form the neural ground of our being from which all other neural firing patterns can build: from plateau to peak and back to plane. This is the home base of tranquility, the openness of possibility, that we can cultivate with our mindsight skills as we become mindful therapists.

MINDSIGHT SKILLS

Deep practice in developing the differentiated hub of the mind is the heart of the training that brings tranquility into our lives as a trait. From the beginning of our conversation we've been exploring how the intentional focusing of attention on the sectors of the rim and distinguishing these from the hub serves to strengthen the ways we can move flexibly from peaks of determined mental activity and plateaus of valenced probabilities of primed states of mind toward the open plane of possibility. Though this may sound abstract to say, and certainly without experiential immersion it would seem quite cold and distant to comprehend in the hearing or reading, it is, at its heart, what I believe equanimity is truly about. Developing the skill of freely moving in and out of the plane of possibility is how brain and mind develop the clarity, balance, and stability of tranquility.

Mindsight skills awaken our lives to tranquility. We face challenges with clarity, remain open to things as they are, and don't identify with mental activity as the totality of who we are. In our triangle, these mindsight skills strengthen the way we regulate energy and information flow, bolstering the mind, and freeing us from the vicissitudes of a busy and chaotic mental world. We literally create an internal sanctuary from which we can experience all that arises, moment by moment. Within our relationships, mindsight permits us to see deeply into the subjective heart of another's life. Others feel felt by us, a deep connection is created, and our relationships become empathic and attuned. This is the ease and fluidity of a "we" that is integrated: Each individual is respected for her uniqueness while becoming intimately embraced by one another. On the brain point of the triangle, the linkage of differentiated circuits creates the neural integration at the heart of harmonious functioning. Neural pathways become coordinated and balanced with the resultant coherence in electrical flow and information processing. Riding the waves of these integrated neural firing patterns, the mind regulates this flow further toward integration as relationships flourish. This is the triangle of well-being with its integrated movement of ease and tranquility.

INTEGRATION, CREATIVITY, AND THE PLANE OF OPEN POTENTIAL

Open systems like us move toward ever more complex states in their flow across time. As Stuart Kauffman (2008) elegantly points

out in his text, *Reinventing the Sacred*, creativity is the natural outcome of complex systems within the universe. For some, this creativity is experienced as divine inspiration; for others, the mathematics
of complexity suggests that creating new combinations is just what
the universe "does." Either way, the majesty of ever-evolving and
increasingly intricate forms fills us with awe. Respecting the wonder of new creations, we sit in amazement that life can become so
rich, so complex, so startlingly new in this freshly alive emergence.

Open systems capable of chaotic behavior move toward maximizing complexity by connecting their differentiated elements.
These are complex systems that are nonlinear, meaning that small
inputs lead to large and unpredictable outcomes. Yet built into the
system is the self-organizational process that pushes the system
toward complexity. These new combinations of linking differentiated elements to one another are, in fact, the outcome of integration. And so we can say, from a strictly mathematical and systems
view, that creativity emerges from integration.

In our exploration of brain basics we have been diving deeply
into the waters of neural integration. In our mindsight skill training we've immersed ourselves in the direct experience of how the
linkage of differentiated aspects of energy and information flow
alter the ways we see and shape our internal world. In many ways,
these ideas and experiences illuminate the path upon which we
can soften our peaks and broaden our plateaus so that they become
more flexible in their flow across time. Life must have manifestations in actualities and moments of propensities in priming: We
need our peaks and plateaus and cannot live in tranquil states of
bliss all the time. But mindsight skills permit us to more freely
move from peak to plateau and return to the flexibility and receptivity of the open plane of possibility. Tranquility can be a ground
of being underlying all our experiences as our lives emerge across
time, a subterranean spring that gives life to all the streams of
awareness and fills our lives with awe and gratitude for all that we
come to know in this precious time we call life.

When we hear the word *no*, we can become stuck in reactivity. We can also reframe that word as *know* and move into a more flexible response—and we can intentionally alter our internal reactivity to become more receptive. From a simple breath awareness practice to the more elaborated hub awareness training, learning to sense and shape our internal world can free us from the constraints of habit and reactivity. This is the way mindsight enables us to create new combinations of response—new peaks and plateaus—so that we are always able to dip back into the underlying open plane of possibility and move again outward with new and fresh approaches even to old situations.

This fluid movement from plane to peak and back again is the essence of tranquility and of creativity. We engage the world, the project we're working on, a relationship, or even ourselves in a way that enables tranquility to be at the heart of our experience. The triangle of well-being fills with harmony as the mind becomes coherent, relationships empathic, and the brain integrated. Creativity flows from this space—a creativity in mind, relationships, and brain. We live life with a deep sense of connection, openness, harmony, engagement, receptivity, emergence, compassion, and empathy. This is coherence in action. And it is from this deep flexibility and engagement that we embrace our interconnected place in the world in which we live.

Chapter 15

TRANSPIRATION

W e've come to our final chapter, and this one is quite simple. As we move forward across the eight domains of integration, what seems to naturally occur is the emergence of a ninth form of "integration of integration," which I have termed a breathing-across, or transpirational integration. Transpiration is the state of awareness of the interconnected nature of reality that places our own identities in the membership of a whole larger than our bodily defined selves.

In moving deeply into mindsight skills, we've learned to sense and shape the flow of energy and information within our relationships, our nervous systems, and our mental experience. We've seen that the linkage of differentiated parts liberates the integrative states of being flexible, adaptive, coherent, energized and stable. As these domains of integration enable us to differentiate hub from rim, left from right, soma from skull-based synapses, and the various layers of memory, narrative, and states, we can then link these specialized functions to one another in achieving higher states of complexity and harmony. When we enable our individual flows of energy and information to be shared by way of our authentic presence with others, we can attune with them and promote the mutual resonance that is at the heart of becoming an interpersonal "we" in the world.

With each of these forms of integration, we move toward deeper states of harmony. In my own experience, personally and with clients in therapy, I have found that there emerges an inner knowing that the boundaries of the body are only a temporary defining set of experiences that construct the notion of a self. This self is reinforced by our contemporary culture and family life to view the "me" of life as confined to our brief time on the planet, our limited circle of people we know, our particular personal concerns. Yet we are widening this bodily defined self to embrace the fuller reality that energy and information flow has been moving through us for millions of years—not just for the century or so that we define as a lifetime. Mindsight promotes integration as we sense the deep nature of this flow; and integration permits us to relax these constrictive definitions of "I" and come to realize we are a fundamental part of a much larger "we" that extends in both time and space beyond what we'll ever know in our bodily shaped lives.

Why would this integration of integration engage such an expanded sense of self? How do our plateaus of probability, the propensities we have in our personalities to define a self as limited to the body, relax with integration? How does our internal topography move from these steep precipices that give rise, repeatedly, to peaks of self-identity that manifest as thoughts, feelings, and behaviors of self-involved preoccupations? How do we come to learn that these repeatedly reinforced thoughts of a time-limited self are but passing peaks from a restrictive and culturally created set of plateaus of personality? How does integration loosen the stranglehold of these peaks and broaden and lower our plateaus as we move toward the open plane of possibility?

BRAIN BASICS

Throughout our journey we've attempted to weave a tapestry that embraces the threads of our two sides of one reality. On the neural firing side, we've seen that top-down constructions of thoughts and ideas emerge from the higher cortical layers of our six cell deep columns. These flows of prior learning, such as that of a bodily defined identity, crash into the bottom-up flow of here-and-now sensation emerging from the lower layers of our cortical columns. Identity likely emerges from the way the top-down flow encounters bottom-up and holds sway over the ultimate internal awareness we have of I and me and mine. Many patients I've seen for couples therapy, for example, have such a constricting sense of identity that they are challenged to even join with a spouse as a part of a collaborative "we," let alone to feel a part of people or purposes beyond their individual concerns. We can imagine in this case that the top-down flow is so strong that it continually reinforces its own constructed view of this limited sense of belonging.

Integration across all of the domains we've been exploring likely releases this stranglehold of top-down to liberate the innate potential of our brains to blend bottom-up and top-down in a more harmonious way. As studies of wisdom and happiness suggest, when we devote our lives to the welfare of others—not abandoning our own needs, but widening our identity to embrace the working for others as a part of who we are—we actually achieve deep states of meaning, connection, and equilibrium. Wisdom, happiness, and compassion, I'll suggest to you, are the products of integration.

And so it is natural to picture the movement toward integration in all its domains as focusing attention to promote differentiation of our various dimensions of neural firing and then to link these functions as we achieve highly complex, integrated circuits. The brain as a complex system self-organizes toward these higher states of harmony. But the details of life may get in the way, and finding a strategy to detect the chaos and rigidity that result from such impediments is the first step toward liberation from such blockages. Our job as mindful therapists is to cultivate mindsight in ourselves so we can detect chaos and rigidity and then identify which neural areas need to be freed to differentiate and link toward integration.

The illusion of our separateness creates suffering and discontent. Even the simplest of studies reveals that when spending money on others or ourselves, those who spend money to benefit others feel better. Compassion and kindness are good for not only our relationships, but our bodies and minds as well. In interactions of clinicians and their patients, those patients who receive caring and empathic attention from their care provider do better as well. We are hard-wired to connect with one another, but modern life makes such connections ever more difficult to achieve. Our goal, as Albert Einstein suggested, is to "widen our circles of compassion" so that we come to dissolve the "optical delusion" of our separateness and embrace the reality of the interconnected nature of our membership in a larger whole.

My own reading of the neuroscience of a self is that the cortex is naturally inclined to create a smaller and limited sense of self. In this way, it may actually take reflective practice to widen these circles of concern. We may need a daily form of "brain fitness" to keep our synapses clear of the optical delusion of our separateness.

MINDSIGHT SKILLS

We can view the world through the lens of the physical domain of reality, noticing only the objects we can touch with our hands or see with our eyes. Throughout our mindsight skill exercises, we've been cultivating the ability to see reality through a different lens. The world of the mind, the subjective inner life of each of us, is as real as that of the physical side of reality. We've worked closely with the visual metaphor of the plane of reality to denote how the two aspects of one reality mutually influence one another. The neural firing and mental experience sides of reality can each drive the other forward. The good news about this truth is that we've seen how we can use our own intention to focus our attention in ways that can create new neural firing patterns in our lives. We can pull ourselves out of unhelpful proclivities of repeating peaks that often arise from high and restrictive plateaus of our states of mind.

The practice of moving our awareness from the rim down into the hub, of differentiating mental activity from awareness itself, is a crucial step of the integration of consciousness. As we differentiate hub from rim, we are freeing our lives to disentangle from automatic pilot as we move into the open plane of possibility. It is this capacity of our minds to move us from peak to plateau and down into the plane that makes transformation possible.

When we come to believe that our peaks and plateaus are the totality of who we are, we are then imprisoned by bodily defined selves and the optical delusion of our separateness. Mindfulness practice is an established mental training that helps us create an approach state in which we have the courage to move toward challenges that might otherwise have us turn away and hide in more comfortable views of reality. One such hiding place is in the notion of a bodily defined separate self. We live in a body, feed our body, spend time and money taking care of our body, and can take on a name, a home address, a Social Security number, each attached to our bodily defined identity. But when we come to feel the transpirational sense of our interconnectedness, when we dissolve the familiar optical delusion of our separateness, we need to let go of this comfort and enter uncharted territory. It is here where the approach state of mindfulness is essential.

Mindful awareness sharpens our executive skills and makes us have better attention and emotion regulation. The power of these exercises is to loosen the hardened and inflexible patterns around our synapses so that we can free the innate drive toward integration. This integration is filled with potential: We free our capacity to make new combinations called creativity and we open our minds to new definitions of who we are. In these ways, using mindsight to open ourselves to ever-deepening layers of integration is an invitation to expand our sense of self. The energy and vitality that emerge from such a new way of living, of selfing, of being, is the life-giving power of presence.

In our journey, we have intentionally stayed close to our own experience—yours and mine. We've traveled to places in the heart of our thoughts and feelings, delved into the spaces in between, and even rested in the wide expanse of open awareness. Through these paths together, who are we? What is this flow of energy and information, really? For me, this journey brings a sense that this flow winds its way through us, through these bodies, in ways that melt the restrictive definitions of our identities. If we do this well, the drive we have to help others and make this world a better place will wind its way toward healing in people and places beyond what these bodies will ever know.

INTEGRATION AND WIDENING OUR CIRCLES OF COMPASSION

With transpirational integration, we come to see ourselves as a part of a whole, a member of a continuity across time and space that grounds us in the present and links us to a larger reality of the flow of life. With the cultivation of mindsight, we see ourselves with an expanded identity. Kindness and compassion are the breath of life, and integration liberates these fundamental ways of linking ourselves to one another. As we cultivate integration in our internal and interpersonal lives, we not only nurture ourselves and our loved ones, but we open the mind to new possibilities. As we strengthen our collective connections through harnessing the power of mindsight, we awaken our minds and widen our circles of compassion to truly embrace the sanctity of this wonder-filled journey of life.

As we come to the end of our journey together, I feel that we are actually just beginning. There is a "hello" deeply embedded in where we've come. When we work on expanding our own levels of inner knowing, cultivating deep ways of sensing our minds, brains, and relationships, we liberate an ability to see the inner world so clearly that our sense of self widens to embrace a much larger core of identity. This widening of our circle of compassion extends beyond our family and friends and opens us to a lifetime membership in a much larger world of we. As mindful therapists, we can harness the power of presence to promote the integration in ourselves and in others that heals ancient wounds and liberates the reality of our belonging to one another. Our clients, our society, our planet are waiting to join us and awaken to this reality of our lives.

Appendix

A DOZEN POINTS ON AN INTERPERSONAL NEUROBIOLOGY APPROACH TO MINDSIGHT, INTEGRATION, AND PSYCHOTHERAPY

(Used with permission from D. J. Siegel, *Mindsight: The New Science of Personal Transformation*, Appendix. New York: Bantam/Random House, 2010.)

Here are a dozen basic concepts and related terms and ideas that form a foundation for our approach of mindsight, integration, and well-being.

1. A *triangle of well-being* reveals three aspects of our lives. Relationships, mind, and brain form the three mutually influencing points of the triangle of well-being. *Relationships* are how energy and information are shared as we connect and communicate with one another. The *brain* refers to the physical mechanism through which this energy and information flows. The *mind* is a process that regulates the flow of energy and information. Rather than dividing our lives into three separate parts, the triangle actually represents three dimensions of one system of energy and information flow.

2. *Mindsight* is a process that enables us to monitor and modify the flow of energy and information within the triangle of

well-being. The *monitoring* aspect of mindsight involves sensing this flow within ourselves—perceiving it in our own nervous systems, what we are calling "the brain"—and within others through our relationships that involve the sharing of energy and information flow through various means of communication. We then can *modify* this flow through awareness and intention, fundamental aspects of our mind, directly shaping the paths that energy and information flow take in our lives.

3. A system is composed of individual parts that interact with each other. For our human systems, these interactions often involve the *flow of energy and information*. Energy is the physical property enabling us to do something; information is the representation of something other than itself. Words and ideas are examples of units of information we use to communicate with one another. Our relationships involve our connection to other people in pairs, families, groups, schools, communities, and societies.

4. We can define well-being as occurring when a system is *integrated. Integration involves the linkage of differentiated parts of a system.* The differentiation of components enables parts to become individuated, attaining specialized functions and retaining their sovereignty to some degree. The linkage of parts involves the functional connection of the differentiated components to one another. Promoting integration involves cultivating both differentiation and linkage. Mindsight can be used to intentionally cultivate integration in our lives.

5. When a system is open to outside influences and capable of becoming chaotic, it is called a dynamic, nonlinear, complex system. When this type of system is integrated, it moves in a way that is the most flexible and adaptive. We can remember the characteristics of an integrated flow of the system with the acronym, *FACES: flexible, adaptive, coherent, energized, and stable.*

6. The *river of integration* refers to the movement of a system in which the integrated FACES flow is the central channel of the river that has the quality of harmony. The two banks on either side of the river's flow are those of chaos and of rigidity. We can detect when a system is not integrated, when it is not in a state of harmony and well-being, by its chaotic or rigid characteristics. Recurrent explosions of rage or terror and being taken over by a sense of paralysis or emptiness in life are examples of these chaotic and rigid states outside the river of integration.

7. In this model, eight *domains of integration* can be harnessed to promote well-being. These include the *domains of consciousness, horizontal, vertical, memory, narrative, state, interpersonal, and temporal integration.* As the mind is an embodied and relational process that regulates the flow of energy and information, we can use the intentional focus of our awareness to direct this flow toward integration in both the brain and relationships. As these domains of integration are cultivated, a ninth domain of *transpirational integration* may begin to emerge in which we come to feel that we are a part of a much larger interconnected whole.

8. Integration in relationships involves the attuned communication among people who are honored for their differences and then linked together to become a "we." Integration in the brain—what we are using as a term for the extended nervous system distributed throughout the entire body—involves the linkage of separate, differentiated neural areas and their specialized functions to one another. The focus of our attention directs the flow of energy and information through particular neural circuits. In this way, we can say that *the mind uses the brain to create itself.* Attention activates specific neural pathways and lays the foundation for changing the connections among those firing neurons by way of a fundamental process called *neuroplasticity.* The function of our mind—the regulation of energy

and information flow—can actually change the structure of the brain itself. Mindsight enables us to create neural integration.

9. One example of neural integration is revealed in the functions that emerge from a highly integrative area of the brain called the *middle prefrontal cortex*. Involving specific parts of the prefrontal region located behind the forehead (including the anterior cingulate, orbitofrontal, and the medial and ventrolateral prefrontal zones), the middle prefrontal integrative fibers link the whole cortex, limbic area, brainstem, body proper, and even social systems to one another. The *nine middle prefrontal functions* emerging from this multidimensional neural integration include: (a) body regulation, (b) attuned communication, (c) emotional balance, (d) fear modulation, (e) response flexibility, (f) insight, (g) empathy, (h) morality, and (i) intuition. These functions would top many people's lists of a description of well-being. They are also the established outcome and process of the reflective skills of looking inward, and the first eight of this list are proven outcomes of secure parent–child relationships that are filled with love. This list exemplifies how integration promotes well-being.

10. Mindsight doesn't just emanate from the middle prefrontal cortex. The reflective practice of focusing internal attention on the mind itself with *openness, observation, and objectivity*—the essentials of a strengthened *mindsight lens*—likely promotes the growth of these integrative middle prefrontal fibers. We use the acronym SNAG to denote how we *stimulate neuronal activation and growth*. This is the foundation of neuroplasticity, of how experiences—including the focus of our attention—transform brain structure. Mindsight SNAGs the brain toward integration, making it possible to intentionally promote linkage and differentiation within the various domains of integration.

11. A *window of tolerance* refers to the span of tolerable levels of arousal in which we can attain and remain in an integrated

FACES flow in which we live with harmony. Widened windows create resilience in our lives. If a window is narrowed, then it becomes more likely for energy and information flow to move outside its boundaries and for our lives to become chaotic or rigid. The integrated states within the window of tolerance are our subjective experience of living with a sense of ease and in the harmonious FACES flow down the river of integration. As we SIFT the mind—tracking the *sensations, images, feelings and thoughts* that dominate our internal world—we can *monitor* energy and information flow moment by moment within our windows of tolerance and *modify* our internal state to remain integrated and in a FACES flow. Ultimately we can use this monitoring and modifying to change not only our present *state*, but also our long-term *traits* that reveal how our windows for various feelings or situations can be widened through changes in our brain's dynamic regulatory circuits.

12. A *wheel of awareness* is the visual metaphor for how we can stay within the open, receptive *hub* of the wheel to sense any mental activities emerging from the *rim* without becoming swept up by them. A strengthened hub permits us to widen our windows of tolerance as we become more observant, objective, and open and attain more resilience in our lives. Mindsight harnesses this important capacity to remain receptive and to be able to monitor the internal world with more clarity and depth. We are then in a position to modify our inner and interpersonal world as we cultivate integration and move our lives toward more compassion, well-being, and health.

REFERENCES
REFERENCES

Allen, J. G., Fonagy, P., & Bateman, A. W. (2008). *Mentalizing in clinical practice.* Arlington, VA: APPI.

Baer, R. A., Smith, G. T., Hopkins, J., Krietemeyer, J., & Toney, L. (2006). Using self-report assessment methods to explore facets of mindfulness. *Assessment, 13*(1), 27–45.

Badenoch, B. (2008). *Being a brain-wise therapist.* New York: W. W. Norton.

Baron-Cohen, S. (2004). *The essential difference: Men, women, and the extreme male brain.* New York: Penguin/Basic Books.

Blakeslee, S., & Blakeslee, M. (2007). *The body as a mind of its own.* New York: Random House.

Brazelton, T. B. and Greenspan, S. L. (2000). *The irreducible needs of children: What every child must have to grow, learn, and flourish.* New York: Perseus Publishing.

Chess, S., & Thomas, A. (1990). The New York Longitudinal Study (NYLS): The young adult periods. *Canadian Journal of Psychiatry, 35,* 557–561.

Coyle, D. (2009). *The talent code: Greatness isn't born. It's grown. Here's how.* New York: Bantam.

Cozolino, L. (2002). *The neuroscience of psychotherapy: Building and rebuilding the human brain.* New York: W. W. Norton.

Cozolino, L. (2010). *The neuroscience of psychotherapy: Healing the social brain* (2nd ed.). New York: W. W. Norton.

Craig, A. D. (2009). How do you feel—now? The anterior insula and human awareness. *Nature Reviews Neuroscience, 10,* 59–70.

Creswell, J. D., Way, B. M., Eisenberger, N. I., & Lieberman, M. D. (2007). Neural correlates of dispositional mindfulness during affect labeling. *Psychosomatic Medicine, 69,* 560–565.

Daniels, D. N. & Price, V. (2009). *The essential enneagram: The definitive personality test and self-discovery guide.* San Francisco: Harper.

Davidson, R. J., Kabat-Zinn, J., Schumacher, J., Rosenkranz, M., Muller, D., Santorellie, S. F., et al. (2003). Alterations in brain and immune function produced by mindfulness meditation. *Psychosomatic Medicine, 65*, 564–570.

Davidson, R. J., & Kabat-Zinn, J. (2004). Alterations in brain and immune function produced by mindfulness meditation: Three caveats: Comment. *Psychosomatic Medicine, 66*(1), 152.

DiNoble, A. (2009). Examining the relationship between adult attachment style and mindfulness traits: A dissertation presented to the faculty of the California Graduate Institute of the Chicago School of Professional Psychology, January.

Doidge, N. (2007). *The brain that changes itself: Stories of personal triumph from the frontiers of brain science.* New York: Penguin.

Dozier, M., Stovall, K. C., Albus, K. E., & Bates, B. (2001). Attachment for infants in foster care: The role of caregiver state of mind. *Child Development, 72*, 1467–1477.

Dutra, L., Bianchi, I., Siegel, D. J., & Lyons-Ruth, K. (2009). The relational context of dissociative phenomena. In P. Dell & J. O'Neil (Eds.), *Dissociation and the dissociative disorders: DSM-V and beyond* (pp. 83–92). New York: Routledge.

Edelman, G. M., & Tononi, G. (2001). *A universe of consciousness: How matter becomes imagination.* New York: Basic Books.

Eisenberger, N., & Lieberman, M. (2004). Why rejection hurts: A common neural alarm system for physical and social pain. *Trends in Cognitive Sciences, 8*(7), 294–300.

Farb, N. A. S., Segal, Z. V., Mayberg, H., Bean, J., Mckeon, D., Fatima, Z., et al. (2007). Attending to the present: Mindfulness meditation reveals distinct neural modes of self-reference. *Journal of Social, Cognitive, and Affective Neuroscience, 2*, 248–258.

Fosha, D., Siegel, D. J., & Solomon, M. (Eds.). (2010). *The healing power of emotion: Affective neuroscience, development and clinical practice.* New York: W. W. Norton.

Freyd, J. J. (1987). Dynamic mental representations. *Psychological Review, 94*, 427–438.

Gazzaniga, M. (1998). *The mind's past.* Berkeley: University of California Press.

Gilbert, Paul (2010). The compassionate mind. Oakland: New Harbinger Press.

Germer, C. K., Siegel, R. D., & Fulton, P. R. (2004). *Mindfulness and psychotherapy.* New York: Guilford.

Goleman, D. (1996). *Emotional intelligence.* New York: Bantam.

Goleman, D. (2006). *Social intelligence.* New York: Bantam.

Goleman, D. (2009). *Ecological intelligence.* New York: Broadway Books.

Greenland, S. K. (2010). *The mindful child.* New York: Free Press.

Hawkins, J., & Blakeslee, S. (2005). *On intelligence: How a new understanding of the brain will lead to the creation of truly intelligent machines.* New York: Henry Holt.

Henry, W. P. (1998). Science, politics, and the politics of science: The use and misuse of empirically validated treatment research. *Psychotherapy Research, 8*(2), 126–140.

Iacoboni, M. (2008). *Mirroring people.* New York: Farrar, Straus and Giroux.

James, W. (1981). *Principles of psychology*. Cambridge, MA: Harvard University Press, 401. (Original work published 1890)

Kabat-Zinn, J. (2005). *Coming to our senses*. New York: Hyperion.

Kagan, J. (1992). *Galen's prophecy*. Cambridge, MA: Harvard University Press.

Kagan, J., & Snidman, N. (2004). *The long shadow of temperament*. Cambridge, MA: Harvard University Press.

Kauffman, S. (2008). *Reinventing the sacred*. New York: Basic Books.

Keltner, D. (2009). *Born to be good: The science of a meaningful life*. New York: W. W. Norton.

Kornfield, J. (2008). *The wise heart: A guide to the universal teachings of Buddhist psychology*. New York: Bantam.

Kornfield, J. (2000). *After the ecstasy, the laundry: How the heart grows wise on the spiritual path*. New York: Bantam.

Kosslyn, S. M. (2005). Reflective thinking and mental imagery: A perspective on the development of posttraumatic stress disorder [special issue]. *Development and Psychopathology, 17*(3), 851–863.

Krasner, M. S., Epstein, R. M., Beckman, H., Suchman, A. L., Chapman, B., Mooney, C. J., et al. (2009). Association of an educational program in mindful communication with burnout, empathy, and attitudes among primary care physicians. *JAMA, 302*, 1284–1293.

Langer, E. (1989). *Mindfulness*. Cambridge, MA: Da Capo Press.

Langer, E. (1997). *The power of mindful learning*. Cambridge, MA: Da Capo Press.

Lazar, S. W., Kerr, C. E., Wasserman, R. H., Gray, J. R., Greve, D. N., Treadway, M. T., et al. (2005). Meditation experience is associated with increased cortical thickness. *Neuroreport, 16*, 1893–1897.

Le Doux, J. (2002). *The synaptic self: How our brains become who we are*. New York: Penguin.

Levine, P. (1997). *Waking the tiger: Healing trauma*. Berkeley, CA: North Atlantic Books.

Levitin, D. J. (2006). *This is your brain on music: The science of a human obsession*. New York: Dutton.

Limb, C. J., & Braun, A. R. (2008). Neural substrates of spontaneous musical performance: An fMRI study of jazz improvisation. *PLoS One, 3*(2), e1679.

Luders, E., Toga, A. W., Lepore, N., & Gaser, C. (2009). The underlying anatomical correlates of long-term mediation: Larger hippocampal and frontal volumes of gray matter. *NeuroImage 45,* 672–678.

Lutz, A., Greischar, L. L., Rawlings, N. B., Ricard, M., & Davidson, R. J. (2004). Long-term meditators self-induce high-amplitude gamma synchrony during mental practice. *Proceedings of the National Academy of Sciences, 101*(46), 16939–16373.

Main, M. (2000). The Adult Attachment Interview: Fear, attention, safety, and discourse process. *Journal of the American Psychoanalytic Association, 48,* 1055–1096.

Main, M., Hesse, E., Yost-Abrams, K., & Rifkin, A. (2003). Unresolved states regarding loss and abuse can have "second generation effects": Disorganization, role inversion and frightening ideation in the offspring of traumatized, non-maltreating parents. In M. Solomon & D. J. Siegel (Eds.), *Healing trauma: Attachment, mind, body, and brain* (pp. 57–106). New York: W. W. Norton.

Neff, K. (2009). Self-compassion. In M. R. Leary & R. H. Hoyle (Eds.), *Handbook of individual differences in social behavior* (pp. 561–573), New York: Guilford.

Nelson, K. (Ed.). (1989). *Narratives from the crib*. Cambridge, MA: Harvard University Press.

Nisbett, R.E. & Miyamoto, Y. (2005). The influence of culture: Holistic versus analytic perception. *Trends in Cognitive Sciences, 9*(10), 467–473.

Norcross, J. (Ed.) (2002). *Psychotherapy relationships that work: Therapist contributions and responsiveness to patients*. Oxford: Oxford University Press.

Norcross, J., Beutler, L., & Levant, R. (2005). *Evidence-based practices in mental health: Debate and dialogue on the fundamental questions*. Oxford: Oxford University Press.

Ogden, P., Minton, K., & Pain, C. (2006). *Trauma and the body: A sensorimotor approach to psychotherapy*. New York: W. W. Norton.

Panksepp, J. (1998). *Affective neuroscience*. Oxford: Oxford University Press.

Panksepp, J., & Biven, L. (2010). *An archaeology of mind: Neuroevolutionary origins of human emotion*. New York: W. W. Norton.

Pennebaker, J. W. (2000). Telling stories: The health benefits of narrative. *Literature and Medicine, 19*, 3–18.

Porges, S. (2009). Reciprocal influences between body and brain in the perception and expression of affect: A polyvagal perspective. In D. Fosha, D. J. Siegel, & M. Solomon (Eds.), *The healing power of emotion: Affective neuroscience, development and clinical practice*. New York: W. W. Norton.

Rakel, D. P., Hoeft, T. J., Barrett, B. P., Chewning, B. A., Craig, B. M., & Niu, M. (2009). Practitioner empathy and the duration of the common cold. *Family Medicine, 41*, 494–501.

Ricard, M. (2005). *Happiness: A guide to developing life's most important skill*. Boston: Little, Brown.

Rodale, J. I. (1978). *The synonym finder*. New York: Warner Books.

Shapiro, F. (Ed.) (2002). *EMDR as an integrative psychotherapy approach: Experts of diverse orientations explore the paradigm prism*. New York: American Psychological Association Press.

Shapiro, S. L., Schwartz, G. E., & Bonner, G. (1998). Effects of mindfulness-based stress reduction on medical and premedical students. *Journal of Behavioral Medicine, 21*, 581–599.

Shapiro, S., & Carlson, E. (2009). *The art and science of mindfulness*. New York: American Psychological Association Press.

Siegel, D. J. (1995). Memory, trauma and psychotherapy: A cognitive science view. *Journal of Psychotherapy Practice and Research, 4*(2), 93–122.

Siegel, D. J. (1999). *The developing mind: Toward a neurobiology of interpersonal experience.* New York: Guilford.

Siegel, D. J. (2001). Toward an interpersonal neurobiology of the developing mind: Attachment, "mindsight" and neural integration. *Infant Mental Health Journal, 22,* 67–94.

Siegel, D. J. (2006). An interpersonal neurobiology approach to psychotherapy: How awareness, mirror neurons and neural plasticity contribute to the development of well-being. *Psychiatric Annals, 36,* 248–258.

Siegel, D. J. (2007a). *The Mindful Brain: Reflection and Attunement in the Cultivation of Well-Being.* New York: W. W. Norton.

Siegel, D. J. (2007b). Mindfulness training and neural integration: Differentiation of distinct streams of awareness and the cultivation of well-being. *Journal of Social, Cognitive, and Affective Neuroscience, 2,* 259–263.

Siegel, D. J. (2009). Mindful awareness, mindsight, and neural integration. *Journal of Humanistic Psychology, 37*(2), 137–149.

Siegel, D. J. (2010). *Mindsight: The new science of personal transformation.* New York: Bantam.

Siegel, D. J., & Hartzell, M. (2003). *Parenting from the inside out: How a deeper self-understanding can help you raise children who thrive.* New York: Tarcher/Penguin.

Smalley, S., & Winston, D. (2010). *Fully present: The science, art, and practice of mindfulness.* Cambridge, MA: Da Capo Press.

Steele, H., & Steele, M. (Eds.). (2008). *Clinical applications of the Adult Attachment Interview.* New York: Guilford.

Stern, D. N. (2004). *The present moment in psychotherapy and everyday life.* New York: W. W. Norton.

Thagard, P. (2000). *Coherence in thought and action.* Boston: MIT Press.

Tronick, E. (2007). *The neurobehavioral and social emotional development of infants and children.* New York: W. W. Norton.

Tulving, E. (1993). Varieties of consciousness and levels of awareness in memory. In A. Baddeley & L. Weiskrantz (Eds.), *Attention, selection, awareness and control: A tribute to Daonald Broadbent* (pp. 283–299). London: Oxford University Press.

Urry, H. L., Nitschke, J. B., Dolski, I., Jackson, D. C., Dalton, K. M., Mueller, C. J., et al. (2004). Making a life worth living: Neural correlates of well-being. *Psychological Science, 15,* 367–372.

Vygotsky, L. (1986). *Thought and language.* Cambridge, MA: MIT Press. (Original work published 1934)

Wallin, D. (2007). *Attachment in psychotherapy.* New York: Guilford.

Wallace, B. A. (2008). *Embracing mind: The common ground of science and spirituality.* Boston: Shambhala.

Wilson, E. O. (1998). *Consilience—the unity of knowledge.* New York: Vintage.

SUGGESTED READING

SUGGESTED READING

Baxter, L. R., Schwartz, J. M., Bergman, K. S., Szuba, M. P., Guze, B. H., Mazziota, J. C., et al. (1992). Caudate glucose metabolic rate changes with both drug and behavior therapy for obsessive-compulsive disorder. *Archives of General Psychiatry, 49*(9), 272–280.

Bechara, A., & Naqvi, N. (2004). Listening to your heart: Interoceptive awareness as a gateway to feeling. *Nature Neuroscience, 7,* 102–103.

Begley, S. (2007). *Train your mind, change your brain.* New York: Ballantine.

Blumberg, H. P., Kaufman, J., Marin A., Charney, D. S., Krystal, J. H., & Peterson, B. S. (2004). Significance of adolescent neurodevelopment for the neural circuitry of bipolar disorder. *Annals of the New York Academy of Sciences, 1021,* 376–383.

Brefczynski-Lewis, J. A., Lutz, A., Schaefer, H. S., Levinson, D. B., & Davidson, R. J. (2007). Neural correlates of attentional expertise in long-term meditation practitioners. *Proceedings of the National Academy of Sciences, 104*(27), 11483–11488.

Brown, K. W., Ryan, R. M., & Creswell, J. D. (2007). Mindfulness: Theoretical foundations and evidence for its salutary effects. *Psychological Inquiry, 18*(4), 211–237.

Carlson, C. E., Asten, J. A., & Freedman, B. (2006). Mechanisms of mindfulness. *Journal of Clinical Psychology, 62*(3), 373–386.

Carr, L., Iacoboni, M., Dubeau, M. C., Maziotta, J. C., & Lenzi, L. G. (2003). Neural mechanisms of empathy in humans: A relay from neural systems for imitation to limbic areas. *Proceedings of the National Academy of Sciences, 100,* 5497–5502.

Cassidy, J., & Shaver, P. (2008). *Handbook of Attachment* (2nd ed.). New York: Guilford.

Cheng, Y., Meltzoff, A. N., & Decety, J. (2007). Motivation modulates the activity of the human mirror-neuron system. *Cerebral Cortex, 17,* 1979–1986.

Cozolino, L. (2006). *The neuroscience of human relationships: Attachment and the developing social brain.* New York: W. W. Norton.

Cozolino, L. (2008). *The healthy aging brain: Sustaining attachment, attaining wisdom.* New York: W. W. Norton.

Craig, A. D. (2002). How do you feel? Interoception: The sense of the physiological condition of the body. *Nature Reviews Neuroscience, 3,* 655–666.

Craig, A. D. (2004). Human feelings: Why are some more aware than others? *Trends in Cognitive Sciences, 8*(6), 239–241.

Critchley, H. D. (2005). Neural mechanisms of autonomic, affective, and cognitive integration. *Journal of Comparative Neurology, 493,* 154–166.

Critchley, H. D., Mathias, C. J., & Dolan, R. J. (2001). Neuroanatomical correlates of first- and second-order representation of bodily states. *Nature Neuroscience, 2,* 207–212.

Critchley, H. D., Wiens, S., Rothstein, P., Ohmnan, A., & Dolan, R. (2004). Neural systems supporting interoceptive awareness. *Nature Neuroscience, 7,* 189–195.

Damasio, A. (1994). *Descartes' error: Emotion, reason, and the human brain.* New York: Grosset/Putnam.

Damasio, A. (1999). *The feeling of what happens: The body and emotion in the making of consciousness.* New York: Harcourt.

Davidson, R. J. (2004). The neurobiology of personality and personality disorders. In D. S. Charney & E. J. Nester (Eds.), *Neurobiology of mental illness* (2nd ed., pp. 1062–1075). Oxford: Oxford University Press.

Davidson, R. J. (2004). Well-being and affective style: Neural substrates and biobehavioral correlates. *Philosophical Transactions of the Royal Society, B, 359,* 1395–1411.

Davidson, R. J., & Hugdahl, K. (1996). *Brain asymmetry.* Boston: MIT Press.

Decety, J., & Moriguchi, Y. (2007). The empathic brain and its dysfunction in psychiatric populations: Implications for intervention across different clinical conditions. *Biopsychosocial Medicine, 1,* 22.

Devinsky, O. (2000). Right cerebral hemisphere dominance for a sense of corporeal and emotional self. *Epilepsy and Behavior, 1,* 60–73.

Dewey, E. M., III, Miasnikov, A. A., & Weinberger, N. M. (2002). Induction of behavioral associative memory by stimulation of the nucleus basalis. *Proceedings of the National Academy of Science, 99,* 4002–4007.

Edwards, B. (1989). *Drawing on the right side of the brain.* New York: Tarcher.

Elbert, T., Pantev, C., Wienbruch, C., Rockstroh, B., & Taub, E. (1995). Increased cortical representation of the fingers of the left hand in string players. *Science, 270,* 305–307.

Elzinga, B. M., & Bremner, J. D. (2002). Are the neural substrates of memory the final common pathway in posttraumatic stress disorder (PTSD)? *Journal of Affective Disorders, 1*(70), 1–17.

Epstein, R. M. (1999). Mindful practice. *Journal of the American Medical Association, 282,* 833–839.

Feinberg, T. E. (2009). *From axons to identity: Neurological explorations of the nature of the self.* New York: W. W. Norton.

Field, D. (2008). White matter matters and myelination: An overlooked mechanism of synaptic plasticity? *Neuroscientist, 11,* 528–531.

Fiske, S. T. (2005). Social cognition and the normality of prejudgment. In J. Dovidio, P. Glick, & L. Rudman (Eds.), *On the nature of prejudice* (pp. 36–53). New York: Wiley Blackwell.

Fogel, A. (2009). *The psychophysiology of self-awareness: Rediscovering the lost art of body sense.* New York: W. W. Norton.

Freyd, J. J. (1993). Five hunches about perceptual processes and dynamic representations. In D. Meyer & S. Kornblum (Eds.), *Attention and performance XIV: Synergies in experimental psychology, artificial intelligence, and cognitive neuroscience—A silver jubilee* (pp. 99–119). Cambridge, MA: MIT Press.

Gallese, V. (2006). Intentional attunement: A neurophysiological perspective on social cognition and its disruption in autism. *Brain Research, 1079,* 15–24.

Gallese, V., & Goldman, A. (1998). Mirror neurons and the stimulation theory of min-dreading. *Trends in Cognitive Science, 2,* 493–501.

Gazzaniga, M. (2004). *The cognitive neurosciences* (3rd ed.). Boston: MIT Press.

Gilbert, D. (2006). *Stumbling on happiness.* New York: Random House.

Goldberg, N. (1986). *Writing down the bones.* Boston: Shambhala.

Hebb, D. (2002). *The organization of behavior.* Mahwah, NJ: Erlbaum. (Original work published 1949)

Jha, A. P., Krompinger, J., & Baime, M. J. (2007). Mindfulness training modifies subsystems of attention. *Journal of Cognitive, Affective, and Behavioral Neuroscience, 7*(2), 109–119.

Kandel, E. (2007). *In search of memory: The emergence of a new science of mind.* New York: W. W. Norton.

Kauffman, S. (1995). *At home in the universe—Self-organization and complexity.* Oxford: Oxford University Press.

Kilgard, M. P., & Merzenich, M. M. (1998). Cortical map reorganization enabled by nucleus basalis activity. *Science, 279,* 1714–1718.

Lieberman, M. D. (2000). Intuition: A social cognitive neuroscience approach. *Psychological Bulletin C, 126*(1), 109–137.

Lieberman, M. D. (2007). Social cognitive neuroscience: A review of core processes. *Annual Review of Psychology, 58,* 259–289.

Lillas, C., & Turnbull, J. (2009). *Infant/child mental health, early intervention, and relationship-based therapies: A neurorelational framework for interdisciplinary practice.* New York: W. W. Norton.

McGowan, P. O., Sasaki, A., D'Alessio, A. C., Dymov, S., Labonté, B., Szyf, M., et al.

(2009). Epigenetic regulation of the glucocorticoid receptor in human brain associates with childhood abuse. *Nature Neuroscience, 12,* 342–348.

McManus, C. (2002). *Right hand left hand: The origins of asymmetry in brains, bodies, atoms and cultures.* Cambridge, MA: Harvard University Press.

Meaney, M. J. (2001). Maternal care, gene expression, and the transmission of individual differences in stress reactivity across generations. *Annual Review of Neuroscience, 24,* 1161–1192.

Miasnikov, A. A., Chen, J. C., Gross, N., Poytress, B. S., & Weinberger, N. M. (2008). Motivationally neutral stimulation of the nucleus basalis induces specific behavioral memory. *Neurobiology of Learning and Memory, 90,* 125–137.

Miller, E. M. (1994). Intelligence and brain myelination: A hypothesis. *Personality and Individual Differences, 17,* 803–832.

Mitchell, J. P., Banaji, M. R., & Macrae, C. N. (2005). The link between social cognition and self-referential thought in the medial prefrontal cortex. *Journal of Cognitive Neuroscience, 17,* 1306–1315.

Moses, J. (2002). *Oneness: Great principles shared by all religions* (rev. expanded ed.). New York: Random House.

Narvaez, D., & Bock, T. (2002). Moral schemas and tacit judgment or how the defining issues test is supported by cognitive science. *Journal of Moral Education, 31*(3), 297–314.

Norton Professional Books. (2008). *Brain model and puzzle: Anatomy and functional areas of the brain* [game]. New York: W. W. Norton.

Pennebaker, J. W. (1997). *Opening up: The healing power of expressing emotions.* New York: Guilford.

Pervin, L. A., & John, O. P. (2001). *Handbook of personality: Theory and research* (2nd ed.). New York: Guilford.

Pfeifer, J., Iacoboni, M., Mazziotta, J. C., & Dapretto, M. (2008). Mirroring others' emotions relates to empathy and interpersonal competence in children. *NeuroImage, 39,* 2076–2085.

Pollatos, O., Klaus, G., & Schandry, R. (2007). Neural systems connecting interoceptive awareness and feelings. *Human Brain Mapping, 28,* 9–18.

Ramachandran, V. S. (2004). *A brief tour of human consciousness: From impostor poodles to purple numbers.* New York: Pearson Education.

Ridderinkhof, K. R., Ullsperger, M., Crone, E. A., & Nieuwenhuis, S. (2004). The role of the medial frontal cortex in cognitive control. *Science, 306,* 443–447.

Rizolatti, G., & Arbib, M. A. (1998). Language within our grasp. *Trends in Neuroscience 21,* 188–194.

Robinson, K. (2009). *The element: How finding your passion changes everything.* New York: Viking/Penguin.

Rock, D. (2009). *Your brain at work*. New York: HarperBusiness.

Schore, A. N. (2003). *Affect regulation and the repair of the self and affect dysregulation and disorders of the self*. New York: W. W. Norton.

Schwartz, J. M., & Begley, S. (2002). *The mind and the brain: Neuroplasticity and the power of mental force*. New York: HarperCollins.

Seligman, M. E. P. (2002). *Authentic happiness*. New York: Free Press.

Seligman, M. E. P., Park, N., Peterson, C., & Steen, T. A. (2005). Positive psychology progress: Empirical validation of interventions. *American Psychologist, 60*, 410–421.

Shapiro, F. (2001). *EMDR*. New York: Guilford.

Siegel, D. J. (1996). Cognition, memory and dissociation. *Child and Adolescent Psychiatric Clinics of North America, 5*, 509–536.

Siegel, D. J. (2000). Memory: An overview with emphasis on the developmental, interpersonal, and neurobiological aspects. *Journal of the American Academy of Child and Adolescent Psychiatry, 40*, 997–1011.

Sigman, M., & Siegel, D. J. (1992). The interface between the psychobiological and cognitive models of attachment. *Behavioral and Brain Sciences, 15*, 523.

Singer, T., Seymour, B., O'Doherty, J., Kaube, H., Dolan, R. J., & Frith, C. D. (2004). Empathy for pain involves the affective but not sensory components of pain. *Science, 303*, 1157–1162.

Solomon, M. F., & Tatkin, S. (2010). *Love and war in intimate relationships: A psychobiological approach to couple therapy*. New York: W. W. Norton.

Springer, S. P., & Deutsch, G. (1997). *Left brain, right brain: Perspectives from cognitive neuroscience*. Cambridge, MA: MIT Press.

Sroufe, L. A., Egeland, B., Carlson, E. A., & Collins, W. A. (2005). *The development of the person*. New York: Guilford.

Uddin, L. Q., Iacoboni, M., Lange, C., & Keenan, J. P. (2007). The self and social cognition: The role of cortical midline structures and mirror neurons. *Trends in Cognitive Science, 11*, 153–157.

Ullen, F. (2005). Extensive piano practicing has regionally specific effects on white matter development. *Nature Neuroscience, 8*, 1148–1150.

van der Hart, O., Nijenhuis, E. R. S., & Steele, K. (2006). *The haunted self: Structural dissociation and the treatment of chronic traumatization*. New York: W. W. Norton.

Vrtika, P., Andersson, F., Grandjean, D., Sander, D., & Vuilleumier, P. (2008). Individual attachment style modulates human amygdala and striatum activation during social appraisal. *PLoS ONE 3*(8), e2868.

Weinberger, N. M. (2003). The nucleus basalis and memory codes: Auditory cortical plasticity and the induction of specific, associative behavioral memory. *Neurobiology Learning Memory, 80*, 268–284.

Zaidel, E., & Iacoboni, M. (Eds.). (2002). *The parallel brain: The cognitive neuroscience of the corpus callosum.* Cambridge, MA: MIT Press.

Zelazo, P. D., Moskovitch, M., & Thompson, E. (2007). *The cambridge handbook of consciousness.* Cambridge, UK: Cambridge University Press.

Zylowska, L., Ackerman, D. L., Yang, M. H., Futrell, J. L., Horton, N. L., Hale, T. S., et al. (2007). Mindfulness meditation training in adults and adolescents with ADHD: A feasibility study. *Journal of Attention Disorders, 11,* 737–746.

THE NORTON SERIES ON INTERPERSONAL NEUROBIOLOGY

Allan N. Schore, PhD, Series Editor
Daniel J. Siegel, MD, Founding Editor

The field of mental health is in a tremendously exciting period of growth and conceptual reorganization. Independent findings from a variety of scientific endeavors are converging in an interdisciplinary view of the mind and mental well-being. An interpersonal neurobiology of human development enables us to understand that the structure and function of the mind and brain are shaped by experiences, especially those involving emotional relationships.

The Norton Series on Interpersonal Neurobiology will provide cutting-edge, multidisciplinary views that further our understanding of the complex neurobiology of the human mind. By drawing on a wide range of traditionally independent fields of research—such as neurobiology, genetics, memory, attachment, complex systems, anthropology, and evolutionary psychology—these texts will offer mental health professionals a review and synthesis of scientific findings often inaccessible to clinicians. These books aim to advance our understanding of human experience by finding the unity of knowledge, or consilience, that emerges with the translation of findings from numerous domains of study into a common language and conceptual framework. The series will integrate the best of modern science with the healing art of psychotherapy.